reflections *on wildness*

reflections
on wildness

WINDHORSE PUBLICATIONS

Published by Windhorse Publications
11 Park Road
Birmingham
B13 8AB
www.windhorsepublications.com

Cover photo Devamitra
Design Marlene Eltschig
Printed by Interprint Ltd, Marsa, Malta

A catalogue record for this book is available
from the British Library

ISBN 1 899579 34 6

contents

INTRODUCTION

This collection was inspired by the efforts of some friends of mine to create a retreat centre, a place where women may prepare themselves for ordination in a Western Buddhist context. The search is on for somewhere wild and remote, a place far from the calls of domestic and professional life where – at least for a while – women can attend to 'what really matters', as Longchenpa, one of the writers in this collection, would say.

My friends have called their project 'Aranya'. This Sanskrit word refers to a place, or state of mind, 'beyond the village' – beyond the safe and secure, the humdrum and everyday. The aranya might be a forest or cave dwelling, or anywhere remote. It is somewhere that is peaceful – and also wild....

This book is offered in support of Aranya – to help with the funding and also to consider the nature, the ethos, of the project. After all, what is aranya, what is wildness?

This collection offers, in its own way, some suggestions.

In a way, reflecting on wildness seems a contradiction in terms. The intentionally reflective nature of this anthology means that there is nothing frenetic here: this is not about having a wild time in the partying sense. It was impossible to resist including a Buddhist story about a young man who is supposed to be meditating in the forest, but is distracted by the sounds of a party happening in the nearby village.

Much closer to the spirit of reflection is the wildness of nature, and this is represented here in many ways — in fact, a veritable jungle of wild animals seems to have prowled into the collection. Many of our writers dwell on the sheer beauty and peace of being in the wilderness, as compared to the stress of city life — reflections that seem poignant in a world in which wild places are fast disappearing. In other extracts, though, we get a sense of the challenges and terrors of life in the wilds, and the courage needed to overcome that fear.

As well as the beautiful and awe-inspiring wildness to be found in the world around us, there is another kind: the wildness within. In this collection we find Walt Whitman exulting in the freedom and spaciousness of life 'loos'd of limits and imaginary lines'. On the other hand, the Buddhist tradition often speaks of taming the mind, calming the turbulence within us, and a number of the writings here reflect this; Milarepa, for example, speaks of the wild horse of the mind, whose bridle is 'ever-flowing inspiration'. And one of the arguably more idiosyncratic selections is 'The Collar', by George Herbert, which seems to say so much about the struggle that taming one's rebellious mind inevitably sometimes is.

I have found it fascinating to reflect on the relationship between the outer wilderness, the deserts and forests that are the traditional domain of meditators, and the inner calm that such places evoke. I am glad to dedicate this book to the attempt to explore that relationship which the Aranya project represents, to the women who are bringing it into being, and to all those women whose lives will be touched by it. I am very grateful to everyone who has worked on the book, and especially Padmavajri, who has handled it with her customary grace.

Vidyadevi

SOJOURNS
IN THE PARALLEL WORLD

We live our lives of human passions,
cruelties, dreams, concepts,
crimes and the exercise of virtue
in and beside a world devoid
of our preoccupations, free
from apprehension – though affected,
certainly, by our actions. A world
parallel to our own, though overlapping.
We call it 'Nature'; only reluctantly
admitting ourselves to be 'Nature' too.
Whenever we lose track of our own
      obsessions,
our self-concerns, because we drift for
   a minute,
an hour even, of pure (almost pure)
response to that insouciant life:
cloud, bird, fox, the flow of light, the
      dancing
pilgrimage of water, vast stillness
of spellbound ephemerae on a lit
      windowpane,
animal voices, mineral hum, wind

conversing with rain, ocean with rock,
   stuttering
of fire to coal – then something tethered
in us, hobbled like a donkey on its patch
of gnawed grass and thistles, breaks free.
No one discovers
just where we've been, when we're caught
   up again
into our own sphere (where we must
return, indeed, to evolve our destinies)
– but we have changed, a little.

Denise Levertov

THE DARKNESS COMES RATTLING

How shall I begin my song
In the blue night that is settling?

In the great night my heart will go out,
Toward me the darkness comes rattling.
In the great night my heart will go out.

Owl Woman

SONG OF THE OPEN ROAD

From this hour I ordain myself loos'd of
   limits and imaginary lines,
Going where I list, my own master total
   and absolute,
Listening to others, considering well what
   they say,
Pausing, searching, receiving,
   contemplating,
Gently, but with undeniable will, divesting
   myself of the holds that would hold me.

I inhale great draughts of space,
The east and the west are mine, and the
   north and the south are mine.

I am larger, better than I thought,
I did not know I held so much goodness.

All seems beautiful to me,
I can repeat over to men and women You
   have done such good to me I would do
   the same to you,

I will recruit for myself and you as I go,
I will scatter myself among men and
    women as I go,
I will toss a new gladness and roughness
    among them,
Whoever denies me it shall not trouble me,
Whoever accepts me he or she shall be
    blessed and shall bless me.

Walt Whitman
'Song of the Open Road'

THE WILDWOOD DELIGHTS

Well, my dear mind, listen to the charms
    of the wildwood:
Precious trees, ready to honor the
    Victorious Ones and
Heavy with fruits, grow splendidly in
    the wildwood,
(With) leaves and fragrant flowers that
    are wide open and
(Graced by) the sweet smell of incense and
    the balminess of a light breeze.

Its waist, on which the drum-beat of
    waterfalls resounds melodiously and
    which is
Bathed in the cool light of the moon,
Is covered by a garment of thick clouds and
In them the crowd of stars adds to the
    encompassing beauty.

Flocks of geese swim on sweet-smelling
    ponds and
Many birds and deer move happily about;

Among lotus flowers and wish-granting
    trees and water lilies,
Bees flit and hum their songs.

Trees seem by their swaying (in the wind)
    to perform a dance, and by
Bending their branches with creepers as the
    tips of their fingers
To invite the guest, saying: 'Please come.'

Cool and clear rivulets blanketed
    by lotus flowers
Seem to be the bright splendor of
    a smiling face.

Wearing diadems of garden flowers and
    evergreens, and
Holding tightly to the azure sky as their
    garments,
The gods, resembling stars in the bright sky,
Seem to shower amorous attentions
    (on each other) in this pleasure grove.

While the cuckoo sings its drunken,
  piercing song
The flowers seem to be buoyed up by the
  cool seasonal wind.

While the cloud-elephants are trumpeting
  their joy
The coming of the rainy season seems to
  pour forth its abundant beneficence.

Roots, leaves, and edible fruits
Are unpolluted in the wildwood and
  available in all four seasons.

Since none is there to speak unpleasant
  words,
In the wildwood emotional outbursts
  decrease;
Since you are far removed from the turmoil
  of the cities,
In the wildwood steady thoughts of
  calmness grow.

Being in harmony with life's true meaning,
  the mind becomes meek and
Comes close to the bliss of inner peace in
  the wildwood.

In brief, the charms of the wildwood are
  unlimited;
Even if you were to talk for aeons, how
  could you ever exhaust (their abundance)?

from 'The Story of the Wildwood Delights'
in Longchenpa's 'A Visionary Journey'
trans. Herbert V. Guenther

FOREST PATH

A moment when, suddenly,
looking back for the way to the future,
you quiver on the edge of yourself.

– All paths panic beneath you,
the motherlode of meaning splits,
gusts east in grits;
the sun throws unmanageable glances
blinding off the choppy water
and spray plumes off, twisting, into empty
    blue.

And you turn, to find yourself
on the winding forest path.
Yes, a violet poses against a leaf
and alarmed wrens flitter in birches.
Now you cling breathless onto
a few memories, a mug of tea,
but you know they are not your home.

Thomas Jones

WIND

This house has been far out at sea all night,
The woods crashing through darkness, the
   booming hills,
Winds stampeding the fields under the
   window
Floundering black astride and blinding wet

Till day rose; then under an orange sky
The hills had new places, and wind wielded
Blade-light, luminous black and emerald,
Flexing like the lens of a mad eye.

At noon I scaled along the house-side as far as
The coal-house door. Once I looked up –
Through the brunt wind that dented the
   balls of my eyes
The tent of the hills drummed and strained
   its guyrope,

The fields quivering, the skyline a grimace,
At any second to bang and vanish with
   a flap:

The wind flung a magpie away and
    a black-
Back gull bent like an iron bar slowly. The
    house

Rang like some fine green goblet in the
    note
That any second would shatter it. Now
    deep
In chairs, in front of the great fire, we grip
Our hearts and cannot entertain book,
    thought,

Or each other. We watch the fire blazing,
And feel the roots of the house move, but
    sit on,
Seeing the window tremble to come in,
Hearing the stones cry out under the
    horizons.

Ted Hughes

'I WANT TO BREAK OUT ...'

I want to break out,
Batter down the door,
Go tramping black heather all day
On the windy moor,
And at night, in hayloft, or under hedge,
    find
A companion suited to my mind.

I want to break through,
Shatter time and space,
Cut up the Void with a knife,
Pitch the stars from their place,
Nor shrink back when, lidded with
    darkness, the Eye
Of Reality opens and blinds me, blue as
    the sky.

Sangharakshita

A REFUGE AND A SANCTUARY

*B*lasts from the Channel, with raining scud, and spume of mist breaking upon the hills, have kept me indoors all day. Yet not for a moment have I been dull or idle, and now, by the latter end of a sea-coal fire, I feel such enjoyment of my ease and tranquillity that I must needs word it before going up to bed.

Of course one ought to be able to breast weather such as this of to-day, and to find one's pleasure in the strife with it. For the man sound in body and serene of mind there is no such thing as bad weather; every sky has its beauty, and storms which whip the blood do but make it pulse more vigorously. I remember the time when I would have set out with gusto for a tramp along the wind-swept and rain-beaten roads; nowadays, I should perhaps pay for the experiment with my life. All the more do I prize the shelter of these good walls, the honest workmanship which makes my doors and windows proof against the assailing blast. In all England, the land of comfort, there is no room more comfortable than this in which I sit. Comfortable in the good old sense of the word, giving solace to the mind no less than ease to the body. And never does it look more homely, more a refuge and a sanctuary, than on winter nights.

George Gissing
The Private Papers of Henry Ryecroft

THE DESIRE TO FLY

*I*t was furthest from the house of all the trees, on a waste weedy spot which no one else visited, and this made it an ideal place for me, and whenever I was in the wild arboreal mood I would climb the willow to find a good stout branch high up on which to spend an hour, with a good view of the wide green plain before me and the sight of grazing flocks and herds, and of houses and poplar groves looking blue in the distance. Here, too, in this tree I first felt the desire for wings, to dream of the delight it would be to circle upwards to a great height and float on the air without effort, like the gull and buzzard and harrier and other great soaring land and water birds. But from the time this notion and desire began to affect me I envied most the great crested screamer, an inhabitant then of all the marshes in our vicinity. For here was a bird as big or bigger than a goose, as heavy almost as I was myself, who, when he wished to fly, rose off the ground with tremendous labour, and then as he got higher and higher and flew more and more easily, until he rose so high that he looked no bigger than a lark or pipit, and at that height he would continue floating round and round in vast circles for hours, pouring out those jubilant cries at intervals which sounded to us so far below like clarion notes in the sky. If I could only get off the ground like that heavy bird and rise as high, then the blue air would make me as buoyant and let me float all day without pain or effort like the bird! This desire has continued with me through my life, yet I have never wished to fly in a balloon or airship, since I should then be tied to a machine and have no will or soul of my own. The desire has only been gratified a very few times in that kind of dream called levitation, when one rises and floats above the earth without effort and is like a ball of thistle-down carried by the wind.

W.H. Hudson
Far Away and Long Ago

THE WORK OF THE FOREST

The Buddha was staying among the Kosalan people in a certain forest thicket, in which, it so happened, the brahmin Navakammika Bharadvaja was working. When he saw the Blessed One sitting cross-legged in the shade of a sal tree, upright, with mindfulness clearly established, the brahmin thought: 'I'm enjoying my work here in the forest. But what is that meditator enjoying?'

So Navakammika came closer to the Buddha and said:

Wanderer, what work are you doing
    here among the sal trees?
    Alone in the forest,
    what gives you delight?

And the Blessed One said:

There is no work left for me to do in the
    forest.
    All the tangles are completely sorted out.
    I am free from all briars
    and, my heart unpierced,
    I delight in being alone,
    all discontent completely gone.

Navakammika Sutta
Samyutta-Nikaya VII.17

THE DESERT
HAS MANY TEACHINGS

In the desert,
Turn toward emptiness,
Fleeing the self.

Stand alone,
Ask no one's help,
And your being will quiet,
Free from the bondage of things.

Those who cling to the world
endeavor to free them;
Those who are free, praise.

Care for the sick,
But live alone,
Happy to drink from the waters of sorrow,
To kindle Love's fire
With the twigs of a simple life.

Thus you will live in the desert.

Mechtild of Magdeburg

THE DAKINI

*T*he groundedness of interconnectedness together with the uncompromising challenge of self-transcendence finds symbolic expression in one of the most positive images of women's evolution known to humankind. In a pantheon of female Buddhas, gods and goddesses, and a host of enlightening beings, we discover the dakini of ancient Tantric Buddhism. The dakini, or sky dancer, expresses a passionate commitment to the truth and symbolizes the transformative energy of the transcendental in female form.

The word 'dakini' comes from a Sanskrit root meaning direction, space, or sky. Dakini is usually translated as sky walker, or sky dancer. The sky symbolizes the open dimension of being, an infinite space in which there is complete freedom of movement. The dakini dances in this open space, enjoying complete spiritual liberation. Her body is naked, symbolizing her uncompromising commitment to truth; nothing about her is veiled or hidden or held back. She may take on any hue of the rainbow, but she is usually depicted as red. Red, the colour of blood, signals the great upsurge of emotional energy that floods through her entire being, and flushes her whole body a bright crimson. She is ornamented with human bones that clatter against each other as she moves. Her long black hair is wild and dishevelled – she cares nothing for appearances. Conventional notions of propriety don't touch her. She is concerned, above all, with direct experience of reality, and a passionate commitment to fully meeting that. As she dances through the sky, she cries out in a deep laugh of utter freedom.

Western women who come into contact with this image of the dakini are very attracted to it. Perhaps this is because of the unrestrained flow of her energy. She is a far cry from the ever-meek and holy Virgin Mary with her downcast eyes, and a real relief from that whited sepulchre known as the Angel in the House. The dakini enjoys life to the full, and refuses to compromise her passionate pursuit of the truth.

Sinhadevi

TO BE A SLAVE OF INTENSITY

Friend, hope for the Guest while you are
    alive.
Jump into experience while you are alive!
Think ... and think ... while you are alive.
What you call 'salvation' belongs to the
    time before death.

If you don't break your ropes while you're
    alive,
do you think
ghosts will do it after?

The idea that the soul will join with the
    ecstatic
just because the body is rotten –
that is all fantasy.
What is found now is found then.
If you find nothing now,
you will simply end up with an apartment
    in the City of Death.

If you make love with the divine now, in
   the next life you will have the face of
   satisfied desire.

So plunge into the truth, find out who the
   Teacher is, Believe in the Great Sound!

Kabir says this: When the Guest is being
searched for, it is the intensity of the
longing for the Guest that does all the
work.
Look at me, and you will see a slave of that
intensity.

Kabir
trans. Robert Bly

THE DISAPPEARANCE OF WILDNESS

Wildness and silence disappeared from the countryside, sweetness fell from the air, not because anyone wished them to vanish or fall but because throughways had to floor the meadows with cement to carry the automobiles which advancing technology produced.... Tropical beaches turned into high-priced slums where thousand-room hotels elbowed each other for glimpses of once-famous surf not because those who loved the beaches wanted them there but because enormous jets could bring a million tourists every year – and therefore did.

Archibald MacLeish
'The Great American Frustration',
in 'Saturday Review', New York, 9 July 1968

THE PANTHER
In the Jardin des Plantes, Paris

His vision, from the constantly passing bars,
has grown so weary that it cannot hold
anything else. It seems to him there are
a thousand bars; and behind the bars, no
   world.

As he paces in cramped circles, over and
   over,
the movement of his powerful soft strides
is like a ritual dance around a center
in which a mighty will stands paralyzed,

Only at times, the curtain of the pupils
lifts, quietly − . An image enters in,
rushes down through the tensed, arrested
   muscles,
plunges into the heart and is gone.

Rainer Maria Rilke
trans. Stephen Mitchell

THE JAGUAR

The apes yawn and adore their fleas in the
    sun.
The parrots shriek as if they were on fire,
    or strut
Like cheap tarts to attract the stroller with
    the nut.
Fatigued with indolence, tiger and lion

Lie still as the sun. The boa-constrictor's
    coil
Is a fossil. Cage after cage seems empty, or
Stinks of sleepers from the breathing straw.
It might be painted on a nursery wall.

But who runs like the rest past these arrives
At a cage where the crowd stands, stares,
    mesmerized,
As a child at a dream, at a jaguar hurrying
    enraged
Through prison darkness after the drills of
    his eyes

On a short fierce fuse. Not in boredom —
The eye satisfied to be blind in fire,
By the bang of blood in the brain deaf the
    ear —
He spins from the bars, but there's no cage
    to him

More than to the visionary his cell:
His stride is wildernesses of freedom:
The world rolls under the long thrust of his
    heel.
Over the cage floor the horizons come.

Ted Hughes

THE TYGER

Tyger Tyger, burning bright,
In the forests of the night;
What immortal hand or eye,
Could frame thy fearful symmetry?

In what distant deeps or skies
Burnt the fire of thine eyes?
On what wings dare he aspire?
What the hand, dare seize the fire?

And what shoulder, and what art,
Could twist the sinews of thy heart?
And when thy heart began to beat,
What dread hand? and what dread feet?

What the hammer? what the chain,
In what furnace was thy brain?
What the anvil? what dread grasp,
Dare its deadly terrors clasp?

When the stars threw down their spears
And water'd heaven with their tears:

Did he smile his work to see?
Did he who made the Lamb make thee?

Tyger Tyger burning bright,
In the forests of the night:
What immortal hand or eye,
Dare frame thy fearful symmetry?

William Blake
'The Tyger'
from 'Songs of Innocence and Experience'

THE WILD HORSE OF THE MIND

A horse of Prana-Mind have I;
I adorn him with the silk scarf of Dhyana.
His skin is the magic Ensuing Dhyana
    Stage,
His saddle, illuminating Self-Awareness.
My spurs are the Three Visualizations,
His crupper the secret teaching of the Two
    Gates.

His headstall is the Prana of Vital-force;
His forelock curl is Three-pointed Time.
Tranquillity within is his adornment,
Bodily movement is his rein,
And ever-flowing inspiration is his bridle.

He gallops wildly along the Spine's Central
    Path.
He is a yogi's horse, this steed of mine.

By riding him, one escapes Samsara's mud,
By following him one reaches the safe land
of Bodhi.

'The Meeting at Silver Spring'
in 'The Hundred Thousand Songs of Milarepa'

THE COLLAR

I struck the board, and cry'd, No more.
    I will abroad.
  What? shall I ever sigh and pine?
My lines and life are free; free as the rode,
  Loose as the winde, as large as store.
    Shall I be still in suit?
  Have I no harvest but a thorn
  To let me bloud, and not restore
  What I have lost with cordiall fruit?
    Sure there was wine
Before my sighs did drie it: there was corn
    Before my tears did drown it.
  Is the yeare onely lost to me?
    Have I no bayes to crown it?
No flowers, no garlands gay? all blasted?
      All wasted?
  Not so, my heart: but there is fruit,
    And thou hast hands.
  Recover all thy sigh-blown age
On double pleasures: leave thy cold dispute
Of what is fit, and not. Forsake thy cage,
    Thy rope of sands,

Which pettie thoughts have made, and
    made to thee
  Good cable, to enforce and draw,
        And be thy law,
While thou didst wink and wouldst not
    see.
        Away; take heed:
        I will abroad.
Call in thy deaths head there: tie up thy
    fears.
        He that forbears
      To suit and serve his need,
        Deserves his load.
But as I rav'd and grew more fierce and
    wilde
        At every word,
  Me thought I heard one calling, *Child*!
        And I reply'd, *My Lord*.

George Herbert

WHY AM I SO LOST?

Where shall we go? Where to direct the mind? We have our theories but maybe they are only so much conceit, only cobwebs thrown to catch a leviathan. Does the world offer us any clues? If we watch and listen intently we may be sure that it does. The woodpecker with its on-and-off knocking, the mix of sun and shadow in the woods, the dry beech leaves buzzing in the wind, the busy water carving earth – they all declare the nature of things; they all preach true Dhamma.

Cut off for now from manufactured comforts, wrenched by the turn of seasons, we cannot suppress the upwelling of a question; we cannot keep from blurting to the unconscious river, Why am I so lost? And with the words loosed and blown across the sky like leaves, we find ourselves already drawn on to track down an answer, as if the admission of our ignorance somehow commits us to the search for wisdom.

Reflecting on all this chaotic chance in nature, we see that the instability runs deeper than we imagined, that we who are wondering about the fleeting show are ourselves rushed on like sticks in the flood.

It becomes impossible – as we scan the distances, as we inspect the spinning flotsam, as we review our thoughts – to find anything which does not change and pass away.

We have till now given so little attention to this universal flux that we have failed to understand the laws that work upon us and, being slothful or indifferent or simply careless, we have again and again crashed against huge, frightening questions of pain and longing.

Now, in this wilderness of time, a flood has orphaned us on a strange beach that is itself crumbling into the stream, and wet nature repeats to our senses what we might have learned long before as doctrine: 'All formations are impermanent.' It was one thing to read the words in the quiet of our rooms and another to stand here cold and beleaguered in the midst of unstoppable change.

Bhikkhu Nyanasobhano
from 'Floodtime'
in 'Landscapes of Wonder'

THE BUDDHA IN THE FOREST

On such specially auspicious nights as the fourteenth, the fifteenth, and the eighth of the fortnight, I dwelt in such awe-inspiring, horrifying abodes as orchard shrines, woodland shrines, and tree shrines. And while I dwelt there, a wild animal would come up to me, or a peacock would knock off a branch, or the wind would rustle the leaves. I thought: 'What now if this is the fear and dread coming?' I thought: 'Why do I dwell always expecting fear and dread? What if I subdue that fear and dread while keeping the same posture that I am in when it comes upon me?'

While I walked, the fear and dread came upon me; I neither stood nor sat nor lay down till I had subdued that fear and dread. While I stood, the fear and dread came upon me; I neither walked nor sat nor lay down till I had subdued that fear and dread. While I sat, the fear and dread came upon me; I neither walked nor stood nor lay down till

I had subdued that fear and dread. While I lay down, the fear and dread came upon me; I neither walked nor stood nor sat down till I had subdued that fear and dread.

The Buddha
in the 'Bhayabherava Sutta'
Majjhima-Nikaya 4

PRINCESS MANDARAVA
GOES FORTH

The next day, at the crack of dawn, as they all looked on, Mandarava went away without the slightest attachment to the king, her relatives, attendants, wealth, or endowments. She remained, however, in her posture of equipoise, seated within the protective net of Guru Padmasambhava of Oddiyana's loving-kindness and compassion. She traversed not one, but two or three valleys and countries, and suddenly found herself in an uninhabited land that was frightful, wrathful, and rugged beyond belief.

For three long days, she remained trapped in a craggy ravine without food, drink, or shelter. She was famished and chilled to the bone. All she could hear were the eerie sounds of many tropical birds and wild animals. Finally, she managed to climb over a peak, only to find herself forced to descend into yet another frightening valley of doom. Then she lost heart and, in a state of disturbed sorrow, went into the depth of her soul, where her spontaneous, fervent devotion remained unaffected. She cried out in urgent despair: 'Kye ma! Kye hu! Lord Guru of Oddiyana! Guru who reveals the path to liberation! Please look upon me now with your merciful compassion! First, I arrived here in this country to the north. Second, I was engulfed by a dense jungle full of wild animals. Third, the sound of water crashing in craggy ravines is piercing my ears. I fear I am in a barbaric country possessed by demons and cannibals! O young man of grace, where can I find you now? Without you my mind is unstable and weak!

'First, I am here in an uninhabited land where the grass is so wild that the wind makes it dance. Second, there is the unceasing sound of ravens crying in the forest. Third, the sun is obscured by the darkness of night. I wonder if I have entered the bardo between this life and the next? Where is the one whose melodious speech is like music to my ears? That you cannot see me now, at this time, fills my mind with chilling sorrow.

'First, I am alone in this country, without a single companion. Second, it resembles a haunted charnel ground. Third, there is the constant eerie din of jungle creatures. It seems that I have arrived in the city of the lord of death! Be quick to look upon me now with your compassionate mercy! Hold me in your heart, O perfect Lord of Dharma!' Then she fell to the ground in tears.

Through his omniscience, the lotus guru knew of her duress and went to her. Mandarava wept in his presence, so over-come with gratitude that she grabbed him and held him tight. He then spoke these words to her: 'What has become of your fearless pledge of courage now that you are confronted by such a malevolent and unruly land? A frightful environment such as this is the catalyst for a practitioner's true practice to emerge. Adverse conditions are the true wealth of a practitioner. Such a supreme place of practice is the most exalted spot for accomplishing the innermost profound Dharma. A frightening, uncomfortable place is the knife that severs discursive thought. The wrathful charnel ground is the environment through which the deceptive view of eternalism is exposed. To discover the illusory nature of the barren, frightening land is to discover the innermost sacred Dharma. The sound of the jungle is the introduction to the bardo. Sadness and elation, truth and deception – these are non-existent. The true practice of guru devotion is the cultivation of undiminishing fervent faithfulness. This is the resting ground where relief from the bardo is sought. In the bardo the terrifying sounds that resemble a thousand roaring dragons are like the sound of the approaching messengers of the lord of death. Such a storehouse of darkness cannot be illuminated in an aeon of light. It is like being trapped in a thick forest where sharp weapons abound, with the eight terrifying narrow passageways and the four wrathful sounds. The suffering is unbearable beyond imagination!'

Instantly, Mandarava's negativities and obscurations were purified. All the noble qualities that develop on the path arose in her mind.

from 'The Lives and Liberation of Princess Mandarava'
trans. Lama Chonam and Sangye Khandro

YESHE TSOGYAL
AND THE WILD BEASTS

*T*hen, like a great army converging upon that place, millions upon millions of worms and insects and other crawling things, such as spiders and scorpions and snakes, swarmed over everything. Some of them filled her sense organs; some bit and stung and scratched her as they crawled onto her. Some jumped upon her; others attacked each other, tossing bits of their bodies about as they ate. All sorts of strange and magical forms appeared.

But mTsho-rgyal just trembled a little and felt compassion rise up in her mind. As the forms became more and more angry and frightful, raging around her, mTsho-rgyal thought:

'Many times I have vowed to be unattached to anything associated with body, speech, or mind. All these sentient beings, worms and other crawling things, arise continuously, increasingly, and abundantly from karmic forces. Why should I tremble with fear before such magical manifestations of the elements? I must remember that all activity is the result of good and bad thoughts. Therefore, whatever may arise, either good or bad, I will recognize as dualistic mental activity and be unconcerned.'

Having come to this profound realization, she said:

'All phenomenal existence
is merely the magical manifestation of mind.
I see nothing to fear in all the expanse
    of space.
Therefore, all of this must be self-arising
    luminance.
How could there ever be anything other
    than this?
All these activities are only ornaments of my
    own being.
Better that I rest in meditative silence.'

After saying this, she entered a meditative state that was completely quiet, without any discrimination of good or evil. And all the apparitions disappeared.

Yeshe Tso-gyal
in 'Mother of Knowledge'

THE WILD SWANS AT COOLE

The trees are in their autumn beauty,
The woodland paths are dry,
Under the October twilight the water
Mirrors a still sky;
Upon the brimming water among
   the stones
Are nine-and-fifty swans.

The nineteenth autumn has come upon me
Since I first made my count;
I saw, before I had well finished,
All suddenly mount
And scatter wheeling in great broken rings
Upon their clamorous wings.

I have looked upon those brilliant creatures,
And now my heart is sore.
All's changed since I, hearing at twilight,
The first time on this shore,
The bell-beat of their wings above
   my head,
Trod with a lighter tread.

Unwearied still, lover by lover,
They paddle in the cold
Companionable streams or climb the air;
Their hearts have not grown old;
Passion or conquest, wander where
   they will,
Attend upon them still.

But now they drift on the still water,
Mysterious, beautiful;
Among what rushes will they build,
By what lake's edge or pool
Delight men's eyes when I awake some day
To find they have flown away?

W.B. Yeats

OWLS

In the night, when the owl is less than exquisitely swift and perfect, the scream of the rabbit is terrible. But the scream of the owl, which is not of pain and hopelessness and the fear of being plucked out of the world, but of the sheer rollicking glory of the death-bringer, is more terrible still. When I hear it resounding through the woods, and then the five black pellets of its song dropping like stones into the air, I know I am standing at the edge of the mystery, in which terror is naturally and abundantly part of life, part of even the most becalmed, intelligent, sunny life – as, for example, my own. The world where the owl is endlessly hungry and endlessly on the hunt is the world in which I live too. There is only one world.

Mary Oliver
'Owls'
from 'Blue Pastures'

INVERSNAID

This darksome burn, horseback brown,
His rollrock highroad roaring down,
In coop and in comb the fleece of his foam
Flutes and low to the lake falls home.

A windpuff-bonnet of fawn-froth
Turns and twindles over the broth
Of a pool so pitchblack, fell-frowning,
It rounds and rounds Despair to drowning.

Degged with dew, dappled with dew
Are the groins of the braes that the brook
    treads through,
Wiry heathpacks, flitches of fern,
And the beadbonny ash that sits over the burn.

What would the world be, once bereft
Of wet and of wildness? Let them be left,
O let them be left, wildness and wet;
Long live the weeds and the wilderness yet.

Gerard Manley Hopkins

OUR LIMITS TRANSGRESSED

We can never have enough of Nature. We must be refreshed by the sight of inexhaustible vigor, vast and Titanic features, the sea-coast with its wrecks, the wilderness with its living and its decaying trees, the thunder cloud, and the rain which lasts three weeks and produces freshets. We need to witness our own limits transgressed, and some life pasturing freely where we never wander.

H. Thoreau
Walden

PEACE IN THE WILDERNESS

Standing to one side of him, a deva said to
the Buddha:

These people who dwell in wild places,
living a life so peaceful and simple,
eating just one meal a day,
how is it that they look so serene?

The Buddha said:

They are not sorrowing about the past,
or longing for the future.
They are living in the present.
That's why they look so serene.
It is by sorrowing about the past
and longing for the future
that foolish people wither away,
like green reeds drying in the sun.

Aranna Sutta,
'The Wilderness'

LIFE IN THE FOREST

There was once a wanderer of the Vajjian clan living in the forest near Vesali.

On one occasion there was an all-night party in Vesali, and the noise – the strumming of stringed instruments, the rhythm of drums, and the sound of people talking – was so loud that the wanderer heard it. He started to lament, saying aloud:

Here we all are, each of us quite alone,
living in the forest,
just like a log left lying among the trees.
On a night like this, with a party going on,
who is worse off than us?

It happened that there was a spirit, a deva, living in the same part of the forest.

Upon hearing the wanderer and feeling sympathy for him, the deva decided to bring him to his senses.

So he came close to him and said:

It's true that you're living alone in the forest,
just like a log left lying among the trees.
But many people would envy your life,
just as beings in hell envy those who are
   heaven-bound.

And the wanderer, brought to his senses
by the deva's words, was very moved.

Vajjiputta Sutta

acknowledgements

The publishers wish to acknowledge with gratitude permission to quote from the following:

p.7:   by Denise Levertov, from *Sands of the Well*, copyright
         © 1996 by Denise Levertov. Reprinted by permission of
         New Directions Publishing Corp.

p.12:   *A Visionary Journey* by Longchenpa, translated by Herbert
         V. Guenther, © 1989 by Herbert V. Guenther. Reprinted
         by arrangement with Shambhala, Publications Inc., Boston,
         www.shambhala.com

p.16:   Subhadassi (ed.), *FWBO New Poetry 1997*, Rising Fire,
         reprinted with kind permission of Thomas Jones.

p.17 and p.34:
         Ted Hughes, *Hawk in the Rain*, Faber and Faber Ltd.

p.26:   'The desert has many teachings' by Mechtild of
         Magdeburg, trans. Jane Hirshfield from *Women in Praise
         of the Sacred* by Jane Hirshfield, editor. Copyright © 1994
         by Jane Hirshfield. Reprinted by permission of
         HarperCollins Publishers, Inc.

p.30:   reprinted from *The Kabir Book* translated by Robert Bly,
         Beacon Press, Boston 1977. Copyright 1977 Robert Bly.
         Used with his permission.

p.33:   *The Selected Poetry of Rainer Maria Rilke* by Rainer Maria
         Rilke. Copyright © 1982 by Stephen Mitchell. Reprinted
         by permission of Random House, Inc.

p.42:   Bhikkhu Nyanasobhana, *Landscapes of Wonder*, Wisdom
         Publications, Boston 1998.

p.45:   *The Middle Length Discourses of the Buddha*, original trans-
         lation by Bhikkhu Nanamoli, translated, edited, and revised
         by Bhikkhu Bodhi, Wisdom Publications, Boston 1995.

p.47:   Lama Chonam and Sangye Khandro (trans.), *The Lives and*

Liberation of Princess Mandarava, Wisdom Publications, Boston 1998.

p.52: Jane Wilhelms (ed.), *Mother of Knowledge: The Enlightenment of Ye-shes mTsho-rgyal*, text by Nam-mkha'i snying-po, oral translation by Tarthang Tulku, Dharma Publishing 1983.

p.55: 'The Wild Swans at Coole', from W.B. Yeats, *Selected Poetry*, published by Pan Books in association with Macmillan, London 1974, seventh printing 1980. Reprinted with the permission of A.P. Watt Ltd. on behalf of Michael B. Yeats.

p.57: Excerpt from *Blue Pastures*, copyright © 1995, 1992, 1991 by Mary Oliver, reprinted by permission of Harcourt, Inc.

Every effort has been made to trace copyright in the following, but if any omission has been made please let us know in order that this may be acknowledged in the next edition.

p.9: by Owl Woman, trans. Frances Denmore, from *Women in Praise of the Sacred*, edited by Jane Hirshfield, HarperPerennial, first edition 1995.

p.38: from 'The Meeting at Silver Spring' in Garma C.C. Chang, *The Hundred Thousand Songs of Milarepa*, Shambhala, Boston and London, 1999, p.163

The Windhorse symbolizes the energy of the enlightened mind carrying the Three Jewels – the Buddha, the Dharma, and the Sangha – to all sentient beings. Buddhism is one of the fastest-growing spiritual traditions in the Western world. Throughout its 2,500-year history, it has always succeeded in adapting its mode of expression to suit whatever culture it has encountered.

WINDHORSE PUBLICATIONS aims to continue this tradition as Buddhism comes to the West. Today's Westerners are heirs to the entire Buddhist tradition, free to draw instruction and inspiration from all the many schools and branches. Windhorse publishes works by authors who not only understand the Buddhist tradition but are also familiar with Western culture and the Western mind. Manuscripts welcome.

For orders and catalogues contact

WINDHORSE	WINDHORSE	WEATHERHILL INC
PUBLICATIONS	BOOKS	41 Monroe Turnpike
11 Park Road	P.O. Box 574	Trumbull
Birmingham	Newtown	CT 06611
B13 8AB	NSW 2042	USA
UK	Australia	

Windhorse Publications is an arm of the FRIENDS OF THE WESTERN BUDDHIST ORDER, which has more than sixty centres on five continents. Through these centres, members of the Western Buddhist Order offer regular programmes of events for the general public and for more experienced students. These include meditation classes, public talks, study on Buddhist themes and texts, and 'bodywork' classes such as t'ai chi, yoga, and massage. The FWBO also runs several retreat centres and the Karuna Trust, a fund-raising charity that supports social welfare projects in the slums and villages of India. Many FWBO centres have residential spiritual communities and ethical businesses associated with them. Arts activities are encouraged too, as is the development of strong bonds of friendship between people who share the same ideals.

In this way the FWBO is developing a unique approach to Buddhism, not simply as a set of techniques, less still as an exotic cultural interest, but as a creatively directed way of life for people living in the modern world.

If you would like more information about the FWBO please visit our website at

www.fwbo.org   or write to
London Buddhist Centre   Aryaloka
51 Roman Road   Heartwood Circle
London   Newmarket
E2 0HU, UK   NH 03857, USA

ALSO FROM WINDHORSE

Compiled by Vidyadevi
REFLECTIONS ON SOLITUDE

Throughout the ages seekers after truth have spoken of the benefits of solitude for reflection, self-examination, and a deeper understanding of life.

This diverse and thoughtful selection of poetry and prose draws on the riches of Western literature as well as the wisdom of the Buddhist tradition, depicting the many delights and challenges of being alone.

Spend a little time with these reflections when life is crowding in on you and find some space...

80 pages
ISBN 1 899579 28 1
£4.99/$9.95

Sangharakshita
THE CALL OF THE FOREST
AND OTHER POEMS

Profound contemplation of nature and spiritual
vision feature prominently in this collection of
Sangharakshita's recent poems. Here we can see
how the practice of Buddhism combines with
the writing of poetry. Both require the cultivation of an intense sympathy with others, which
forms the basis of the essential Buddhist virtue of
loving-kindness.

56 pages
ISBN 1 899579 24 9
£7.99/$15.95

Sangharakshita
COMPLETE POEMS 1941–1994

Sangharakshita has dedicated himself to helping people transform their lives not only through his work as a Buddhist teacher but also through the medium of verse, for in his poetry he combines the sensitivity of the poet with the vision born of a life of contemplation and uncompromising spiritual practice.

Here we have the opportunity to listen to a unique voice and to be uplifted by the reflections of an extraordinary person and an accomplished teacher.

528 pages, hardback
ISBN 0 904766 70 5
£17.99/$34.95

Sir Edwin Arnold
THE LIGHT OF ASIA

This inspiring poem by Sir Edwin Arnold
(1832–1904), though written more than a
hundred years ago, retains the power to move us
in a way that no prose rendering of the life of the
Buddha can. We cannot but admire the courage,
determination, and self-sacrifice of the Indian
prince who, out of compassion, left his palace to
find a remedy for the sufferings of the world.

192 pages, hardback, with glossary
ISBN 1 899579 19 2
£9.99/$19.95

Sangharakshita
PEACE IS A FIRE

This collection of aphorisms, teachings, and poems by the pioneering Western Buddhist Sangharakshita offers instant inspiration to anyone who is ready to have their views challenged and their minds expanded.

The breadth of the author's thought is well represented in these sayings which range from art and literature, through sex and relationships, to philosophy and religion. His words point beyond themselves to Reality itself, to the freedom accessible to all who dare to change.

160 pages, with photographs
ISBN 0 904766 84 5
£6.99/$13.95

Sangharakshita

A STREAM OF STARS:
REFLECTIONS AND APHORISMS

This is a collection of aphorisms, poems, and
writings by the eminent Western Buddhist
teacher, Sangharakshita. Encompassing culture
and society, relationships and the human
condition, these incisive teachings illuminate
many aspects of life.

With clarity, insight, and flashes of humour,
Sangharakshita provokes us to thought and then
to aspiration: an aspiration to true happiness and
freedom.

136 pages, with photographs
ISBN 1 899579 08 7
£6.99/$13.95

ArtScroll Series®

Rabbi Nosson Scherman / Rabbi Meir Zlotowitz
General Editors

ASCENDING JACOB'S LADDER

Published by

Mesorah Publications, ltd

in conjunction with
Ahavat Shalom Publications

Essays on the Fundamentals of Jewish Life —
Shabbat, Festivals, Prayer, Teshuvah, Torah Study,
the Jewish Home and the Wisdom of Kabbalah

By
Rabbi Yaakov Hillel
Rosh Yeshivat **Ahavat Shalom**, Jerusalem

FIRST EDITION
First Impression … January 2007

Published and Distributed by
MESORAH PUBLICATIONS, LTD.
4401 Second Avenue / Brooklyn, N.Y 11232
in conjunction with
YESHIVAT AHAVAT SHALOM

Distributed in Europe by
LEHMANNS
Unit E, Viking Business Park
Rolling Mill Road
Jarow, Tyne & Wear, NE32 3DP
England

Distributed in Australia and New Zealand by
GOLDS WORLDS OF JUDAICA
3-13 William Street
Balaclava, Melbourne 3183
Victoria, Australia

Distributed in Israel by
SIFRIATI / A. GITLER — BOOKS
6 Hayarkon Street
Bnei Brak 51127

Distributed in South Africa by
KOLLEL BOOKSHOP
Ivy Common
105 William Road
Norwood 2192, Johannesburg, South Africa

ARTSCROLL SERIES®
ASCENDING JACOB'S LADDER
© Copyright 2007 by MESORAH PUBLICATIONS, Ltd. and RABBI YAAKOV HILLEL
4401 Second Avenue / Brooklyn, N.Y. 11232 / (718) 921-9000 / www.artscroll.com

ISBN-10: 1-4226-0227-3
ISBN-13: 978-1-4226-0227-0

Printed in the United States of America by Noble Book Press Corp.
Bound by Sefercraft, Quality Bookbinders, Ltd., Brooklyn N.Y. 11232

Dedication

It is clearly through the *hesed* of *Kudsha Brich Hu* that the *hacham* has become so closely involved in the lives of our entire family. His wise counsel and his *tefillot* on our behalf are with us every day. We hope and pray that with the help of the *Ribono shel Olam*, he will continue to spread the light of Torah through his army of *talmidim*, enriching our people with his vast treasures of *hochmah*.

We dedicate this volume in honor of our dear parents, Mr. and Mrs. **Eli and Susan Mirzoeff.** Thanks to their untiring efforts on behalf of their children and their wonderful example, we can truly understand the importance of Torah and of *kavod* for *hachamim* and *tzaddikim*. We love them dearly, and can never thank them enough for all they do for us.

In the *zechut* of these sacred writings, may Hashem grant them health, wealth, *nahat*, and *arichut yamim*.

Adam and Chavie Mirzoeff
Bilhah and David Moradi
Esther and Reuven Rosenkrancz

Preface

First and foremost, I must express my deep gratitude to Hashem for having given me the opportunity to study and teach Torah my entire life, and especially, to have been privileged to author many books, both on the revealed aspects of our holy Torah and on its secrets, which have been widely accepted around the world, and have brought much benefit and insight to many people.

I am also grateful for the fact that in addition to publishing and disseminating Torah works in Hebrew, I have merited publishing a number of books in English, thus allowing me to transmit Torah ideas to a new and broader audience.

The history of this book begins with my visits to Jewish communities in America and England over the past eighteen years. During those visits, I often spoke and lectured on a variety of topics. Many of these lectures were tape-recorded, to become much sought-after and popular. Thus, I decided to transcribe and compile them into one volume.

Because the lectures were delivered to a wide variety of audiences, the reader might find here several approaches to a single topic – at times more conservative, at other times more moderate. This is due to my audience at the time, and what I felt they needed to hear. However, having carefully reviewed all the essays in this book, I believe they will be of benefit to people on all levels.

I believe that the reader will find many new and exciting ideas in these essays. There is a great deal here that is inspiring, as the teachings often contain Kabbalistic insights that are incorporated in very subtle ways. These always have a powerful and profound effect on people.

One of the most acute problems of our generation is a lack of clarity and understanding about the underlying concepts of Torah and *mitzvot*. There is a need to clearly distinguish between good and evil in life, and the many gray areas that lie between them. Our generation is characterized by confusion, unclear opinions, and a general lack of guidance. True understanding, which follows from a clear and deep appreciation of the Torah in all its facets and dimensions, is necessary for leadership; yet this is very rare in our time. As a result, *da'at Torah*, or the true Torah outlook (*hashkafa*), is hard to attain. I thank Hashem for having allowed me to study under great Torah figures since my youth – to view, firsthand, living examples of authentic *da'at Torah*, and to build on those foundations through my own studies and experiences. I hope and pray that this book will introduce its readers to a correct and structured perspective on life, particularly concerning our personal responsibility in this world.

I have called the book *Ascending Jacob's Ladder*, for its ultimate purpose is to guide and encourage people to improve their spiritual lives, and ascend the ladder of perfection which links us to our Creator. This ladder must be climbed one step at a time, in a gradual, structured way, for jumping or skipping steps usually results in a fall at some later stage. Rather, each level of ascent has its own, particular challenges, achievements and rewards – both in this world, and in the World-to-Come. Really, the ladder is our own Jewish soul, and the rungs are its different levels. For while our feet must be grounded in this world, our souls must stretch upward to our Creator. Thus we ascend, stage after stage, always yearning for perfection and closeness to Hashem.

Thus, I offer you here "Jacob's (Yaakov's) Ladder." It is a system of advice and guidance that I have formulated over many years. I hope that many of our dear and precious brethren will ascend this ladder with me, for the journey is ultimately one of great joy, as each level opens new horizons of understanding and appreciation of God's closeness to us and the depth of His Torah. As a result, we will perform *mitzvot* with greater depth, understanding and enthusiasm, with love and fear of our Creator.

I hope and pray that the spiritual journey of ascending Jacob's ladder will benefit many people, and that each chapter of this book will serve as another rung to bring the readers closer to Hashem. If so, this will be my reward and fulfillment in both this world and the next.

This book has been sponsored by my dear friend, Adam Mirzoeff of Lawrence, New York. Adam and his parents and their family have been close friends and dedicated supporters of Yeshivat Ahavat Shalom for many years, devoting heart and soul to strengthening the Yeshivah and widening its circle of friends and donors. I hope that the merit of this great *mitzvah* will bring him and his family abundant blessing for continual success and happiness, both materially and spiritually. May Hashem grant them all long lives, full of Torah and *mitzvot*, good health, prosperity and happiness. Amen!

With gratitude and humility,

Rabbi Yaakov Moshe Hillel

Contents

Ascending
Jacob's Ladder

The Value of Time

The Seven Days of Creation

Hashem created the world with ten utterances.[1] He said, "Let there be light," and there was light. He said, "Let there be a firmament," and the heavens came into being. Yet the process of creation was not a one-time event occuring some six thousand years ago. For even after creating all the worlds – the spiritual, physical, down to the one we live in – Hashem remains connected to them, continuously infusing His light into creation. Every one of Hashem's utterances still reverberates high in the heavenly spheres. His words "Let there be light" remain the source of light forever, and all light that exists comes from that ongoing utterance.

We can compare this to a heart continuously pumping blood. The blood reaches every part of the body. If the flow were to stop, the body would perish. So, too, the Creator continuously gives of His light and radiates the forces of creation into the world, renewing existence every second.

Why don't we see the constant renewal of creation on the physical realm? Maybe reality is similar to a movie. Though each single frame is a separate picture on its own, when the film moves fast, the human eye cannot detect the subtle changes between one picture and the next, and it all appears as one continuously unfolding scene.

---

1. *Pirkei Avot* 2:1.

Yet this is not the real reason why we cannot perceive the renewal of creation. Rabbi Hayyim Volozhin asks this question in *Nefesh HaHayyim*,[2] and explains that we do not see this effect because it is transpiring in the root of creation, which is God's four-letter Name.

Our physical world is a reflection of what is transpiring in the higher, spiritual world. Just as the physical world is composed of four basic elements: fire, air, water, and earth, so that everything that exists is a mixture of these four components, so the spiritual forces behind these four elements are the four letters of Hashem's Name, *Yud-Kay-Vav-Kay*,[3] the "*Shem Havaya.*" Hashem is the source of all life, and the four letters of His Name are the four basic elements of all the spiritual worlds that were created by Him. They give life to everything.[4]

Now, not only does Hashem's Name gives existence to creation, it also accounts for its constant renewal. This is because the order of the letters of the Name changes from moment to moment. The four letters and the nine vowels (*kamatz, patah, tzere, segol, shva, holam, hirik, kubbutz,* and *shuruk*) can be arranged in a multitude of combinations. Some *siddurim* note which combination of letters of Hashem's Name applies to each month. Furthermore, not only does each month have its own combination of letters, but each week, day, hour, and second has its own combination, according to the special *tikun* (spiritual rectification) possible to do at that moment. There are kabbalistic principles that allow letters to be changed for others; or, letters can be "expanded" to reveal yet other, hidden letters.[5] Thus, the possible letter combinations that derive from God's Name are infinite.

2. *Nefesh HaHayyim, shaar* 1, chapter 2.

3. The letter *hay* in Hashem's Name is written here *kay*, to avoid spelling out the holy Name needlessly.

4. *Shaarei Kedushah*, part 1, *shaar* 1.

5. For instance, the letter *yud* can be spelled out *yud-vav-dalet,* thus revealing two additional letters.

Thus, each moment of existence has its own special significance unlike any other moment that will ever exist. The arrangement of the letters at any given moment represents the special and unique way that Hashem reveals Himself to the whole of creation at that particular time.

We may not see this happening, but some opinions hold that the great prophets were able to comprehend the changes in the various combinations of Hashem's Name at any given time, and they could therefore perceive the renewal of creation at each and every moment.

Why Ten Utterances?

The sages ask why Hashem needed to speak ten separate times when He could have created the whole world with one phrase: "Let there be a world."[6]

The kabbalists explain that the ten utterances signify Hashem's ten basic attributes, which are the ways He relates to us and reveals Himself to us. Like the letters of Hashem's Name, the attributes manifest themselves in infinite combinations, depending upon the person, the situation, or the time. This is a very deep concept, but basically, Hashem created the world in order to relate to us through it. For example, He relates to us through the attribute of *hesed*, loving kindness; through *din*, judgment; through *rahamim*, mercy, which is *hesed* and *din* combined, and so on.

When Hashem planned His creation, He knew how he wanted to relate to the world He was about to create. Since He wanted to relate to the world and rule over it with these ten attributes, He created the world within that same system of ten.

---

6. *Pirkei Avot* 2:1.

As human beings created in the Divine image, we too have the capacity to express these same ten attributes.

Three of the attributes relate to intellect: *hochmah*, *bina*, and *da'at*. *Hochmah* is the capacity to absorb knowledge; *bina* is the ability to understand that knowledge deeply; and *da'at* means knowing how to apply both knowledge and understanding. A person can be brilliant, yet not know how to say the right thing to the right person at the right time. That is a function of *da'at*.

In addition, we have another seven attributes through which we interact with the world. These are called "*middot*," or character traits. We are commanded by the Torah to model our *middot* after Hashem's: just as He is kind, so, too, we must be kind; just as He is merciful, so, too, we must be merciful, and so on.[7]

Rabbi Hayyim Vital asks a very deep question about this: Why isn't *middot* development included in the 613 commandments?[8] There is no commandment not to lose your temper or to be humble, though we know such things are important, as our sages tell us: "Insulting someone publicly is like spilling his blood";[9] "being arrogant pushes away the Divine Presence";[10] "losing one's temper is like worshiping idols."[11] There are many character traits that span a broad range of behavior, from negative traits, such as pride, anger, stinginess, and cruelty, to positive ones, such as humility, tranquility, generosity, and kindness. Our sages also tell us the great reward for developing good character traits and the terrible punishment for negative behavior. Why, then, are they not listed as *mitzvot*.

---

7. *Shabbat* 133a.
8. *Shaarei Kedushah*, part 1, *shaar* 2.
9. *Baba Metzia* 58b.
10. *Sotah* 5a.
11. *Shabbat* 105b.

The answer is that improving our behavior is included in the broader commandment to emulate Hashem.[12] The verse says that Hashem created man in His image. However, since Hashem has no physical form, a different type of resemblance must exist between man and his Creator. The answer is that we can "resemble" Hashem through our behavior. When we model our behavior after Hashem's and act in a Godly way, then we are His image.

The physical part of a human being is composed of the four basic elements mentioned above. These physical elements have a very rudimentary form of spiritual energy that enlivens them. This is called the *nefesh behamit* (animal soul) or the *nefesh yesodit* (basic soul). It's a very low form of spirituality, which, because of its attachment to the physical, is similar to that of animals. Nonetheless, it is a source of life.

Beyond that, we have the soul that is *helek Eloka mima'al*, a portion from Hashem above. This is the soul that Hashem breathed into Adam. Hashem made Adam's body out of dust of the earth and then breathed into him the Godly spirit.[13] It is, so to speak, a part of Hashem Himself, because, as the *Zohar* explains, when you blow, you blow from inside yourself.

When we say that a person has 248 limbs and 365 sinews, we are talking primarily about a person's spiritual form. The 248 spiritual limbs of the *neshamah* (soul) correspond to the 248 positive commandments we perform, and the soul's 365 spiritual sinews correspond to the 365 negative commandments that we avoid transgressing. Furthermore, these correspond to the number of limbs and sinews of the human body.

With every *mitzvah* we do, whether a positive or negative commandment, we open a channel to allow Hashem's *kedushah*

---

12. *Devarim* 11:22.
13. *Bereshit* 2:7.

(holiness) to flow into a particular limb or sinew – both physical and spiritual. In this way, we perfect ourselves and attain a higher level of *kedushah* by bringing the *Shechinah* into our lives.

In general, the *middot* stem from the *nefesh behamit*. A person can be very animalistic. However, with conscious effort and through *mitzvah* performance, we can uplift our actions until we fulfill our role as human beings.

Perfecting one's *middot* is the work of a lifetime. The Vilna Gaon draws insight on this topic from the verse: "My words are like the stormy rains and drops of dew...."[14] The Torah is compared to rain and dew, both of which cause plants to grow. However, what grows depends largely on what you plant. If you plant good things like wheat, barley, fruits and vegetables, the rain will make these things grow and goodness will increase in the world. But if you sow bad things like poisonous plants and weeds, that is what will grow.

The same holds true for Torah, says the Gaon. If you learn Torah, it will make you big. But in what it will make you big depends upon what you plant. If you plant seeds of good *middot*, Torah will make you a great *tzaddik*. If you don't work on your *middot*, Torah will make you big – but you will be a big monster.

It's frightening but true. Without working on our character traits, we can never improve.

Why Seven Days?

Ten signifies perfection and completion, the closing of a circle. Of our ten attributes, three correspond to the intellect, which is the link

---

14. *Devarim* 32:2.

between us and our Creator. These three attributes are beyond the limitation of time.

Our other attributes, the *middot*, are seven in number. Seven represents a system that operates within time, such as the natural world. Within the realm of nature, everything is bound by time. The number seven has special significance in Judaism. We have seven days of the week, seven years for the *shemittah* cycle, and forty-nine (seven times seven) days of the *omer*. All these cycles of seven connect to periods of time.

The creation of the universe was accomplished with ten utterances, corresponding to the ten attributes, which are the totality and perfection of the channels through which Hashem relates to us. We have these ten attributes within us as well, because we are also created in the Divine image. On the other hand, time, which relates to the lower worlds, is measured by seven.

The main purpose in Hashem's creating the world in seven days is to teach us the relevance of functioning within time. Time is the most important thing in the world. Time is everything. The nations say "time is money," but time is much more than money. Time is life itself. Every single tick of the watch is one more second of our life gone by. If we understood the value of time, we would know how to properly utilize every second of life Hashem gives us to do what we are expected to do. Hashem created the world in seven days to teach us that the way to bring the world to perfection and its final correction is through serving Him within the limits of time, according to the situation in each time, according to each individual and his personal situations and trials, according to the source of his soul.

Dividing Up Our Time

Each of us has a different *tikun*. Each of us has a different purpose in this world, and each one of us must perform that which he came to fulfill, utilizing his life and everything Hashem has given him – his talents, his wealth, his strengths.

When a person is born, it is already decided how long he will live. Hashem gives him a lifespan according to what he has to accomplish, and what he has to accomplish is reflected in what he lacks. It might be that a person's *neshamah* has already been in this world a few times and performed certain *mitzvot*, but it still lacks others, and it needs more time to complete itself. A new *neshamah* might need more time. Each person is given a lifespan long enough to attain completion. In fact, not only does one receive life and time, but enough intellect and capabilities necessary to do everything one must. As a person's life progresses, he will be given all he needs, including the financial support, to complete his mission.

Similarly, every generation has its own problems, and Hashem expects each generation to complete its unique mission. Hashem gives us the trials and tribulations and all the situations necessary for us in our times.

Sometimes we have tremendous opportunities to do *hesed*; sometimes we live in a time frame when the ultimate necessity would be to strengthen the study of Torah. We can see that the generations go according to the Divine plan and follow a pattern. Each generation is unique, just as each individual is unique. For example, the Sages say, "If you see a generation where people want to learn Torah, give yourself up to it.[15] Give your time, your money, your life. And if you see a generation where people are not interested in Torah, don't give." What does "don't give" mean? It means "*kanes*," go into yourself. There are certain generations when people work on their own perfection, striving to attain very high levels of spirituality, to

---

15. *Berachot* 63a.

come closer to Hashem. And there are certain generations where you're not allowed to do that. We have to give ourselves up to the mission.

The watch is ticking away, the seconds are passing by. Another second is going by, but where is it going? Every second of our existence is a speck of our spirituality, and not only of our spirituality but of all our mental and physical capability that we should have used at that moment for a particular service incumbent upon us – whether it was to study Torah, to pray, to do a *mitzvah*, to be nice to the people close to us, or whether it was to offer others good advice, to give a loan, help someone who is weak, or anything helpful you can imagine. Of one thing we can be sure: it was given to us to do good.

Just as the second hand sweeps across the face of a clock leaving numbers behind, so, too, with each passing second we leave behind some of our spirituality, our mind, and our physical strength. It is gone, but where did it go? It depends on what we did with it. If we did a *mitzvah*, the second goes to *Gan Eden* where it waits for us. If we did something wrong with that second, it goes down somewhere else, where it also waits for us.

Eventually, a person is going to discover how he divided up his life. He will look for his years, his weeks, his days, his hours, his minutes and his seconds. And he will find them. How many went up and how many went down?[16]

The kabbalists tell us that each person creates his own *Gan Eden* from the good deeds he does in this world.[17] Each and every good deed creates a spiritual force that goes up and waits for us. After 120 years, we come and receive that reward. And with each sin, we create

16. *Arvei Nahal, parashat Vayakhel.*
17. *Ruah Hayyim, mishnah 1.*

an accuser. A person is literally dividing himself up day by day, second by second.

The *Zohar* finds this concept alluded to in a verse:[18] "Avraham was old, coming with days." Literally, this verse doesn't make sense. Of course, if you're old in years, you're coming with days, because time-wise, many days add up to years.

Yet a person can live to a ripe old age but have done nothing with his life. He was given years, but what happened to his days? Were they full days that he utilized properly, or did he waste them?

Avraham was not only old in years, but when he came up to *Gan Eden*, he came with all his days. His days were perfect. His life was like a beautiful diamond necklace. Most people's necklaces are incomplete. Some days were wasted in idle pastimes or wrongdoing, others were only partially utilized as they should have been. The diamonds are missing or flawed. Such people will need to repair their necklace to bring it to perfection. Avraham, though, came up with all his days, each one a flawless diamond.

You can live many years, but that number has no significance. The question is, how long did you serve Hashem?

We have to know the value of time. Hashem has given us time. Hashem has given us life. Hashem has given us intelligence. Hashem has given us all sorts of talents. Hashem has given us power, wealth. Whatever Hashem has given us is supposed to be used to serve Him.

Life is holy. How is a person going to feel if, God forbid, he wasted his life? The hours went by, and he didn't achieve anything. This is what we have to understand. We are going to give an account. It is written that Hashem will ask us why we wasted time from Torah study

18. *Bereshit* 24:1.

even for the brief moment it takes to swallow our saliva.[19] We will have to answer for each moment.

Making a Tikun

This is life. We have to know how to relate to life according to the importance of what we can achieve. You take one second of life, of existence, you invest it with your intelligence, with your physical strength, with your talents, and you uplift it to spirituality and it becomes *netzah* – it exists forever. If you wasted it, it's gone forever.

Now, I hear people saying, "Why are you telling me this now? It's too late. Had I known this twenty or thirty years ago, I would have acted differently. But what can I do now to repair the damage I caused myself?" There is only one thing that can console us. We have a *mitzvah* called *teshuvah*.

Repentance is not an accurate translation for *teshuvah*; it has a much deeper meaning. *Teshuvah* means returning. When a person does *teshuvah* and returns to the way of Torah, he brings back with him all the lost seconds, hours, days, weeks, and months. He brings it all back. *Teshuvah* can correct everything, even the past, and bring it back and return it to its source perfected.

But how does this work? How can a moment used properly correct what we didn't do right ten minutes or ten years ago? Don't the repercussions of that moment belong to it alone?

Hashem is kind to us. If you regret the past with all your heart, Hashem considers it as if you served Him all your life. The good path which you are following now will change everything, even your past. This is the power of the *mitzvah* of *teshuvah*.

---

19. *Iyov* 7:19.

The *Gemara* says that "one who did not see *simhat bet hashoeva* never saw joy in his life."[20] The festival of Sukkot is a time of happiness, and the water-drawing event added even more joy. People danced and sang with great happiness. The *Gemara* tells us that the *tzaddikim* – people religious from birth – would declare, "Thank God our later years did not shame our youth. Just as we were righteous when we were young, so we are righteous when we are old. We are continuing on the right path. We started on the right track and didn't become lazy." The *baalei teshuvah* say, "Thank God that our later years have atoned for our youth." In conclusion, they all said together, "Happy is the person who never sinned."

Undoubtedly, it is best not to sin in the first place. No one should think that because a *baal teshuvah* is so precious in Hashem's eyes it might be better to sin and then repent. No, it is always better not to sin in the first place. When it comes to our children, we want to make sure they never sin. We want them to be totally righteous.

Teshuvah corrects what was done wrong. Without that, we have no *simhah*. What is there to be happy about in this world, if not the fact that we have the honor and the possibility of serving Hashem always – even in the moments we thought we had lost?

If a person does not realize the significance of what Hashem expects from him, life is meaningless. Hashem expects each of us to attain our ultimate level in serving Him. The more He has given us, the more He expects from us. When a baby makes his first sounds, his parents are thrilled. But when parents ask an older child what he learned in school, they would be very upset if he makes sounds like a baby. Similarly, Hashem expects more from a person who is capable of learning and understanding than from one who is not. If we don't learn, we are going to remain ignorant, and we will lose – our life, our

---

20. *Sukkah* 5:1.

time, ourselves. Moment by moment, our soul is going. Every second, part of it is gone. But where did it go?

That's the big question we have to ask ourselves.

Let us hope that our seconds will tick away with us moving in the right direction, and that Hashem will help us all to correct our ways, to change for the better. If Hashem has given us this golden opportunity called life, we must use it as a springboard to ascend. It's time to stop playing games and to get serious about our lives. If we do, Hashem will help us complete our designated task in a good way, happily and successfully. Eventually, we will arrive in the *Gan Eden* we created ourselves, with all our days sparkling like diamonds.

Elul

Elul Is Our Opportunity to Change

E ach wonderful day is a gift from our Creator, Who knows we will have to face Him on the days of judgment – Rosh Hashana and Yom Kippur. But because He loves us so much, He gives us a month to prepare, to mend our ways and improve ourselves.

To make the most out of these days of *teshuvah* (repentance), we must understand exactly what is involved. The first step in doing *teshuvah* is to truly regret any wrongs we have done. The second step is to commit ourselves not to repeat those same mistakes. This includes taking precautions to avoid situations conducive to making such mistakes. The third and main component of *teshuvah* is to confess our sins to Hashem.

To do all this, we must first admit to ourselves that we have sinned. The evil inclination works hard to get us to avoid admitting any wrongdoing on our part. We either ignore our wrong behavior or do our best to overlook it. If neither of those tactics works, we justify what we did – anything to avoid admitting we were wrong. Yet, as it says in *Mishle* (28:13), a person who tries to hide his sins will not succeed, while the person who admits his wrongdoings will be treated mercifully by Hashem. Before we can even begin to repent, we must admit to ourselves that we erred.

This brings us to a very basic point. The only way we can know that we erred is if we know the difference between right and wrong.

Knowing Right from Wrong

The *Shemoneh Esre* is divided into three basic sections. The first three blessings praise Hashem; the last three thank Him for listening to us and answering our prayers. The thirteen blessings between them are requests, the first of which is, "You have given us intelligence," by which we mean the wisdom of Torah, the knowledge of Torah, the depth of Torah and, ultimately, an understanding of the practical application of Torah. Before we can ask for anything else, we must have Torah, because without Torah, there is no way we can achieve our goal.

Without Torah, admitting our wrongdoing is impossible, because to recognize what is really right or wrong, we need the light of Torah. The Ramhal, Rabbi Moshe Hayyim Luzzatto, builds his famous book *Mesillat Yesharim* on Rabbi Pinhas ben Yair's nine-step guide on how to serve Hashem.[21] He explains how a person should ascend level by level – constantly improving and purifying himself – to become increasingly devoted to Hashem. The first stage in this upward progression is Torah, because only through Torah study can we reach the next level, which is "awareness." The only way to accurately assess our actions is by scrutinizing them according to the Torah's standards.

The story is told that once, the Vilna Gaon picked up a crust of bread from the table on Shabbat. He was about to eat it when he saw that it was moldy and inedible. Shocked that he had moved *muktzeh* on the holy day, he dropped the bread on the floor and fainted. Just then, his wife came into the room, saw the bread on the floor, understood what had happened, picked it up, and ate it. At that, the Gaon was revived. If the bread was still edible, it was not *muktzeh*, and he had committed no sin by moving it.[22]

---

21. *Avodah Zarah* 20b.
22. See *HaGaon*, vol. 1, pp. 215–216.

The more Torah a person knows, the more he realizes the severity of a sin, and the greater is his fear of transgressing it.

One *tzaddik* was so afraid of transgressing the detailed laws of Shabbat that his hands began to shake as Shabbat drew near. He trembled from the beginning of Shabbat to the end, just thinking of what he inadvertently might do wrong with his hands. Such a level is attained only through study. The more a person understands what Hashem expects of him and how seriously He relates to each action, the greater the person becomes. Most people are not on this high of a level. But someone like the Vilna Gaon, with his level of understanding, could faint at the thought that he had moved *muktzeh*.

This is the awareness we strive for, and without studying Torah, we can never attain it.

Climbing the Ladder

Following our request to Hashem for Torah wisdom, we ask Him to help us repent: "Return us, our Father, to Your Torah." The *mitzvah* of *teshuvah* begins with a request for Torah, because without knowing Torah, our repentance will be flawed. As our sages tell us, "An ignorant person cannot be pious."[23]

The blessing continues, "Bring us back, our King, to Your service." After we learn what we are supposed to do, we ask that we be drawn back into serving Hashem the right way.

The third stage of *teshuvah* is beyond this. After learning to come closer to Hashem, after becoming as perfect as we can in keeping *mitzvot*, we progress to total *teshuvah*. We ask Hashem: "And bring us back in perfect repentance before You." Having learned Torah, we already know what we have done wrong, and we truly regret it. Also,

---

23. *Pirkei Avot* 2:5.

we have corrected and improved our actions and deeds. Now we can bring our *mitzvah* of *teshuvah* to a higher, more spiritual plane. Through living a life of *teshuvah*, a person can literally wipe his slate clean. He can erase all the blemishes his sins caused, whether in himself, in his soul, or in the root of his soul, which exists in a higher spiritual world. This is the highest level of *teshuvah*.

Unfortunately, many people today want to start the process of repentance, which is called *teshuvah shelema* – "perfect *teshuvah*" – with this third and final stage. They go around looking for a *tikun*. They come to the *hachamim* and ask, "Should I say *Tehillim*? Should I immerse myself in an ice-cold *mikveh*? Should I sit on an anthill? What can I do? What suffering can I take upon myself?" But you cannot skip over any of the earlier levels to jump to a higher one. It's impossible.

When Yaakov Avinu, who represents all *bnei Torah*, set out from his parents' home to begin his life in the world, he had a dream. In the dream, Hashem showed him a ladder that stood on earth and extended into the higher worlds. The lesson to Yaakov – and to us – is that serving Hashem is like climbing a ladder: you have to take it one rung at a time to move from one level to the next. Furthermore, unless you realize where you are on the ladder, you can't climb to the next rung. Not admitting where we are – which includes realizing which areas need improvement – is our greatest mistake.

Someone once asked me, "Why do we have to verbalize our mistakes by reciting *vidui*? It's enough that we wholeheartedly regret what we did and take steps to avoid repeating the sins. What more do we need?"

I answered him, "Verbalizing one's sins is part of the *mitzvah* of *teshuvah*, and there's no getting around it. Take, for instance, *teshuvah* for speaking *lashon hara* (defamatory speech). While saying *vidui* for *lashon hara*, a person would have to think, 'I regret that I spoke *lashon hara*.' Secondly, he has to think as he recites it, 'I'm going to be careful not to speak *lashon hara* in the future.' He should further think, 'I'm friendly with So-and-so, but every time we meet he pulls me into this type of conversation. From now on, I'm going to avoid his company.' That would be full and perfect repentance."

Your heart and mouth have to be equal partners when you say this confession, as our sages tell us on the verse: "For the matter is very close to you, in your mouth and in your heart to do it."[24] The *mitzvah* of *teshuvah* is not somewhere "out there." "It is not in the heavens or across the seas."[25] We don't have to walk with the angels or go to the far ends of the earth to repent. "It is in your mouth" – by saying the *vidui*; and "in your heart" – by feeling sincere regret as you verbalize your sins and make plans to avoid such transgressions in the future.

Levels of Repentance

To what extent do we have to do *teshuvah*?

There is no limit.

We can understand this concept through a story about Rav Hai Gaon, one of the last *Geonim* in the era after that of the *Amoraim* and the Talmud, which places him even before the *Rishonim*. He was a leading *rosh yeshivah* in his generation and head of the academy at Pumbedita, Babylonia.

Once, Rav Hai Gaon arrived alone at a city where no one recognized him. He went to the synagogue and prayed *Minhah* with

---

24. *Devarim* 30:14.
25. *Eruvin* 54a.

the congregation. Afterward, one of the local people invited him home. Rav Hai Gaon accepted the offer. The host offered to carry one of the stranger's bags and led him to his house.

The host treated his guest with all the courtesy he would accord any visitor. He graciously served him a meal and gave him a comfortable place to sleep.

The next morning, people started streaming to the man's home. Word had gotten around that the leading Torah sage of the generation – Rav Hai Gaon himself – was in town. Ordinary people crowded outside to catch a glimpse of the great man. They were soon joined by yeshivah students, judges, rabbis, and sages.

When the host saw so many people outside his house, among them the most distinguished people in the city, it dawned on him that his guest was no ordinary traveler but none other than the Torah giant of that era.

The man was in shock. He fainted, regained consciousness, and promptly fainted again. When he finally came to, he apologized profusely to Rav Hai Gaon.

"Please forgive me," he begged. "I didn't know who you were. I thought you were just an ordinary guest. I had no idea you were the illustrious Rav Hai Gaon!"

From this experience, Rav Hai Gaon drew an important personal lesson, one that he taught others and that has been passed down through the generations. We are like that host. We have no idea of Hashem's greatness. The teshuvah we do today is not the same teshuvah we can do tomorrow. With the knowledge, appreciation, and depth that we have at this moment, we can express regret and make a commitment about future behavior. But tomorrow, we are going to be on a higher spiritual level. Our understanding of what it means to sin in Hashem's presence will be deeper.

It's like a foolish person who is caught running a red light.

"What's the big deal?" he asks the patrolman who stops him. He thinks it is a matter between him and the policeman. Okay, so this time he was caught; maybe next time he won't be.

But the patrolman writes a ticket, and that ticket will bring the matter to the courts. In court, the errant driver will have to face a judge, who represents the law of the land. At the top of this judicial pyramid is the Supreme Court. When the speeder thought he was in a game to outsmart the policeman, it was one thing; when he finds himself standing in court, the picture will look a lot different.

Teshuvah works the same way. At first, a person may think, "It's no big deal. I sinned against Hashem, and now I'll do *teshuvah*" – and he will do *teshuvah*, on his level. But the next day, it will suddenly hit him. "How could I have sinned against Hashem, the Creator of the world?" Yesterday's regret doesn't measure up to today's understanding. He repents all over again.

A week later, he's on a higher level. "Now," he tells himself, "I really understand how wrong it was to do that. How could I have sinned against Hashem, the Creator of the world, Master of the universe?" Looking back, his previous *teshuvah* nowhere near repented for the transgression as it now appears to him. Before, he had not felt enough anguish. Now, he feels deep regret and remorse at what he did.

Throughout life, says Rav Hai Gaon, we rise from one level of understanding to another. Whatever *teshuvah* you have done in the past is nothing compared to what you must do now, when you have a clearer appreciation of the One against Whom you sinned.

The Reckoning

One of the great rabbis had a custom to make a daily reckoning of his sins. He would do this in the presence of an elderly rabbi. Every night, the elderly rabbi would come and sit in his room for half an hour and listen to him enumerate the day's transgressions. The rabbi did this as part of a personal development program. Knowing he would have to confess his sins to another person would spur him to be more careful about his actions and would develop his humility as well.

There was nothing half-hearted about the way the rabbi fulfilled his resolution, either. He'd throw himself down, bang his head against the floor, beat his chest, and scream, "I've done this! I've done that!" He mentioned every transgression he had committed that day. Of course, the transgressions he was crying over were those of a person on his level. For instance, he might bemoan learning only twenty-nine *blatt* of *Gemara* that day instead of thirty, saying two words of the *Shemoneh Esre* without proper intention, or being unable to speak to someone when that person approached him. His regret was sincere. He felt he should have tried harder. These were the types of transgressions he confessed to, these very fine points he felt were mistakes for someone on his level.

One day, the elderly rabbi who used to come and listen to the confessions didn't arrive. Since the rabbi had made a resolution to confess his sins daily, he looked for someone to take the elderly rabbi's place. He went outside and found the night watchman standing guard in the freezing cold.

"Would you please do me a favor?" he asked the watchman. "All you need to do is come inside and sit in my room for half an hour. You'll drink something hot and rest awhile."

The burly watchman readily agreed, and followed the rabbi inside. All of a sudden, the rabbi fell to the floor. He started screaming and banging his head on the floor while confessing his terrible sins in a loud voice.

The watchman was shocked. After listening for a few minutes, he said, "Rabbi, take it easy. Believe me, I've sinned ten times more than you, and I don't feel like that."

On a more serious note, a contemporary example of this type of intense personal scrutiny can be found in the story told of Rabbi Moshe Feinstein, *ztz"l*. In his later years, Reb Moshe had a pacemaker inserted to regulate his heartbeat. The operation and the device caused him much pain and suffering. He made a spiritual reckoning, reviewing his life to see if he could pinpoint the need for this specific suffering. He wondered what he had done wrong with his heart, in his behavior toward his fellowman, to deserve this particular experience. He reviewed his life, going back year by year, until he reached his childhood. As a little boy in *heder*, he was always the first one to raise his hand and answer when the rebbe asked a question. He now realized this behavior contained an element of *hitnasut*, raising oneself up at the expense of one's fellowman.[26] By repeatedly showing that he knew the right answer when the other boys didn't, he gained honor for himself at their expense. That, Reb Moshe said, was why he was undergoing the suffering.

The message is simple: We can never finish the *mitzvah* of *teshuvah*. We have to live a life of *teshuvah*.

---

26. *Midrash Rabbah, Bereshit* 1:5.

Preparing for Rosh Hashana

On Rosh Hashana, the books of life and death, health, livelihood, and success – everything! – are open. At this time, Hashem decides, based on our actions of the previous year, what will happen to us in the coming year. The weeks preceding the Day of Judgment are filled with wonderful days of opportunity to put things right. How can we make maximum use of this time?

We are like prisoners in a dungeon, says Rabbeinu Yona.[27] As we sit in the dark confinement, some prisoners dig a tunnel and make their escape. Everyone runs away except one man.

When the jailers return and find him, they beat him, saying, "You fool! Why didn't you escape with the rest of them when you had the chance?"

Some people wonder why the one who didn't escape is taken to task. Maybe he should be rewarded for not running away. It depends on how you look at it. If you think jail is a place where bad people are sent to pay for their crimes, you're right. In that case, maybe the prisoner who stayed should be given a prize.

But we're talking about a different jail altogether. We're talking about being imprisoned by our evil inclination. In this sense, the whole world is a jail where we are continually drawn toward evil. And so, when a golden opportunity to run away from that situation presents itself, when we have a chance to run closer to Hashem, if we don't make use of the tunnel of escape – these days of opportunity – then the jailer is right to hit us for our stupidity.

---

27. *Shaarei Teshuvah, shaar* 1.

Hashem's Kindness

It says in *Tehillim*: "It is a kindness You do, Hashem, for You will pay a person according to his deeds."[28] What kind of a kindness is it to reward a person for his deeds? Isn't this just paying him what he deserves?

Say, for instance, you hire a painter to paint your house. He does the job, and you pay him the price you both agreed the job was worth. You are paying for the value of his labor, not doing him a favor. What's the kindness? You're only paying him what you owe him.

Similarly, what big kindness is Hashem doing when he pays us for work we did? Isn't He just giving us what we deserve?

The *Gemara* brings one answer to this question.[29] Usually Hashem judges the world according to His attribute of judgment. In this system, which is impartially fair but not lenient, Hashem rewards a person according to his actions. However, if Hashem sees that a person cannot stand up to this type of strict judgment, He turns to kindness. Instead of judging a person according to the strict letter of the law, He judges him more leniently, giving him more reward and less punishment than is due him. This, says the *Gemara*, is what is meant by Hashem's kindness. Hashem looks at our actions and pays us more for them than what they would be worth if judged against a higher, more impartial standard.

Since the Torah is a precious jewel with seventy facets, we can explain this concept of Hashem's kindness in another way. *Midrash Tanhuma* comments on the verse, "When you light the lights [of the Bet HaMikdash],"[30] that Hashem's command stemmed from His

---

28. *Tehillim* 62:13.
29. *Rosh Hashana* 17b.
30. *Bamidbar* 8:2.

desire to make the Torah greater and more wonderful.[31] Hashem said to Moshe, "Not because I need these lights – which are lights for human beings – did I ask you to light the lights in the *Bet HaMikdash*, but only to give you the merit of this *mitzvah*." As the source of all light in existence, Hashem has no need for light prepared for Him by human beings.

The *Midrash* continues: "When a person builds a home, he makes the windows narrow on the outside and wider on the inside." Nowadays we don't build like this, but such windows are common in old European castles. The narrow outer opening was to protect the occupants from attack, and the wider inner dimension was, as the *Midrash* tells us, to allow the light coming from outside to spread inward. In contrast, "When King Solomon built the Temple, he didn't build it that way." King Solomon did just the opposite: he made the windows broad on the outside and narrower on the inside. Why? "So that light would shine from within the Temple to the outside." The holy Temple, where the Divine Presence dwelt, was the source of light, and King Solomon wanted that light to spread from the Temple outward to illuminate the world. The *Midrash* then tells us that King Solomon made these special windows to teach us that Hashem is light itself and doesn't need any light human beings can offer Him.

We cannot bring Hashem any benefit through our actions. Hashem commanded us to light the Temple lights so that we could gain merit by doing His will. He created the world to impart His goodness to us. By obeying His commandments, we make ourselves capable of receiving His goodness and His kindness.

We can also learn this principle from what we know about the holy Ark. The Ark was carried by four Levites. An onlooker would see four people, two on each side with a pole on their shoulders. In the middle

---

31. *Behalotcha, siman 2.*

was the Ark, being held up by the two poles. However, we are told *ha'aron noseh et nosav*, "The Ark carries its bearers."[32] What we see is an illusion. We see the four Levites carrying the Ark, but the Ark is really carrying them.

We see this type of miracle even today. A brilliant businessman who was worth millions once said to me, "I don't understand it. There are so many expenses involved in maintaining a yeshivah, but there's no income. How can it exist?"

He's speaking like a businessman. He knows you have to watch the bottom line and ask the right questions: "What's your investment?" "How much is the overhead?" "How much do you pull in?"

"How can you run the yeshivah," he repeated, "if you don't pull in anything?"

"You're right," I said. "It doesn't make sense."

Every yeshivah has to depend on contributions from philanthropists kind enough to give charity to the organization. We imagine that they support the yeshivah, but the truth is that the yeshivah is supporting them. Hashem allows it to appear as if those who support Torah are carrying the yeshivot, but it's not so. The Torah is carrying not only itself, but them too.

This principle holds true for everything we do. Hashem created the world in such a way that anything spiritual carries itself. What we have is the opportunity to do the right thing in this world. If we do, Hashem rewards us as if we are controlling events. However, in truth, He is the source of light, and the Torah supports the world. Even evil is only an illusion.

In our generation, the world is running after all kinds of craziness. Hashem is presenting us with that test. But if a person really wants to

---

32. *Sotah* 35a.

do the right thing, if he wants to do Hashem's will, any spiritual action he takes will uplift him to the point where it is as if he is not doing it himself. He'll be carried along, almost like the holy Ark. The Torah itself will solve his problems, and he will reach tremendous heights in a way that cannot be logically explained.

When Pharaoh's daughter saw a basket carrying a baby floating on the Nile, she sent her *amah* to bring it. The word *amah* can mean a maidservant, in which we understand that she sent a maidservant to bring the basket to her. Alternatively, *amah* can mean arm. In this case, the meaning would be that she stretched out her arm. Moshe's basket was ten to fifteen feet away. What good would it do for her to reach out for it? No one's arm is that long.

The sages tell us that her arm miraculously extended all the way to the basket, enabling her to take it.[33]

We see similar miracles every day. When a person is involved in spiritual pursuits, he can reach far beyond his capabilities, both mental and physical. If we do the right thing, Hashem will help us.

One example is success in Torah study. *Torat Hashem temima... mahkimat peti,* "Hashem's Torah is perfect...and makes a stupid person wise."[34] Rabbi Hayyim Vital comments on the words *mahkimat peti,* "*yesh me'ayin,*"[35] which means "something from nothing." In other words, you don't need to be brilliant to become great in Torah. Even a dull mind will become extraordinarily sharp if a person makes a full effort. If you learn Torah in the right way, the Torah itself will build up your intelligence. Nothing else can do this.

There is no guarantee that someone who is highly intelligent is going to be successful in learning Torah. It is likewise true that you

---

33. *Ibid.* 12b.
34. *Tehillim* 19:8.
35. *Etz Hada'at Tov.*

don't necessarily need a high IQ. Sometimes brilliant graduates of top universities are not successful in learning Torah. Other times, *baalei teshuvah* who were failures in their previous life – drug addicts, dropouts – become outstanding Torah scholars. How is this possible? Hashem's Torah has the power to turn even a *peti*, someone who is stupid, into a wise man.

We can achieve nothing on our own other than the basic good intention to do Hashem's will. Beyond that, Hashem makes us successful and gives us the ability to do wonderful things.

The *teshuvah* movement is a good example of this success. Otherwise, it's hard to explain. Contemporary society lacks basic ethical and moral values. Lust for money and power, a breakdown of traditional standards, perverse lifestyles – it's a world gone crazy. In the midst of all this, you see people who leave it all for Torah. They give up a bad way of life to live a good spiritual life, and they succeed. It's unbelievable that people are willing to give up success, money, fame, prosperity, and all the supposedly good things in this world to live a very secluded life devoted to Torah study. Not only that, but we ourselves are bringing up children to live a life where they willingly give up these things – sports, entertainment, movies – to live just for Torah. How is it possible?

We can't explain it except to say, that's the power of Torah. Torah elevates. It pulls people up to a higher level where they willingly forsake those other things so they can lead a holy life.

This is the meaning of "It is a kindness You do, Hashem." Torah and *mitzvot* are the source of life and the light in our lives. Though it seems we are the ones making the effort, the truth is, the Torah is giving us everything. If we are stupid, the Torah will give us intelligence. If we are poor, Hashem will give us what we need. If we try to do something to serve Hashem, He will make a miracle, and it will come to be.

Then Hashem comes along at the end of the day and rewards us for our deeds. This is a big kindness, because actually we have done nothing. He did it all.

The Impact of Our Actions

Our every action has serious repercussions throughout the world. The familiar parable likens our situation to that of passengers in an ocean liner. Suddenly, they hear the sound of drilling. When they investigate, they find a man drilling a hole in the floor of his cabin.

"What are you doing?" they shout at him. "You're going to sink the ship!"

"What do you care about what I do in the privacy of my own cabin?" he replies. "It has nothing to do with you."

People sometimes think that whatever they do affects only themselves. However, according to *halachah*, all Jews are responsible for one another. The actions of each person influence the general situation of every other Jew and of all humanity. The Rambam says a person should always see the whole world as if it is hanging in the balance.[36] If he does a good deed, he tilts the scales to the side of merit and reward. If he does even one bad deed, he could bring the whole world to punishment and destruction.

The Netziv, Rabbi Naftali Tzvi Yehuda Berlin, once told his students, "When you study the *Gemara*, and one of you doesn't extend himself to his maximum capacity to understand a *Tosafot* but just studies it in a shallow, superficial way, he commits a grave sin." This in turn, said the Netziv, affects the whole world. At the far end of the scale, it could cause a totally assimilated Jew to fall one step lower and convert to Christianity. Between these two levels, thousands of

---

36. *Hilchot Teshuvah* 3, *halachah* 4 on *Kiddushin* 40b.

people will be pulled down one level. For example, a person who was studying Torah a full day will only study half a day. One who had a set study session will stop going to it and instead study at home. Someone who usually studied a little at home won't study at all. A person who prayed in a *minyan* will start praying by himself, while someone else, who usually prayed at home, won't pray at all. How did all this come about? Because one student in the Volozhin Yeshivah didn't learn a *Tosafot* well enough.

Everything we do has an effect on Jews everywhere.

In a letter, the Hazon Ish, Harav Avraham Yeshaya Karelitz, *ztz"l,* wrote about a situation when many new immigrants were arriving in Israel.[37] He was asked if yeshivah students could help outreach organizations in their work to get the newcomers into religious educational frameworks and so save them spiritually. Since there were not enough activists to do all the work, were the yeshivah *bachurim* allowed to leave the yeshivah for a week or month to help save these people?

The Hazon Ish forbade it. He explained that although each one of us is an individual, together we are like one body. "Those who are activists," said the Hazon Ish, "should go out and work with the people. They are the legs of the Jewish people. Others are the hands of the Jewish people. The yeshivah students are the brain of the Jewish people – and you're not allowed to take the brain to do the work of the legs."

Also, said the Hazon Ish, the activists who do all the running around should not think they are achieving anything. They are only successful thanks to the yeshivah students sitting and learning, because we are all one. If the brain is functioning properly, the rest of the body can carry on with its tasks; if there is no brain, though, nothing else can function either.

---

37. *Collected Letters of the Hazon Ish* 8, חלק חדש.

Everything is intertwined. If we learn Torah well, it purifies the air we breathe and makes the whole world a better place in which to live. The physical world is elevated through its connection with the spiritual world. One example of this is the field Avraham Avinu bought from Ephron. The Torah says, "Ephron's field went up."[38] Rashi explains that the field "left the possession of a commoner to become the possession of a king." The field became more spiritual.

Another example: At the time of the flood in Noah's era, water covered the earth to a depth of three *tefahim*, the width of three closed fists, obliterating everything. Why to that depth? Because the sins of the people who lived in the pre-flood era profaned and contaminated the earth to exactly that depth.

Inanimate objects can be affected by sin and elevated by *mitzvot*. A field can go up, and the ground can go down.

Another example: When Yaakov Avinu was about to take a stone on which to rest his head, all the stones fought for the privilege. The whole physical world seeks connection with the spiritual world so that the spiritual world can lift it up.

We see that actions have an effect on all creation, not only on human beings. If a person sins, the whole world can suffer because of him. On the other hand, if he does something good, he can bring good to the whole world.

Why Judge Us on Rosh Hashana?

Part of Hashem's kindness to us is making Rosh Hashana, which is the Day of Creation, the Day of Judgment.

On Rosh Hashana, all the people in the world pass before Hashem one by one, like sheep being led to pasture. This could have taken

---

38. *Bereshit* 23:17.

place on any day of the year. Why on the day when the world was created?

To understand this, we must ask another question: Why did Hashem create the world? Obviously, He lacked nothing, so what did creating the world add to the picture?

Let us imagine a very learned rabbi who is fluent in all parts of Torah. This rabbi sits and learns by himself and doesn't teach anyone. Is he any less great a rabbi? Is he any less knowledgeable? Of course not. He may not have fulfilled his obligation to pass on his Torah, but he is still a great rabbi who knows everything.

Similarly, Hashem is perfect in every form of perfection we can imagine, as well as those we can never imagine. He lacks nothing, and He did not have to create the world. However, Hashem had the desire to give of His perfection, and you cannot give unless there is a recipient. Hashem thus created the world so there would be someone to whom He could give. This is the purpose of Creation, as the Ramhal explains it from kabbalistic sources, including the *Zohar*.

While we cannot understand the full depth of this reason, we know that the ultimate perfection of goodness comes through giving. Being good within oneself is not the perfection of goodness. The perfection of goodness comes through being able to give. As it says, "You built a world of kindness."[39] The world was created so that Hashem could give His goodness and kindness to His created beings.

Every single day of the year, the forces that brought a specific day into being return. It is a yearly cycle. This means that Rosh Hashana, year after year, is the eternal day of kindness, the day of giving, the day of *hesed*. In order to judge with mercy and kindness, Hashem chose as the Day of Judgment this most wonderful day of the year, when the kindness of Creation came into being.

---

39. *Tehillim* 89:3.

Hashem's judgment is not cruel or vengeful. He does not say, "Aha! You didn't do my *mitzvot*, so now see what I'm going to do to you." Nothing like that, God forbid. Hashem created us so that He could give us wonderful, beautiful things. By "wonderful, beautiful things," we mean spirituality. This is the true reward in both this world and the next.

Our ability to sense and appreciate spirituality is very limited. In this world, the physical part of us is like a barrier blocking us from the spiritual. Studying Torah and doing *mitzvot* slowly purify and refine the physical until it becomes as spiritual as possible. In this way, a person can become very close to Hashem in this world, and much more so in the next. This is the kindness, the goodness for which Hashem created us.

Because He loves us so much, He chooses to judge us on the day of the year that is filled with the most mercy and kindness: Rosh Hashana.

It All Depends on Us

There is an even deeper idea, a kabbalistic idea and one mentioned by Rabbi Yonatan Eibeshitz: Once Hashem created human beings, He made everything conditional on their behavior.

The whole known universe today is only the lowest part of the lowest world. Beyond it, there are more spiritual realms, and beyond those, others. The vast universe, with all the planets, stars and galaxies, the ends of which scientists cannot see, is only the lowest part of the lowest world – the physical part of Creation.

Hashem created the entire universe, and He continues to sustain it. He keeps all these worlds alive, but He made them conditional on the actions of human beings. This means that when we act as we should, when we study Torah, pray, and do *mitzvot*, Hashem sends more and more life force into this world. When a person sins, God forbid, he causes Hashem's light to leave this world.

Rabbi Yehuda Hanasi tells us, "Know what is above you."[40] The Baal Shem Tov interprets this to mean, "Do you know what goes on upstairs? It's all because of you. You cause it."

Rabbi Meir said, "If you stop learning Torah, you will be faced with many reasons to stop."[41] If you stop today because of a football game, tomorrow you will stop because of a trip to the beach. A thousand and one distractions can stop you from learning Torah. This is the literal meaning of this phrase. However, Rabbi Hayyim of Volozhin, the chief disciple of the Vilna Gaon, explains it this way: "When you stop learning Torah, all the angels, all the higher worlds will cease to function and will become static. Only when we are active in serving Hashem are all the higher worlds actively performing their duties."

Our sages teach us that Hashem created the angels to praise Him. They have set times when they sing songs of praise to Him, and they can't start until we do. Once we begin, they get the green light to go ahead. In the opinion of most sages, they are like automatons – beings that have no freedom of choice. That is why it says, "I have given you" – a human being – "the power of movement among these standing ones."[42] The angels are the standing ones; they don't go up, and they don't go down.

When we do a *mitzvah*, you might say we start the ball rolling from our lower world upward and onward. The angels, who are, in a way, our emissaries, take our *mitzvot* up to Hashem and present them, saying, "Look at these wonderful *mitzvot* Your children have done."

---

40. *Pirkei Avot* 2:1.
41. *Ibid.* 4:12.
42. *Zecharia* 3:7.

Then Hashem, through them, sends down blessings into this world for all the good things, such as wisdom and spirituality.

Whatever we do has repercussions in the higher worlds. As it says in the *Zohar*, before performing a *mitzvah*, we should concentrate intently on what we are about to do and put our whole heart into it. This will arouse all the higher worlds to serve as conduits to bring our *mitzvot* up to Hashem and bring blessings down.

Rabbi Hayyim of Volozhin explains this idea in great depth. He asks, "Why does it say that a person is created *b'tzelem Elokim?*"[43] The literal meaning is seemingly that we are created in the image of God. However, we know that God has no image, so what does this expression mean?

He explains it like this: King David, when exiled and moving from place to place, likened himself to a migratory bird.[44] Does this mean he sprouted wings and grew a beak? Obviously not. He compared himself to a bird because his actions were similar to the actions of a bird. "Just as the bird migrates from place to place," he said, "so, too, I move around from place to place."

Similarly, when it says we were created in the image of God, it doesn't mean a physical image. It means that Hashem gives us the capacity to act and, in so doing, to emulate His attributes. In this way, we become similar to Him, so to speak. Just as He does acts of kindness, so can we do acts of kindness – and so on for each of His attributes.[45] We can form our character and develop ourselves according to His attributes and His actions. This is what it means to be created in Hashem's image. It is not a physical image but a spiritual concept.

---

43. *Nefesh HaHayyim*, beginning of *shaar* 1.
44. *Tehillim* 102:7.
45. *Shabbat* 133b.

Rabbi Hayyim of Volozhin then asks a question: "Why does it say we were created in the image of *Elokim?*" Hashem has many names, and this one refers to His attribute of *din*, strict judgment. Why were we created according to this attribute?

He explains this according to the *Shulhan Aruch*,[46] which says that when you say Hashem's Name *Elokim*, you must be conscious of the fact that Hashem is all-powerful, that He is the source of all power in the world and that He can do anything. Being created in this image of Hashem indicates that we have been given those powers. A human being is also powerful, and there is no end to the force of his actions.

Hashem created all the myriad spiritual and physical worlds, thousands upon thousands of them, and rules over them all with absolute power to create, destroy, and sustain. A human being is similarly all-powerful. These worlds were given into his hands. If he sins, God forbid, he can destroy all these worlds. If he does *mitzvot*, he brings more and more of Hashem's light, goodness, and blessing into our world. Through his actions, a person can uplift the whole of creation – or destroy it.

"If so," someone is bound to ask, "how can I ever right all the wrongs I have done in the past? Who knows how many people I harmed all over the world! We're told we should ask forgiveness during the days and hours preceding Rosh Hashana, but I don't even know whom I harmed. Who knows how much of the world I damaged and contaminated by my actions? Worse, you're telling me that my actions have an effect on the higher worlds, from the angels on up to the spiritual world that is the source of my soul! How can I ever fix it all?"

Rabbi Hayyim of Volozhin explains that when Titus desecrated and destroyed the Holy Temple, his actions affected only its physical

---

46. *Orah Hayyim* 4.

aspect.[47] As a gentile, his actions had no effect on the higher worlds. That is why the sages told him, "Don't think you have achieved anything. You ground flour that had already been ground."[48] Someone who grinds flour that was already ground hasn't achieved a thing. It started out as flour, and it ended up as flour.

If so, who did destroy the Temple?

The Jewish people. Their actions destroyed the spiritual force underlying the Temple. Only then could the physical entity, the wood and stones, crumble and fall. The ostensible cause could have been Titus or a different insignificant creature. It doesn't make a difference who did it in the end. The destruction was the outcome of our sins.

How are we going to put all this right? How can we purify all those blemishes we have made in the higher worlds and restore all the worlds our actions have destroyed?

The answer is through *teshuvah*. *Teshuvah* means not only to come back to Hashem, but to bring back with you all the "missing parts" that fell from the higher spiritual worlds into the depths of evil. The *mitzvah* of *teshuvah* causes all those "parts" to ascend to their proper place and become once again a part of the Divine chariot. *Teshuvah* is repentance on our part, but it is also the correction and perfection of all the higher spiritual worlds.[49]

"I Will Always Be There"

How did the system work before Hashem created human beings? It couldn't operate from below to above – there was no one below to initiate the process. It had to work the other way around – from

---

47. *Nefesh HaHayyim, shaar* 1:4.

48. Rashi, *Sanhedrin* 96b.

49. See the end of Chapter 4: *"Teshuvah*: The Battlefield of Our Heart."

above to below. Whatever Hashem willed came into being. The one and only time in the entire existence of the universe that everything came into being without first starting below in our world was the first Rosh Hashana, and this process repeats itself *every* Rosh Hashana.

On Rosh Hashana, instead of *everything depending on us* to make the first move, it comes down to us. Our job is to open ourselves to the spiritual outpouring from above at this time.

In the *Haftara* reading for *Shabbat Shuvah*, we find this verse: "I will be like dew to the Jewish people."[50] The Jewish people asked Hashem, "Come to us like rain," and Hashem answered, "I will come to you like the dew."[51] Isn't dew less than rain?

Rabbi Yonatan Eibeshitz explains it this way: The Jewish people asked Hashem to come to them like rain, which falls in abundance. Hashem responded, "If I come to you like rain, you will not benefit as much. I will come to you like dew."[52]

Rain falls from clouds in the sky, but its formation does not begin there. The sun's heat causes water on earth to evaporate into the atmosphere, where it forms rain clouds. Rain has its source down here in our world. If, for some reason, water on earth did not evaporate one year, there wouldn't be any clouds or rain. Hashem said, in effect, "You are asking Me to come to you like rain, but do you realize what that means? That means that I can never come to you unless you first send up what you have to send up, because that's how it is with rain. I'll come in a better way. I'll come like the dew. Dew doesn't depend on evaporation; it comes out of the earth, summer and winter. In other words, I will always be there for you."

This is what Hashem is saying to us. If I come to you as dew, I am

---

50. *Hoshea* 14:6.
51. *Ta'anit* 4a.
52. *Yaarot Devash* 1:1.

always there. It's not dependent on your actions toward Me. This is why we say this particular verse on the Shabbat between Rosh Hashana and Yom Kippur.

To avoid becoming overwhelmed by all we have to correct in ourselves, it's best to pick one small point on which to work. Once we have made a sincere resolution, it is considered as if done, and we can face Rosh Hashana. Then Hashem will treat us as true penitents, and He will reward us by helping us bring our resolution to fruition.

Teshuvah

The Battlefield of Our Heart

I n the days leading up to Yom Kippur, all of us would like to be able to set our sights more clearly on what Hashem expects of us. We can learn a lot from *parashat Ki Tetze*, which is read at this time of the year.

Many topics in the Torah of great depth are misunderstood by the average person. War is a prime example. The real war is not fought over land and territories, as many people think; it is fought within us. The spiritual battle between our good inclination and our evil inclination is what really determines the outcome of all battles in the physical world. As the prophet Yeshaya said, "It shall be on that day that Hashem will deal with the hosts of heaven in heaven and with the kings of the earth on the earth."[53] The day referred to is the great day of redemption. On that day, Hashem will eliminate the guardian angels of each of the seventy nations. Each nation has its own spiritual representative in the heavens, the source from which it derives its strength. Once these representatives are eliminated in the higher world, the outcome of the battle down here on earth is a foregone conclusion. Where is that spiritual battlefield? In our heart.

King Solomon tells us that "a wise man's heart is to the right, and a fool's heart is to the left."[54] What does that mean? Don't we all have our hearts more or less in the same place? It means that a person's

---

53. *Yeshaya* 24:21.
54. *Kohelet* 10:2.

yetzer hatov, his good inclination, is on the right side of his heart, while the *yetzer hara*, the evil inclination, is on the left. The wise person listens to the advice of his good inclination, while the fool acts according to his evil inclination.

If we overcome our evil inclination in the battlefield of our heart, we give tremendous strength to the Jewish people, and no one can harm us. Once we deprive the nations' spiritual forces of their power – as Yaakov did when he defeated Esav's guardian angel – we take away their ability to harm us.

The following first verses in *parashat Ki Tetze*, in their literal meaning, offer advice about how a Jewish soldier should behave in time of war:

> When you go out to wage war against your enemy, and Hashem lets him fall into your hands and you take captives, and you see there among the captives a good-looking woman, and you desire her and take her as a wife, you bring her into your home, and she should cut off her hair, and cut[55] her fingernails, and she should take off her garments of captivity, and she should sit in your house, crying for her parents, one month; then, if you would like to take her, you may marry her, and she will be your wife. However, if you decide not to marry her, you must send her off free; you're not allowed to sell her into slavery; you may not make use of her in any way, because you have caused her this suffering. [56]

The passage is familiar, and Rashi explains it. However, I'd like to expand on this according to the great kabbalist Rabbeinu Yitzhak Luria Ashkenazi, known as the Ari *z"l*.

The war spoken of here is the inner war between a person's good

---

55. Rabbi Eliezer, *Yevamot* 48a.

56. *Devarim* 21:10–14.

and evil inclinations. Our sages are telling us clearly that it's a constant battle.

"Against Your Enemy"

For our first insight, we must look at the original *lashon kodesh*. "Against your enemy" is a translation of *al oivecha*. The word *al* is used instead of the more common *im*. *Im* would translate as "going out to war *with* your enemy." *Al*, which means *upward*, implies that the real war is up above in heaven. It may appear that we are fighting forces on the ground, but we are actually battling the *sarim*, the guardian angels of our enemies, and the only way we can defeat them is with spiritual force. This verse is telling us that to win the war, we must battle what is *above* our physical enemies.

Who is our enemy? The *yetzer hara*, the evil inclination. We have no other real enemy except the *yetzer hara*. The *yetzer hara* wants to destroy us in this world and to rob us of our portion in the next. And he will never make peace with us under any condition.

So what strategy should we use? Taking it easy won't work. We may fall asleep on him, but he stays awake, constantly plotting ways to trap us and pull us down. Our sages call the *yetzer hara* "an old and stupid king." The Hafetz Hayyim wondered how they could call him stupid when he is constantly coming up with new tactics to pull us down. He answered that "a tradesman is called after his trade." Someone who deals with electricity is called an electrician; one who puts on a roof is called a roofer. The *yetzer hara's* trade is to make us stupid. That's his job, and he does it well. For this reason, he is called a stupid king.

Our sages say that a person would never sin unless a spirit of foolishness entered him, because if he had any sense, he would see that it's not worth his while to sin. If he sins, it can only be out of stupidity. Yet how can a person who may be brilliant in many areas suddenly become stupid? That's the *yetzer hara* at work. It made him stupid.

So, the advice is, don't let yourself fall asleep and don't wait for the *yetzer hara* to attack. You have to go out to fight him. That's why it says, "*When* you go out to wage war...." Not *if* you go out. You don't have an option. You won't win the war by waiting inside. Go out and fight. "A person should always arouse his good inclination to fight the evil inclination."[57] You have to be aggressive, alert, and awake, constantly attacking, not waiting for the evil inclination to attack you on your turf. Go out and fight him on his turf to make sure he doesn't get near you. Keep him far away from your home territory.

"You Take Captives"

Next we question why Hashem lets the enemy fall into our hands and be taken captive. Who wants him anyway? Wouldn't it be better to kill him and be done with it?

No. We need him, as we learn in the first paragraph of the *Shema*. We are commanded to love Hashem "*b'chol levavcha*," "with all our hearts." The Hebrew word for heart is *lev*; why *levavcha*? Our sages derive from the extra letter *bet* in *levavcha* that we should serve Hashem with both our inclinations, the good inclination and the bad.

We can understand how we should serve Hashem with our good inclination. But how can we serve Him with the bad?

The answer is that sometimes we need to harness our evil inclination to serve Hashem. For example, a person must always be humble and avoid all forms of arrogance, which he knows is damaging. However, the verse says: "Take pride in following

---

57. *Berachot* 2a.

Hashem's path."[58] Those who study Torah must take pride in being *bnei Torah*. Some people in yeshivah walk around broken and shy, looking ashamed. This is not the correct way. A *ben Torah* should take pride in having the merit to be a guardian of the Torah.

Pinhas serves as another example of how the evil inclination can be used in the service of Hashem. Pinhas killed Zimri, a great prince of the Jewish people, and the woman he was with by stabbing them with a spear. Taking a person's life is an expression of the evil inclination. But in this instance, the *yetzer hara* was controlled and used in Hashem's service, and Pinhas was rewarded by God for his action.

In the context above, what does "you take captives" mean? The Ari *z"l* explains that Hashem gave us freedom of choice. To do so, He had to create the whole system of good and evil in the world. He created evil forces for the sole purpose of being a stumbling block for us. The *Zohar* speaks of the *Sitra Ahra*, "the Other Side." This is the bad side, the side of *tumah*, impurity. Hashem created good and evil in the world, and He put us right in the middle. Our physicality feels a stronger pull to evil; our spiritual side is drawn more toward the good. This is the continuous battle a human being faces.

A *mitzvah* is always a *mitzvah* no matter who does it, and it always has spiritual repercussions in the higher worlds. However, the kabbalists tell us that if a sinner does a *mitzvah*, he feeds the *Sitra Ahra*. If a person doesn't repent for sins he has committed, and continues doing *mitzvot*, all his *mitzvot* go to the evil side. When a person finally does *teshuvah*, he "takes captives," i.e., he takes back from the *Sitra Ahra* all the *kedushah* generated by the *mitzvot* he did when he was a sinner, which was devoured by the forces of evil.[58a]

---

58. *II Divrei Hayamim* 17:6.

58a. This is not to imply that a sinner should not perform *mitzvot* lest he strengthen the *Sitra Ahra*. To the contrary, failure to perform the commandments is a far greater sin. Rather, one should learn from this how important it is to repent, and for one to

The forces of the *Sitra Ahra* feed off holiness, and they can capture any act of holiness that is not done in the proper way. If a person is not yet fully on the side of *kedushah*, even his *mitzvot* can become captured by the *Sitra Ahra*. When he does *teshuvah*, however, he brings back all these captured forces of holiness into the realm of *kedushah*.

What does it mean to do *teshuvah*, to return? To what do you return?

You return not only yourself to be close to Hashem, but you bring back to the side of holiness all that you damaged and caused to fall into the clutches of the evil side. Imagine a war between the king's forces and the enemy's forces. When you sinned, you were not faithful to the king. You worked for the enemy. Whenever the enemy forces defeated the king's forces, they took spoils. Now, when you realize you did something very wrong, you repent. You go back and fight that enemy. You defeat him and bring back all that was stolen from the king. With *teshuvah*, you bring back all that you destroyed and gave over to the forces of evil.

"You Bring Her into Your Home"

All of a sudden, having reached this stage, a person now sees "a good-looking woman." This refers to his soul. For the first time, he comes face to face with his soul, and he is overwhelmed by her beauty. All at once, he realizes the greatness of his soul and desires to subjugate his body to it. He wasn't aware of this before, but now he would like to stay close to his soul forever, so he brings her into his "home," his body. He has repented and reached the level where he

---

reflect on the need to repent before he studies Torah or performs a *mitzvah*. I have discussed this in my commentary, *Amudei Horaah*, to *Morah B'Etzba* (1:1) and in my work, *Haven B'Chochmah, siman* 4.

realizes that his soul is the main thing. He judges every action based on whether or not it will benefit or harm his soul.

When you care for someone, you want only the best for him, and that's how it should be with your soul. You must set aside time to think about what life is all about, to think seriously about important matters, to feel Hashem's closeness, and to realize what you've done wrong and how you must do *teshuvah* to put things right.

The first step is that the captive soul must cut off her hair. The Ari z"l explains this to mean that a person must change his outlook on life. His whole way of thinking must be transformed. Only then can the body be controlled. If a person really wants to control himself, his mind must become the stronger part of him. If a person is very superficial, the desires of his heart will lead him astray. But if he is strong, his mind will guide him, and his heart will follow suit. So the first thing a person must do is purify his mind by immersing it in Torah.

It says in the *Zohar* that a Jew, the Torah, and Hashem are one. How? Hashem is like a fire, so how can we even come close to Him? The answer is through immersing ourselves in His Torah, which is His word. To make ourselves a fitting receptacle for Torah and holiness, we have to purify our minds and change our way of thinking. We have to throw out of our minds all the bad thoughts and unclean things that have penetrated into our Holy of Holies. And, obviously, the more Torah that goes in, the more the bad things will go out.

"And Cut Her Fingernails"

The next step for our captive soul is to "cut her fingernails." Fingernails symbolize a person's tendency to reach out and grab what doesn't belong to him. Cutting the fingernails alludes to curbing this inclination and repairing any damage one might have caused. If you have harmed anyone or done something wrong in your life, you have to do *teshuvah* for those deeds. Though Hashem forgives us for our sins against Him, if we have harmed anyone financially or in any other way, we must ask that person for *mehila*. If we've stolen something, we have to give back what we took. If we don't put that right, Hashem won't forgive us, because the wrong took place between one human being and another, and must be corrected on that same level.

"She Should Take Off Her Garments of Captivity"

The soul must then "take off her garments of captivity." Rabbi Hayyim Vital writes that every soul has a spiritual garment.[59] We know that the body is like a garment to the soul, as it says, "Do not anoint the flesh of a man."[60] Why not just say "Do not anoint a man"? Why "the flesh" of a man. The wording implies that man himself is really the spiritual part of the human being. The flesh, the body, is an exterior shell, like a garment to the soul.

The body is divided up into 248 organs and 365 sinews. These correspond to the 248 and 365 spiritual organs and sinews of the soul. When you order a suit, the tailor takes measurements and sews the suit accordingly. So, too, when Hashem created the human form, He tailored it according to our soul. Each *mitzvah* we do has an organ that corresponds to that particular *mitzvah*. A person will not be spiritually and physically perfect unless he has fulfilled every *mitzvah* he can do.

---

59. *Shaarei Kedushah* 1:1.
60. *Shemot* 30:32.

Today, many *mitzvot* no longer pertain to us, but whatever we can do, we must do. The *mitzvot* which we cannot do physically can be fulfilled by learning the laws about how to do them. For instance, our sages say that one who studies about how to offer sacrifices is considered as if he actually offered a sacrifice.[61] This holds true for all the *mitzvot* we cannot fulfill in actuality. If we learn about them, Hashem regards it as if we fulfilled them.

When a person dies, he leaves behind his body, the physical part, the more exterior "overcoat," and rises to heaven with his more spiritual garment. This cloak, which you weave from the *mitzvot* you fulfill – because each *mitzvah* is like another thread, another button, another part of this beautiful cloak – is really each person's *Gan Eden*.

The soul itself cannot enter *Gan Eden* without this cloak, and this cloak is literally the personal *Gan Eden* of each individual. When a person sins, he is dirtying this garment and tearing it to shreds. He becomes clothed by unclean forces of the *klipah*, the *Sitra Ahra*. But when he does *teshuvah*, he pulls away from these evil forces. Then the soul takes off the unclean garments that were given to her by the *Sitra Ahra*, and she receives her own "*haluka d'rabbanan*," as our sages call it, a spiritual cloak woven by the Torah and *mitzvot* one does.[62]

"She Should Sit in Your House"

Then the soul will "sit in your house," which means your body, and cry over her father and mother. Her father is *HaKadosh Baruch Hu*, and her mother is *Knesset Yisrael*. The soul will cry over the sins she committed and all the wrong things she did. She will cry for

---

61. *Menahot* 100a.
62. See *Ruah Hayyim* 41, ‎כל ישראל יש להם חלק לעולם הבא.

causing so much suffering to our Father in heaven. She will cry for "one month." The Ari z"l says this month is the month of Elul, the month of *teshuvah*. This is the time when a person should set aside a few minutes a day to think about what he's done in the past, and to decide what he can do to improve and become better a better person. It is a time to cry for past wrongdoings.

We know that the letters of the world *Elul* stand for **ani leDodi veDodi li**, "I am for my Beloved (Hashem), and my Beloved is for me."[63] Note that we initiate the connection. Rabbi Hayyim of Volozhin, in his teaching for the month of Elul, speaks about a disagreement that's been going for two thousand years. Hashem says to us, "Come back in repentance to Me, and I'll come back to you,"[64] but we say, no, "You bring us back in *teshuvah*, and we'll come back."[65] Rabbi Hayyim concludes that it is time to end the argument. We've been stubborn for two thousand years, not accepting Hashem's will, let's agree to do it His way. If we start doing what we have to do in our own hearts, then it will all work out upstairs as well. And this is the message of Elul. Elul means "*Ani leDodi.*" I'm going to reach out to Hashem first. Then, "*veDodi li,*" Hashem will respond to me.

It's up to us.

"She Will Be Your Wife"

Once we've gone through these stages, the conclusion of the verse becomes understandable: "Then...you may marry her, and she will be your wife." If you've done *teshuvah* the right way, then your soul, with your body, will be together forever.

---

63. *Shir Hashirim* 6:3.
64. *Malachi* 3:7.
65. *Eicha* 5:21.

People always want to know what the difference is between *olam haba*, the World–to–Come, and *la'atid lavo*, the time of the resurrection of the dead.

When a person passes away today, in our times, the *neshamah* goes through a special hall of souls. There are many different levels, each progressively higher, and a soul that has fulfilled its mission on earth will have great reward, which means closeness to Hashem. As the *Zohar* says, it is *olam haba*; literally, the "coming world." It is coming, because it already exists.

On the other hand, *la'atid lavo* is when the dead will be resurrected. Then, each soul returns to its own body to receive eternal, everlasting reward, spiritually as well as physically. Just as the soul and the body were together in this world to fulfill the *mitzvot* and to pass tests, so they will be together in receiving the final reward, which comes after the resurrection of the dead. For this reason, this time is called *la'atid lavo*, "the future to come." As the Ramhal explains at the end of *Derech Hashem*, the reward experienced then will be on a much higher level, because even our physical side will be so greatly purified as to become almost spiritual. Body and soul will exist forever in a situation of unending reward.

This is the meaning of "then…you may marry her, and she will be your wife." If you've done *teshuvah* in this way, then your body and soul will be united, like a husband and wife. Your soul will be part of your body in the resurrection of the dead, like a husband and wife, who will be together when the dead are resurrected.

One Minute of Teshuvah

The *Gemara* tells us about Rabbi Elazar ben Durdaya who spent his life pursuing physical pleasure.[66] He went from one bad woman to the next, and that was his entire life. One day, a casual comment by one of these women brought him to realize that he was living his life the wrong way. He was overcome with remorse and wanted to repent. He sat down to ponder his fate and cried out for help. He first turned to the surrounding mountains and hilltops, then to heaven and earth, the sun and the moon, the stars and the constellations, and begged each in turn to seek mercy for him. They all replied that they were unable to do so. Finally, he realized that only he could seek mercy for himself.

At that moment of realization, Elazar ben Durdaya put his head down between his knees, and sobbed to the extent that his soul left his body. When he died, a heavenly voice proclaimed, "Rabbi Elazar bar Durdaya is welcomed into life in the next world!" The heavenly voice declared that he was now "Rabbi" Elazar bar Durdaya. He received *semichah* (rabbinical ordination) on the spot, and this was in the time of the Talmud, when such ordination was tremendously significant.

When Rabbi Yehuda Hanasi heard what happened, he cried and said, "Some people acquire their world [to–come] in just a minute!"

We learn from this story that even a person who lived his whole life in the most evil way, had his sincere repentance accepted by Hashem. He went straight up to *Gan Eden*, and was seated in a distinguished place along with the rabbis and the righteous people of the highest caliber.

Rabbi Hayyim Shmuelevitz, the Rosh Yeshivah of Mir, used to say, "Why did he get *semichah*?" You can only get *semichah* if you learn,

---

66. *Avodah Zarah* 17a.

and he didn't learn. He answers that Rabbi Elazar ben Durdaya taught us a fundamental principal of *teshuvah*, and this is enough to grant him *semichah*. He taught us that even if you did wrong, you can correct yourself – but only you can do it.

But why was Rabbi Yehuda Hanasi envious of Elazar bar Durdaya? Rabbeinu HaKadosh, as he is called, was the prince of Israel at the time, the greatest rabbi of his time. He wrote the *Mishnah*, he was a multi-millionaire who owned extensive property, and he lacked nothing. Yet the *Gemara* states that before he died, he lifted up both hands and said, "Master of the Universe, it is well known to You that I used my ten fingers to exert myself in the Torah, and I didn't take pleasure from this world even with my little finger." He didn't allow himself to benefit in any way from this world. In other words, everything he did was for Hashem.

The life of Rabbeinu Hakadosh was one chain of outstanding deeds. His father and grandparents were great rabbis who sent him to the best yeshivot where he rose to become the teacher of *Klal Yisrael*. How could he possibly be envious of Elazar ben Durdaya's one minute of *Yiddishkeit*?

Rabbeinu HaKadosh realized that though he had used every single moment of his life in the service of God, he had never attained Rabbi Elazar bar Durdaya's level of intensity. He had never used just one minute of his life with such complete depth of feeling and such regret of sin as did Rabbi Elazar bar Durdaya. And that's what he was envious of.

We see how important just one minute of our life is. If we're not alert, Yom Kippur can pass by just like that, leaving us wondering what we accomplished.

The Power of Teshuvah

The Torah tells us that after the destruction of the Temple and the exile of the Jewish people, after millennia of dispersal among the nations, at the end – in the times leading up to *Mashiah* – we will wake up and realize the truth. The *teshuvah* we are seeing in our time is the return alluded to.

The Torah goes on to say: "This *mitzvah* that I command you today is not beyond you, nor is it far away from you. It is not in the heavens above that you should say, 'Who will go up for us to the heavens and bring it down to us and teach it to us, that we should do it?' And it is not something across the sea that you should say, 'Who will go to the ends of the earth to bring it us and teach it to us, that we should do it?' For the Torah is very close to you, in your mouths and in your hearts to do it."[67]

A person comes to do *teshuvah* and feels overwhelmed. He says, "How can I possibly repair the damage I did in the higher world. What am I going to do? And who knows who I harmed down here in this world. Who knows what damage and destruction I caused! One person got an illness because of me, another went bankrupt, and that one has no children. What can I possibly do now?"

HaKadosh Baruch Hu tells us that this *mitzvah* – the *mitzvah* of *teshuvah* – is not beyond you, and it's not far away from you. You don't have to ascend to the heavens. True, when you sinned, you blemished the higher worlds, but you don't have to go up there to repair the damages.

Nor do you have to travel to the far corners of the earth. Not at all. It's very close to you. It's in your mouth and in your heart. The essence of *teshuvah* is *vidui*. All of Yom Kippur from beginning to end is one long *vidui*. In every prayer we say, we admit our sins to

---

67. *Devarim* 30:11–14.

Hashem. We do this verbally. According to the Rambam, the *mitzvah* of *teshuvah* is the *mitzvah* of *vidui*, no more and no less.

Obviously, when we say *vidui*, it can't be just lip service. You must feel sincere regret for the bad you did, and make a commitment never to sin again. With *teshuvah*, you can repair all the damage you did to the higher worlds, and all the damage you did in the four corners of the earth. How? By admitting your sin verbally by saying *vidui*, and by putting your heart into it when you regret the past and make a commitment for the future. *To do it* – just as when you sinned you didn't need to go up into any higher worlds or reach the ends of the earth for your transgression to have repercussions, you can repair the damage from right where you are.

On Yom Kippur, we say *vidui* ten times. Maybe we'll say it at least once with all our hearts, and really regret what we've done. We should at least try to understand what we're saying. We should know what each point means and think about each point, about how much we regret it and how hard we will try to avoid such actions in the future.

For example, consider, *"Viy'adnu atzmeinu lidvar aveira."* What does that mean? It means that we availed ourselves of the possibility of committing a sin. For example, if a person knows that a certain street contains a lot of immorality, but he decides to walk down that street, he's availing himself of the possibility of sinning. But if he says, "No, I'm never going to go that way. I can take a longer route. True, it will take me more time, but at least I won't have to go by the particular street where there's a lot of *pritzut* (immorality)." In making this decision, he is taking steps to avoid transgressing the prohibition of "availing himself of the possibility of committing a sin." So, a person must know what he's saying, and understand, and regret what he's done wrong, and put some thought into how to avoid getting into those situations again and sinning. Once you've committed yourself, it's considered *teshuvah*, though you haven't faced the test yet. You're still in *shul*, it's Yom Kippur, and you're saying *vidui* like an angel in heaven. Even so, Hashem will accept your promises – if your heart is with you.

Sukkot

Sukkot is the culmination of the judgment process begun on Rosh Hashana. On Rosh Hashana, the totally righteous and the totally evil have their judgments signed and sealed. Between these two absolutes, people who are neither one hundred percent righteous nor completely evil have their judgment finalized at *Neilah* on Yom Kippur.

Yet, as the *Zohar* explains, this is only the first signature. Just as an official document may require a second signature by a higher authority before it becomes valid, so too this document of judgment must be signed at a higher spiritual plane. The second signature occurs on Hoshana Rabba, which the *Zohar* calls the time of *mesirat hapitkim*, "handing in the notes," referring to the notes of judgment. Running the world according to what is written on those notes, which contain the judgment and decisions of the next year, begins on Simhat Torah, after the *Kedushah* of *Mussaf*.

The commentators ask why the process doesn't end at *Neilah* on Yom Kippur. By that point, we have reached a peak of *teshuvah*, and the gates of repentance are closed, as the word *Neilah*, which means, "locked," tells us. What is gained by waiting to finalize the judgment until the end of Sukkot? What can we possibly achieve in the realm of repentance during these days that we couldn't before? The mood of *teshuvah* changes after Yom Kippur, while the mood of Sukkot is one of joy and merriment, so how do we connect them with repentance?

The answer is that to be complete, our repentance must be motivated by both fear and love. Until Yom Kippur, our motivation is primarily awe of Hashem's Omnipotence and fear of the judgment we face. After Yom Kippur and until Simhat Torah, the driving force behind our sincere repentance is love for Hashem and a desire to draw closer to Him.

When a person's repentance is motivated by fear, his intentional sins are downgraded to the level of unintentional sins. However, when he returns to Hashem out of love, his sins are turned into credits in his favor. This is something we have to understand and contemplate. A person who sinned and then repented out of love is going to have his whole list of sins credited to him as if they were *mitzvot*. This is the highest level of *teshuvah*, *teshuvah m'ahava*, repentance motivated by love.

During the Ten Days of Repentance, the atmosphere is serious, and we feel the weight of judgment upon us. Through the study of *mussar* and contrite confession of our misdeeds, we work on ourselves, adding up the entries in our spiritual ledger. We go over what we did wrong, feel sincere regret for our sins, express this regret verbally, and take it upon ourselves not to repeat the wrongdoing. This is the essence of *teshuvah*, and it is how repentance driven by fear of punishment works.

To get a sense of what this really means, imagine a terrorist bursting through the door right now and saying, "Anyone who moves is going to be shot." Would anyone move? No. No one would move, because no one wants to be shot.

The Torah is speaking to us all the time, literally shouting at us, "Watch out! Someone who does this is doing wrong. He'll be punished." We know it, too, yet people still transgress. Why? Because we're lacking in *yirat Shamayim*, the reverent awe and fear of our Creator that would lead us to obey His laws.

Our problem is that the machine-gun-toting terrorist bursting through the door is more real to us than belief in reward and punishment. A kernel of skepticism in a person's heart keeps him from full belief in Divine justice in this world and the next. We need to work on ourselves to make our fear of heaven real.

Don't Expect a Plea Bargain

Sin has serious consequences, and our life depends on our understanding of this. It's reality, plain and simple. A person should never say to himself, "I'm not worried. Hashem will be lenient in my case. I'll make amends, and we'll make a deal, some sort of a compromise." Hashem expects the maximum from us, far more than we imagine ourselves capable of. Most of us use less than twenty percent of our potential – and don't even believe we have the other eighty percent.

Hashem expects the whole one hundred percent. That's why He created us. Yet a person can be so busy patting himself on the back that he misses the point. He congratulates himself on performing the basics. "I'm a good Jew," he says to himself. "I get up in the morning, wash my hands, and say *birkot hashahar*. I go to *shul* and pray, put on *tallit* and *tefillin*, make a blessing before and after I eat. Why, I even study Torah all day!" The Ramhal warns against this superficial approach. "Scrutinize your actions," he says. "Check to see if what you did was good or bad, and examine the good you did to see if there was no admixture of bad within it."[68]

Most of us are first-class actors. Our public behavior is usually better than our private actions. If someone learns Torah all day, he should compare the way he learns when he's alone, with how he learns when he knows he's being observed. When Rabbi Yohanan ben Zakai was on his deathbed and his students asked him for a blessing, he said, "Would that your fear of heaven be as great as your fear of flesh and blood."

---

68. *Mesillat Yesharim, Zehirut* 3.

We all know what Rabbi Yohanan ben Zakai meant. In public, when it's a question of making a good impression, people are on their best behavior. But in private, it's a different story.

It all boils down to *emunah*, belief. Our belief in Hashem must be so vivid that we know that *every* sin will be punished. This is the basis for repentance out of fear.

Repentance out of love is different. We fulfill the *mitzvot* out of a desire to do Hashem's will, out of love for Him, which brings us to *simhah*, happiness, the peak *mitzvah* fulfillment.

It's How You Do It

The kabbalists tell us that each *mitzvah* has five levels.

1. The first level is the action of the *mitzvah* itself.

2. The second level is the power of speech relating to that *mitzvah*, which divides into two sections: (a) learning the *halachot* of the *mitzvah*, and (b) saying a preliminary passage declaring your intention to perform the *mitzvah*. According to the kabbalists, when you do a *mitzvah*, you should say the relevant verse. For instance, if you see someone struggling with a suitcase, as you help him, you say, "*Azov ta'azov imo.*"[69] If you give charity, you say, "*Patoah tiftah et yadecha.*"[70] Doing the *mitzvah* should include activating the power of speech as it applies to that particular *mitzvah*.

3. The third level is *kavanat halev*, intention. You must realize that Hashem commanded you to do this, and that you are doing the *mitzvah* because He commanded you to do it.

---

69. *Shemot* 23:5.
70. *Devarim* 15:8.

4. The fourth level on this ascending scale is *mahshava*, thought. This is beyond what *halachah* demands, as explained by the *Shulhan Aruch*.[71]

According to *halachah*, even if we are distracted while performing a *mitzvah*, we are credited with having performed it (save for several exceptions). For example, if a person said to himself, "I am going to do this *mitzvah* because my Creator commanded me to do so," and then, as he started doing the *mitzvah*, his mind wandered, he still fulfilled the *mitzvah*.

According to the kabbalists, though, we have an obligation to think about the *mitzvah* as we do it. This is a step beyond intent. Thought brings a person to contemplate the reasons behind the *mitzvah* and to consider what he is achieving by doing that particular *mitzvah*.

According to *halachah*, we must have this full awareness while saying the first verse of the *Shema*. If our mind wanders, we haven't fulfilled the *mitzvah* of saying the *Shema*. The same applies to the first blessing of the *Shemoneh Esre*. The Bach[72] says intent must be present to properly fulfill the *mitzvot* of *tzitzit*, *tefillin*, and sitting in the *sukkah*, because the Torah specifically mentions the reason and intention behind these *mitzvot*.

5. The fifth and highest level in performing a *mitzvah* is, as the Ari *z"l* explains, with *simhah*, happiness. It's how you do a *mitzvah*. If you do a *mitzvah* like someone carrying a sack of potatoes on his back, the whole *mitzvah* is lacking. Your deed can be the most wonderful in the world, but without *simhah*, it's not complete

Imagine if the greatest Torah sage of our time would ask us to bring him a cup of tea. How happy we would be to have the privilege of serving him! We'd be telling the story for years to come. "He asked

---

71. *Shulhan Aruch* 60:4.

72. Rabbi Yoel Sirkis (1570-1641), author of the *halachic* commentary *Bayit Hadash*.

me for a cup of tea. I had the *zechut* to bring a cup of tea to the *gadol hador*." How would we feel? Unbelievably honored, uplifted and happy beyond bounds. Similarly, when we do a *mitzvah* with great happiness, it shows we realize the privilege we have in serving Hashem. Our *simhah* demonstrates our full belief that what we're doing is Hashem's will. We're so happy to have the opportunity to serve Him that we do the *mitzvah* with great enthusiasm.

We reach this peak on Sukkot. It's a festival filled with *mitzvot* and a time of rejoicing. On Sukkot, we are happy to serve Hashem and feel privileged to fulfill His commandments. This is complete *teshuvah m'ahava*, repentance out of love, which is the highest level of repentance.

Just Passing Through

At the time that the Temple still stood, the highlight of the Sukkot festival was *simhat bet hashoeva*, the water libation ceremony. The *hachamim* tell us that anyone who never saw this event never saw real rejoicing. When the *Gemara* talks about the ceremony, it says, "Praiseworthy is he who has not sinned, but he who has sinned should repent, and he will be forgiven."[73] We are all familiar with the *Gemara*'s teaching that "even the perfectly righteous cannot stand in the place where the penitent stands."[74] The simple meaning is that when a person repents, all his previous transgressions are transformed into *mitzvot*, which add enormous credit to his spiritual account.

When a person repents and says to himself, "If I had known, I never would have done it," he nullifies his deed, much the same way other transactions and vows are deemed invalid if the participant later reveals that he was not fully aware of all the facts. Following this

---

73. *Sukkah* 53a.
74. *Berachot* 34b.

sincere regret comes a strong desire to draw close to Hashem, to become beloved to Him through serving Him. The penitent feels boundless love for his Creator and takes great pleasure in doing His will. In response, "as water reflects the image of someone who looks into it,"[75] Hashem reflects the penitent's love back to him and draws him close.

Full happiness on Simhat Torah is only felt when a person completes the whole spiritual ascent that begins on Rosh Hashana. Some people think Simhat Torah is all about dancing, but that's missing the point. They're like a man who disappears from his home all year and doesn't visit his wife or family. He's no Rabbi Akiva, and he's certainly not in a yeshivah. Then, once a year, on his wedding anniversary, he comes home and makes a big party. "It's great to be home," he declares – before disappearing for another year. His happiness is superficial, and he has nothing to dance about. You only can dance on Simhat Torah if you worked the whole year, especially during the days leading up to the holiday.

Studying Torah connects us to life, as it says, "wisdom gives life to one who possesses it."[76] People who don't have Torah are like dead. Their whole way of life, with its worthless pursuits, reflects emptiness. On Simhat Torah, when we surrender ourselves totally to Torah, we realize how privileged we are to be Hashem's servants.

The four days between Yom Kippur and Sukkot have a unique dimension to them. Rabbeinu Tam used this time to write inspired poetry. The Ari z"l explains that during these days, when everyone is purified from the repentance they did and busy with mitzvot, people are on a higher level. These four days are so crammed with activity – building a sukkah, buying the four species, and all the other myriad details of getting reading for the holiday – that

---

75. *Mishle* 27:19.
76. *Kohelet* 7:12.

everyone is just too busy to do bad things. As soon as the holiday starts, though, people tend to relax their guard and to become caught up in transgression again. That's why the first day of Sukkot is called *rishon leheshbon avonot*, "the beginning of the new accounting period for sin."[77] Until then, the purity of Yom Kippur still holds sway.

The question is asked, why, out of all the *mitzvot* of the holiday, such as *lulav* and *etrog*, is the holiday named after the *sukkah*?

Our sages define the essence of the holiday as, "Leave your permanent dwelling, and sit in a temporary dwelling (*sukkah*)...."[78] The Tur explains that Sukkot is the time of harvest, when people reap the fruits of their labor. With the granaries full of wheat and other crops, a person feels strong, powerful, and wealthy. This type of test is spoken of in the verse: "Yeshurun became fat and kicked."[79] Even an upright person runs the risk of becoming filled with pride at the thought of his own success. If he's not careful, he can imagine himself to be a self-made man who doesn't need Hashem anymore. The granaries are full because he's a smart businessman. He knows how to wheel and deal, he knows when to raise prices and when to lower them, and whatever he has achieved is due to his own talents. The Torah comes along and tells us, "Leave your permanent dwelling." It is not yours to begin with. Your home and everything you have is a gift from Hashem. There are people who are smarter than you, better businessmen than you, stronger than you, better looking than you, and they have nothing to eat. Moreover, there are people who are not as smart as you and far less talented, and yet they're multi-millionaires.

---

77. *Vayikra Rabbah* 30:7.
78. *Sukkah* 2a.
79. *Devarim* 32:15.

King David states it clearly: Hashem "raises the poor from the dust and lifts the needy from the garbage dumps."[80] It's no problem for Him. He can lift someone from the gutter and make him into a huge success, or topple a man from the pinnacle of power. We have to know that everything we achieve is from Hashem. How does the Torah want us to come to this realization? By leaving our homes for the *sukkah*. In our home, we feel secure. A *sukkah*, no matter how beautiful and comfortable we make it, is obviously a temporary residence. This is to stress the point that the world we live in is also only a temporary residence. We are just passing through on our way to the next world. It doesn't pay to feel too established in this world or to be too involved in worldly matters.

An American who visited the Hafetz Hayyim in Radin was shocked at what he saw. No rugs, no pictures on the wall, only a wooden table and chairs – how could the leader of the generation live in such poverty?

"Where is all your furniture?" the guest asked in shock.

"Where is yours?" his host asked in reply.

Puzzled at the question, the visitor answered, "I'm just passing through. I don't live here."

To which the Hafetz Hayyim responded, "I, too, am just passing through."

His answer has become famous because it succinctly sums up the attitude we should have. We are here for a purpose. To fulfill our purpose, we are given certain tools. Everything we have is given to us by Hashem to help us fulfill our purpose in life, not to "become fat." This is the lesson of Sukkot.

---

80. *Tehillim* 113:7.

Know Your Potential

People think the physical and spiritual realms are totally separate. This is how some other religions see things. If you want to become a priest, you can't get married. The Torah doesn't teach that. A person only becomes complete, spiritually as well, when he marries. Before he marries, he is only half of a whole. With marriage, he becomes complete and achieves sanctity.

This is the exact opposite of the worldview that a man-woman relationship is inherently less spiritual, as Aristotle claimed. The Rambam, in *Moreh Nevuchim*, more or less followed the philosophy of Aristotle on this point. The Ramban wrote a whole epistle, "*Iggeret HaRamban*," disagreeing with the Rambam to prove that the Torah's approach is the exact opposite. There is sanctity in the physical world. We take something which you cannot conceive of as a *mitzvah*, and we make it holy. That's the whole idea.

The Vilna Gaon and the kabbalists discovered deep meaning in the *gematria* of the word *sukkah*: *samech-vav-kaf-hay*. The letter *vav* equals 6 and *kaf* equals 20; together they add up to 26, which is the *gematria* of *Yud-Kay-Vav-Kay*. This is the *Shem Havaya* – the Name that represents God's utter transcendence of the physical world. *Samech* equals 60 and *hay* equals 5; together they add up to 65, the *gematria* of *aleph-dalet-nun-yud*, A-do-nai,[81] which is the Name that represents God's Presence within the world. Both these names come together in the *sukkah*, which symbolizes the perfect synthesis of the spiritual and mundane.

The *sukkah* not only teaches us that this world is a temporary residence and that everything is from Hashem, it teaches us that whatever Hashem gives us in the physical world – including all our wealth and success – is not meant to remain as it is. We are here to uplift it into a higher realm.

What is a *sukkah*? The *Zohar* says the *sukkah* is a holy place, like a

---

81. We caution the reader not to read this sacred Name aloud.

mini-sanctuary ("רזא דמהמנותא").[82] The *halachot* of what you can and can't do in a *sukkah* are similar to those of a synagogue, with certain exceptions to allow for normal life. A husband and wife can live together in a *sukkah*, and it is permitted to eat in a *sukkah*. On the other hand, you can't bring a pot of food into the *sukkah*. It's not respectful of the *sukkah's* sanctity to bring that type of utensil into it, so you bring food in on a serving platter. When you're in the *sukkah*, you are literally under the Clouds of Glory. We don't see them, but there are many things we don't see. We don't see the spiritual world, but it's there.

On the first day of Sukkot, Avraham Avinu is our guest; on the second day, Yitzchak Avinu; on the third day, Yaakov Avinu. Each of the seven days is honored by the presence of one of the *ushpizin*. The *Zohar* says that when we make a *brit milah*, we must declare, "This is the chair of Eliyahu...." Otherwise, he won't come. The sages learn from this that the same holds true for inviting the *ushpizin* to the *sukkah*. We must prepare a special chair and say, "This is the chair of Avraham Avinu," or "This is the chair of the *ushpizin*." There we are, sitting in the *sukkah*, surrounded by the Divine Presence with Avraham Avinu as our guest! It's unbelievable! This is the whole idea of, "Just as the Name of Heaven rests on the sacrifice of the holiday, so does the Name of Heaven rest on the *sukkah*."[83]

What is a *sukkah*? The essence of a *sukkah* is the *schach* with which we cover it. And what is *schach*? Nothing more than leaves, branches, or palm fronds, the most readily found material in the world. Yet these leaves become sanctified through their use in the *sukkah*. They are now elevated to a higher level and must be treated with the respect due them. It is forbidden, for example, to tread on them after the holiday; instead, we save them for use in baking *matzot* on *erev Pesah*.

---

82. *Zohar* 103.
83. *Sukkah* 9a.

The message of the *sukkah* is clear. Hashem is telling us, "Use everything I give you to serve Me." Wealth is for increased service of Hashem through supporting Torah and giving charity. Our minds are to be used for Torah; our strength, for studying harder and doing *mitzvot*. Whatever we do must be done in the most elevated way possible. We have to transform and raise the physical into the spiritual realm.

"The Name of Heaven rests on the *sukkah*." The Torah is saying to us, "Look what you can do. With a few leaves and branches, you can make a mini-sanctuary, an abode for the Divine Presence. All it takes is a few leaves." Know your potential as a Jew. The *sukkah* teaches us what our whole approach to life must be.

You're the Boss

What about the person inside the *sukkah*? It's not enough to have the right approach; a person must work on himself and strive to improve. The *mitzvot*, done with love for Hashem and great joy, point him in the right direction. On Sukkot, we are told to take four species: the *etrog* (citron), *lulav* (palm branch), *hadassim* (myrtle leaves) and *aravot* (willow branches). Our sages say the *etrog* resembles the heart; the *lulav*, the spine (and, according to the kabbalists, the *brit kodesh*); the *hadassim*, the eyes; and the *aravot*, the lips.

On the first day of the holiday, new ledgers are opened for us. On their blank pages, any new sins and transgressions we commit will be written. To keep a clean slate, we need a guaranteed way to make sure we don't stumble. The four species tell us: Take charge of your heart, and control your eyes, your lips, and your sanctity. Walk straight, like the *lulav*, and don't be crooked. If you take these things in hand on the first day of the holiday, you are going to be the boss. You'll be in charge of yourself and in charge of your life. Everything will be under control, if you take control from the beginning. Why? Because "sin crouches at the door."[84] The evil inclination lurks at the threshold, waiting to trip us up right at the beginning. He knows that if he can gain control at the outset, he'll be the boss. However, if we take charge from the beginning, we will be in charge forever. That's why the *Zohar* comments on the commandment, "Take for yourselves on the first day....":[85] Make sure to take hold of your heart and take charge of your eyes on the very first day. Know what is permitted to you and what your desire should be for. Your heart should be full of desire for greatness in Torah and serving Hashem.

Take for yourselves...myrtle leaves.... Watch your eyes. Watch where you look.

Take for yourselves...willow branches.... Watch what you say and what you eat. If a person wants to succeed in Torah study, he must first be careful about what he eats and, even more so, what he says.[86] Rabbi Shimon bar Yohai said, "If it were up to me, I would say a person should have two mouths, one for mundane tasks like talking about business, eating and drinking, and another mouth especially for words of Torah and prayer."[87] Hashem gave us only one mouth, however, because He wants us to learn to control ourselves.

Take for yourselves...a palm branch.... If you're spineless, you have no character. If you're honest and ethical, you are considered to have a strong backbone.

A businessman once asked Rabbi Yehezkel Abramsky, *av bet din*

---

84. *Bereshit* 4:7.
85. *Vayikra* 23:40.
86. *Tosafot, Ketubot* 104a.
87. *Yerushalmi Berachot* 8a.

of London, whether a certain shady business deal he was considering was permissible or forbidden.

Rabbi Abramsky understood that the businessman was interested in making the deal, as long as he would not be transgressing *halachah*.

Rabbi Abramsky looked into the *Shulhan Aruch* and then said, "I can't say it's forbidden, but I wouldn't do it."

The man was surprised. "I don't understand," he said. "If it's not forbidden according to *halachah*, why wouldn't you do it?"

To this Rabbi Abramsky replied, "When you do crooked things, your mind becomes crooked. There's no way to act crooked and keep your mind straight. If my mind were to become crooked and warped, God forbid, then my Torah would be warped, and my *shiurim* would be warped. So I certainly wouldn't do it."

This is the whole idea of the *lulav*.

Our sages also tell us that the four species represent four types of people. Some people are like an *etrog*: they have both flavor, symbolic of Torah, and fragrance, symbolic of *mitzvot*. Others are compared to the *lulav*, which has flavor from its fruit, the date, but no fragrance; these people learn a lot of Torah but their *mitzvot* fall short of their learning. The third group of people is likened to *hadassim*, which are fragrant but have no flavor, for they have no edible part; these people do much but don't learn enough. The fourth group is like *aravot*, which lack both flavor and fragrance. These people have neither Torah nor *mitzvot*.

These four types of people are found in the Jewish population in direct proportion to the quantity and value of their comparable species. Of the four species, the *etrog* is the most expensive. If there were more people with both taste and fragrance, we would have more *etrogim* in the marketplace. Next in price is the *lulav*, followed by the *hadassim*. The *aravot* are cheap. Why? Because most people, unfortunately, fall into the "no taste, no fragrance" category. That's why there are plenty of *aravot* on the market. Exceptional people with both taste and fragrance are rare.

A World of Hesed

Yom Kippur's influence continues to flow over the days between Yom Kippur and Sukkot. The spiritual progression is from repentance out of fear to repentance out of love.

Then we have Sukkot, which gives us the proper Jewish outlook on life, that it is not due to our own strengths or talents that we have achieved what we have, but that everything is from Hashem. We have to keep in mind that this world is only a temporary dwelling for us, and that our job is to uplift the physical-material to the spiritual level. The message of the *sukkah* is that twigs and leaves can have the highest spiritual value, and so, too, can a true penitent transform himself from being despised by his Creator to being loved and exalted – even to become a chariot for the Divine Presence to rest upon, just as the Divine Presence rests on a *sukkah* and the *schach*. Then we have the four species to teach us how to work on ourselves, especially our character improvement.

Hashem wants us to do *hesed*, so a person must develop his ability to give – both materially and spiritually. For instance, you can study with someone who is weak in learning and uplift him, or talk to someone who is depressed to cheer him up. Sukkot is a time of *hesed*. The *hesed* culminates in Simhat Torah, which is the peak of what we want to attain: the realization that the only life we have in this world is Torah.

Hanukah

When Yaakov left Lavan, as we find in *parashat Vayishlah*, which we read just before Hanukah, he sent angels ahead of him to meet his brother Esav. They bore a message explaining his twenty-two year absence.

"Tell Esav in my name," Yaakov instructed the angels, "that I have been dwelling (*garti*) with Lavan until now…"[88] Rashi comments that the *gematria* of the word *garti* is 613, "As if to say, 'Although I [Yaakov] lived with the evil Lavan, even so, I kept all six hundred and thirteen *mitzvot*.'"

Rashi's comment, though, does not end there. He continues: "…and I didn't learn from his evil ways." This is surprising. We know that Rashi wrote very concisely, with every word carefully chosen, yet this phrase seems to add nothing new to the previous thought. If you say, "I lived with Lavan, who is a notorious evildoer, and even so, I kept all six hundred and thirteen commandments," then it certainly follows that you didn't learn from his evil ways. Of course you didn't if you kept the commandments!

The second part of Rashi's explanation points to a deep message conveyed to us by Yaakov Avinu: a person can keep all the *mitzvot*, even study Torah, yet still be influenced by the non-Jewish culture around him. Yaakov was really warning future generations: If you aren't careful, you will incorporate into your way of life their customs, their mannerisms, their behavior, the way they speak, the way they sit, the way they stand, the way they walk, play and enjoy life –

---

88. *Bereshit* 32:5.

everything. You may eat kosher, put on *tefillin*, pray with a *minyan* and fulfill all the six hundred and thirteen commandments, yet still learn from their bad ways. The danger is real, and it is the path to assimilation. Yaakov wanted to make it clear to each and every Jew who followed him that he kept the six hundred and thirteen commandments not just nominally, but fully. He was not influenced by Lavan in the slightest, not by the way he thought, nor by the way he acted.

People assume that the danger of straying from Judaism lies in not being Torah and *mitzvah* observant. We congratulate ourselves on doing *mitzvot* and feel that as long as we continue to do so, we're fine. From Yaakov's statement, though, we learn that even if we keep the *mitzvot* but lack the right thoughts and feelings, we can become lost.

If we go through the motions of living a Jewish life without knowing why, our *mitzvot* lack their full value. It's a sign that we already have been influenced by the surrounding culture. This should not surprise us. Anyone who has had the privilege of observing *hachamim* has surely noticed their humility, their manner of speech, their consideration for others, their kindness and love – all the unique and exemplary qualities of a Jew. It is all too easy to absorb the mannerisms – the vulgarity, the cheapness, the rudeness, and the lack of morality – of the surrounding culture. Yaakov was telling us, "Though I lived with Lavan, I stayed deeply Jewish in every way."

Staying Jewish

In the Egyptian exile, our forefathers were on the verge of assimilating. Even so, they did not change their language, their names, or their style of dress.[89]

---

89. *Vayikra Rabbah* 32:5.

Jewish names have an influence. If the name is a good one, it brings the child good fortune. If you name a child after a film star or a famous baseball player, it does nothing for him; if you name the child after Moshe Rabbeinu or Avraham Avinu, the name itself will have a good influence. The same is true if you name a child after a righteous grandparent.

Nowhere among the six hundred and thirteen *mitzvot* is there a commandment to use only Jewish names or to speak only Hebrew, yet it is to our ancestors' eternal credit that they clung to these practices during the harsh Egyptian exile.

As for dress, the Torah says, "Do not follow their traditions,"[90] which teaches us that we should dress a little differently from the nations of the world. Fashion was a big problem then, and it's a big problem now. Once a year, some degenerate in Paris decides what's "in." Ties have to be narrow, belts wide, pants need five pleats, and shoes must have pointy toes. Everyone throws away last year's clothes and races to get the latest fashions. Next year, the man in Paris changes direction. Now ties have to be wide, belts narrow, pants need three pleats and shoes have a square toe. The public rushes to throw away yesterday's fashions to buy the latest. It's crazy, but that's what people do – and it's a very bad influence on us. We are not supposed to follow gentile fashions. Maybe we can fight the trend and keep the *mitzvah* by wearing last year's fashions. We can be one year behind just to be different.

The Greek Agenda

What did the Greeks want from us?

There is a difference between Purim and Hanukah. On Purim, it is

---

90. *Vayikra* 18:3.

a *mitzvah* to enjoy a festive meal, and drink to the point of inebriation. On Hanukah, however, there is no *mitzvah* to make a festive meal, and wine is not part of the commemoration.[91] Why not?

Haman wanted to kill us physically. Men, women, children – it didn't make a difference to him. He wanted to annihilate all the Jews. Since he wanted to destroy us physically, we commemorate the Purim miracle of our salvation physically, by making a feast.

The Greeks, on the other hand, didn't want to kill us; they wanted us to assimilate. They wanted to cool down our religious fervor. They wanted us to study their philosophies and indulge in their sports. Until this day, Greek philosophers are studied in the halls of academia, and the Olympic games, started by the Greeks, are a regular event. The Greeks wanted us to be like them, not a holy nation that believes in a spiritual dimension to existence. "Keep everything down to earth," they said. "What you see, exists; what you don't see, doesn't exist. Be scientific, logical, and academic. Don't get involved in all those deep spiritual concepts like the Divine Presence. Don't think that by doing *mitzvot*, you become holy and your homes become holy. Don't believe the Sabbath is a holy day, and all the other days are mundane. Don't believe that certain times of the year, like the first of the month and the festivals, are unique. Don't believe that any success that comes your way is from God.

"Life isn't like that," the Greeks claimed. "If you're smart, and you work hard, you'll make money. Then, find a girl you like, marry her and enjoy life. It has nothing to do with sanctity or connecting to the Creator. Why all these silly restrictions on pleasure. They make no sense. If you Jews believe all that stuff, you're behind the times."

Had we agreed to assimilate into Hellenist society and culture, the Greeks would have left us alone. "Go ahead and run your country,"

91. The *Levush* on *Orah Hayyim* 670:2.

they would have said. "You can be in charge. We'll just leave a few soldiers here and there to make sure you don't rebel. Pay your taxes once a year, and you can live in peace. You can even keep *mitzvot* or learn Torah as long as you keep spirituality out of it. We don't like all those supernatural things.

"As far as we are concerned," said the Greeks, "your Torah is a beautiful book of historical and cultural value, just like the history books of other nations. We shall recommend that it be translated into the Greek language. It will become a best-seller. But just take it at face value and leave out the spirituality. The same goes for *mitzvot*. They should be seen as nice Jewish customs, just like the customs and folklore of other nations, nothing more. What we are against is the spiritual interpretation which you apply to those customs. Do away with all those abstract concepts, and your religion becomes logical and acceptable to us."

The Romans expressed similar objections. The wicked Turnus Rufus, a Roman general, once asked Rabbi Akiva, "What is the difference between one day and the next?"[92] The implication was that there is no difference; all days are alike. The sun rises and the sun sets, and that's it, so how can you claim that Shabbat and holidays are holier than other days?

Turnus Rufus was trying to prove to Rabbi Akiva that the Jews are no different than anyone else. He was in effect saying, "You Jews say you're the chosen people, that you're different. But what makes you different? All human beings are the same. We all have two eyes, a nose, two ears, two arms, and two legs. Do you think that just because you make a *brit milah* it changes anything? What does cutting off a piece of flesh have to do with spirituality?"

Turnus Rufus then asked Rabbi Akiva, "Whose works are more perfect, man's or God's?"

---

92. *Sanhedrin* 62b.

Most people would say that Hashem's creations are more beautiful than anything humans can produce, but Rabbi Akiva answered, "Man's handiwork is more beautiful than God's." How could he say that?

Rabbi Akiva knew the question was a trap. Had he said that Hashem's handiwork was perfect, Turnus Rufus would have countered, "Then why do you interfere with His creations? He created you with a foreskin. Why do you cut it off?" Rabbi Akiva blocked this line of questioning by going straight to the truth. "Hashem creates the raw material," he said, "and we bring it to perfection." A person with a foreskin is imperfect. *Brit milah* perfects the creation.

The spiritual dimension, which cannot be seen, infuriated the Greeks. They decreed that the Jews couldn't keep Shabbat or circumcise their sons.[93] Incredibly, they insisted that the Jews hang between the horns of their oxen a sign stating, "I have no share in the God of Israel."[94] They wanted this message to be a constant reminder to every Jew while he plowed his fields or drove his wagon. They wanted to hammer home the distorted message that a person's actions have nothing to do with God. "Do you think God has time to waste with your petty human activities?" they mocked. "He is beyond all this. Stop believing that He runs the world." That's Greek philosophy in a nutshell.

As Jews, we believe that Shabbat is distinct from the other days of the week and is holy, not mundane. We also believe that a Jew is holy. We believe that the relationship between husband and wife is holy, too, that the Divine Presence is with them, and that the children they bring into the world are holy. We believe that even our work to earn a living serves God. We tithe our earnings and give the money

93. *Megillah* 17a.
94. *Bereshit Rabbah* 2:4.

to charity, donate a *sefer Torah*, build a synagogue, support Torah institutions, or do any number of good deeds, believing that any success we have, any income and all blessing comes from Hashem. The Greeks didn't believe in any of this.

With every *mitzvah* we do, we say, "Who has sanctified us with His commandments." Hashem imbues us with sanctity each time we do a *mitzvah*. The Greek decrees were designed to uproot this belief, to uproot the holiness of the Jewish people.

Greek Philosophy

Yaakov Avinu was telling us, "In all the years that I sojourned with Lavan, I never forgot the Torah's connection to Hashem." The Greeks believed in wisdom. The sciences, including mathematics, geometry, and astronomy, were part of Greek wisdom. As far as the Greeks were concerned, the Jews could study Torah as much as they pleased, as long as they didn't say it came from Hashem and connects them to Him.

According to the Greeks, God was not interested in running the daily lives of human beings. Whether He did or did not create the world made no difference to them. Like the other nations of the world, they envisioned a Creator Who was above it all, somewhere far away in the heavens with no connection to our world. For this reason, *brit milah* infuriated them. Yet we know it would be impossible for a Jew to keep the laws of family purity and maintain proper behavior between husband and wife without this *mitzvah*. Even to understand Torah in depth would be impossible for a person with a foreskin, because the Torah, being spiritual, demands that those who study it be pure and holy.

The *mitzvah* of *brit milah* prepares us for learning Torah. We offer thanks to Hashem in the blessing after bread "for the *brit* you cut into our flesh and for the Torah You taught us." Man is made from the dust of the earth. What transforms him into a vessel fit to receive Torah, which is spiritual, is this *mitzvah* done to his flesh. There is no way the holy Torah could descend and become part of us without our bodies first being sanctified through a *brit*.

The Greeks harshly enforced their decrees against our religious beliefs and practices. The penalty for disobedience was death.

Now we can understand the special addition to the *Al Hanisim* prayer we say on Hanukah. It states that the Greeks wanted "to make them forget Your Torah," and through that, "to take them away from Your *mitzvot*." Note that the Greeks had nothing against studying Torah as history or literature. They were against "*Your* Torah," Hashem's Torah. Once you can make the Jews forget it is Hashem's Torah, you can slowly draw them away from the understanding that the *mitzvot* are a connecting link between a Jew and his Creator.

Yaakov's message was: I lived with Lavan, I kept the *mitzvot*, and I didn't learn from his ways. Had I learned from his ways – to see the Torah as man-made wisdom – I would not have continued doing *mitzvot*, and the link between me and Hashem would have been severed.

Victory or Oil?

When we recount the miracles of Hanukah in *Al Hanisim*, we say nothing about the jar of pure oil found by the Maccabees. *Al Hanisim* is all about the war: "You delivered the strong into the hands of the weak, the many into the hands of the few, the impure into the hands of the pure, the wicked into the hands of the righteous, and the wanton into the hands of those who study Torah." *Al Hanisim* goes on to tell us that after the Jews conquered the Greeks, they purified the Temple, lit the *menorah*, and established the eight days of

Hanukah as a time of praise and thanks to Hashem. What about the miracle of the jug of olive oil that had only enough oil for one day but burned for eight?

On the other hand, the *Gemara* asks, "What is Hanukah?"[95] The *Gemara* doesn't ask, "What is Purim?" "What is Pesah?" "What is Shavuot?" "What is Sukkot?" All the other holidays are mentioned in the *Tanach*, even Purim, which was the last to be included. Nowhere in the twenty-four books of *Tanach* is Hanukah mentioned, hence the *Gemara*'s question.

Rashi explains that the *Gemara* is asking, "For which miracle did the *hachamim* establish the festival of Hanukah?" and he answers, "For the sealed jar of oil, hidden and untouched." The *Gemara* goes on to say that when the Jews drove the Greeks out of Yerushalayim and regained the Temple, they looked around for oil to light the *menorah*. The only oil that could be used in the Temple was oil made by people who were ritually pure. Such oil itself had ritual purity. If a person who was ritually pure became defiled, through contact with the dead, for instance, it took him seven days to regain his pure status.

When the Jewish victors looked for oil in the Temple, they discovered that the Greeks had tampered intentionally with all the oil to make it impure. Were the Greeks out of their minds? Didn't they have anything better to do? They had captured the Temple, which was filled with treasures. Instead of busying themselves with the gold and silver, they ran around looking for little jugs of olive oil. Instead of gathering precious stones, they took the time to open the jugs and pour out the oil. It doesn't make sense.

After a thorough search, the Jews found one jug of pure olive oil still sealed with the seal of the *kohen gadol* (high priest). Though this

---

95. *Shabbat* 21b.

jug contained only enough oil for one day, it burned for eight days. This, the *Gemara* tells us, is the miracle of Hanukah. For this reason, it was established as a Jewish festival.

If this is what Hanukah is all about, why isn't it mentioned in *Al Hanisim*? Who are the warriors? Matityahu, the *kohen gadol*; his five sons, all *roshe yeshivot*, and those who joined them. These pious, holy scholars battled for the sake of our religion and defeated the Greek legions, whose trained warriors were heavily armed. The Jewish victory was a tremendous miracle. In *Al Hanisim*, we mention only the victory, but the *Gemara* says Hanukah is about the jug of pure oil. It seems to be a contradiction.

The answer is that the victory alone was not enough to establish Hanukah as a holiday for all times. Emphasis on the military victory could have seriously misled us into thinking it was a war of one country against the other, like any other war. Today, Israel is fighting the Arabs. How many Arabs are there? Two hundred and fifty million. How many Jews? A handful. Some Jews say, "We're better armed, more intelligent, and braver because we believe in the fight to save our homeland." This is a nationalistic approach, not necessarily a religious one. Thinking that the power and ability to win is in our hands, and not in Hashem's, is dangerous. If commemoration of the Hanukah miracle had stopped at recounting battlefield victories, it would not only be a distortion of history, but a dangerously wrong interpretation of what actually took place. People could then say, "We've always been stronger, and we've always fought with greater conviction for our cause. That's why we won then, and that's why we'll win now." Unfortunately, some people today commemorate Hanukah and the victory of the Maccabees by making a Greek-style sports event called "The Maccabiah Games," which is sometimes referred to as the "Jewish Olympics." This is the exact opposite of what Hanukah is all about.

The real battle was a battle of the spirit. The Greeks opposed the Jewish belief in spirituality. Hashem made the miracle of the oil to teach us the truth. "Don't be fooled," the oil comes to say. "You won on the battlefield, but the real battle was light against darkness." The light of Torah fought and triumphed over the darkness of Greek wisdom. That was the real war. One tiny flame of pure light dispelled vast expanses of darkness.

No Extra Miracles

Hashem only makes a miracle when necessary. At first glance, it seems there was no need for the miracle of the oil since *halachah* states that if everyone is ritually impure, ritually impure oil may be used. We can only conclude that Hashem made the miracle of the oil for a reason, the main reason: so that we will never make the mistake of thinking it was just another patriotic, nationalistic battle. It justified performing an extra miracle to teach us that it was a battle of light against darkness.

This gives us deep insight into Hanukah. The danger still exists. We are surrounded by the Greeks and their culture even today. They want us to give up our religion, our way of thinking, our ways of feeling and acting, our customs – everything. We have to know that we must give our lives for these things. Without that attitude, we can even keep the *mitzvot* but still be in danger of assimilating. We have to know that the Torah changes us and makes us into holy people. "You are a holy nation to the L-rd, your God."[96] We are different. Shabbat is different. We work for our living differently. We behave differently. We marry differently. We live differently. The *mitzvot* change us; they bring sanctity into us.

---

96. *Devarim* 7:6.

"There is no light other than Torah."[97] Only the light of Torah can battle and overcome the darkness of evil. The light from the *menorah* shone outward through the narrow slits King Solomon built into the Temple walls. The wider part of the openings was on the outside, contrary to the way such windows were usually built, to emphasize that Hashem is the source of light, and His light shining forth from the Temple lights up the world.[98]

The seven branches of the *menorah* symbolize the seven days of the week. The central branch of the *menorah* represented Shabbat, with the three branches on each side representing the three days of the week before Shabbat and the three days of the week after Shabbat. Every day, the *kohen gadol* would pour equal amounts of oil in all seven lamps.[99] By the next day, though, the six lamps that branched out on either side were extinguished, while the center flame still burned. To relight the center flame, the *kohen gadol* first had to extinguish it, then put in oil and a new wick. This miracle, which took place in the *Bet HaMikdash* every single day, proved to the whole world that the Divine Presence was with the Jewish people.[100]

The nations of the world mock our observance of Shabbat and think we lose out by not working on that day. The opposite is true. Shabbat is the source of all blessing for the week. What you are given during the week is according to how you honored Shabbat. Instead of us losing on Shabbat what we gain on the weekdays, actually we earn on the weekdays what we invested in Shabbat. The *menorah* sends the message to us and to the whole world that the Divine Presence dwells with the Jewish people.

For exactly this reason the Greeks made a point of contaminating

---

97. *Ta'anit* 7b.
98. *Midrash*, beginning of *parashat Behalotcha*.
99. *Shabbat* 22b.
100. *Ibid.*

the oil. They knew its significance, and it infuriated them. They sought to extinguish the holiness of the Temple, which is precisely why Hashem brought about the miracle specifically through Matityahu, the *kohen gadol*, and his five sons.

We are still fighting this battle. Our duty is to bring light, the light of Torah, into the world and to disperse the darkness that the nations and assimilated Jews, the inheritors of the Greek tradition, bring into the world. And our message remains: a small flame of light will dispel vast expanses of darkness.

Purim

The arch villain of the Purim story is Haman, who sought to annihilate the Jewish people and wage a personal vendetta against Mordechai, their leader.

Haman's anti-Jewish vehemence was nothing new. He was a direct descendent of Amalek, who sought to wipe out the Jewish people as they left the Egyptian bondage. The Purim story begins a thousand years before the events in Mordechai and Esther's time. It begins with Amalek.

"Amalek battled Israel at Refidim."[101] The word *refidim* conveys two messages: (1) because the Jews loosened their grip (*rafu yadehem*) on Torah, Amalek was able to attack them; and (2) due to divisiveness (*perud levavot*) caused by bad character traits such as jealousy and hatred, the nation became vulnerable to attack.

The two are intertwined: Bad character traits weaken the connection to Torah. This is the basic theme of the *Megilla*, and, you might say, of all Jewish history.

"Jealousy and hatred" does not necessarily mean out-and-out fighting. Competing with others, trying to keep up with the Joneses, never being satisfied with what you have – this approach to life eventually leads to hatred.

"They left Refidim and came to the Sinai Desert."[102] The Jews left behind their divisiveness, symbolized by "Refidim," and achieved

---

101. *Shemot* 17:8.
102. *Ibid.* 19:2.

unity as a people with love for their fellow Jews. Now they could come to the Sinai Desert to receive the Torah.

It is significant that the Torah was given in the desert. A desert is empty – a bare and barren place devoid of commerce, competition, material gain, wealth, and pleasure. To merit Torah, collectively and individually, we must make ourselves like a desert.[103] When a person becomes like a desert, others have no reason to envy him, compete with him, or hate him. Such conditions are ideal for learning Torah.

When the Jewish people were in the desert, Hashem sustained them, giving them all they needed. This is always the case. If you rely on Hashem instead of putting all your efforts into material success, your basic needs will always be met. This is the simple meaning of the teaching that "the Torah is given only to those who eat manna."[104] Just as the Jews in the desert were sustained by manna from heaven, any Jew who forgoes materialistic ambitions and relies solely on Hashem will be taken care of by Him. Like the Jews in the desert, he will be sustained by Hashem. This applies to all generations, including our own.

Being in the desert enabled the nation to reach a level of unity so unprecedented that the Torah actually uses the singular form *vayihan* as opposed to the plural of *vayahanu* to describe their encampment at Sinai.[105] This absolute unity, *k'ish ehad belev ehad*, "Like one man with one heart,"[106] was a prerequisite for receiving the Torah. Wherever there is hatred, jealousy, or competition, there is *bitul Torah*, slackening in Torah, which makes us vulnerable to attack by Amalek. On the other hand, *ahavat Yisrael*, love between Jews that is devoid of jealousy and competition, brings the greatest blessing for learning Torah.

---

103. *Eruvin* 54a.

104. *Mechilta, Beshalah* 16:4.

105. וַיִּחַן שָׁם יִשְׂרָאֵל נֶגֶד הָהָר – *Shemot* 19:2.

106. *Mechilta, Yitro* 19:2.

Torah Study and Unity

The same Amalek who attacked us in the desert due to our divisiveness reappeared at the time of Mordechai and Esther as Haman. This is alluded to in Haman's petition to King Ahashverosh to destroy all the Jews. "There is one nation," Haman said to the king, "that is scattered and dispersed among the peoples in all of the provinces of your kingdom."[107] The best time to destroy the Jews, Haman said, is now, when they lack unity.

The Jews of that time are criticized for attending and enjoying the banquet held by King Ahashverosh.[108] Even though they were forced to attend, how could they witness the immodesty and impurity at the event? More, how could they see Ahashverosh dressed in the sacred garments of the *kohen gadol* and still enjoy themselves? This indicates not only extensive divisiveness among them, but also their distance from Torah.

Therefore, when the time came for Esther to approach the king and petition him for her people's salvation, she asked Mordechai to "go and gather all the Jews."[109] Only unity similar to that achieved at Sinai would set the stage for Divine intervention.

At the same time, Mordechai taught Torah. Haman himself realized the power of Torah when he saw Mordechai teaching his disciples the *mitzvah* of *kemitzah* – the handful of flour that the *kohen* would scoop up for the *minhah* offering in the Temple.[110] Haman told Mordechai that the slight movements he made with his fingers when demonstrating the *mitzvah* to his students were more powerful than the ten thousand *shekels* he himself had given Ahashverosh to destroy the Jews.

---

107. *Esther* 3:8.
108. *Megillah* 12a.
109. *Esther* 4:16.
110. *Megillah* 16a.

That was Mordechai and Esther's strategy to avert the evil decree: unity and Torah study.

All the wealth, honor and power given Haman by the king meant nothing to him, though, whenever he saw "Mordechai the Jew sitting at the king's gate."[111] Rashi explains that this refers to the *tallit* and *tefillin* that Mordechai wore. What upset Haman was to see Mordechai the Jew – Mordechai acting like a Jew, wearing *tallit* and *tefillin*. The Ben Ish Hai adds that Mordechai had a long beard and *peyot* as well. Haman realized that as long as there are people like Mordechai, who fulfill the *halachot* of the Torah down to the smallest detail, no plan to destroy the Jews can ever succeed.

The renewed unity and Torah study of the Jewish people in Mordechai and Esther's time did much more than foil Haman's scheme to annihilate them; they caused the plan to boomerang (*vanahafoch hu*), destroying the Amalekites.

Having regained their unity and their attachment to Torah, the Jewish people rose to a higher level of inspiration and dedication than before. They wholeheartedly reaffirmed their acceptance of the Torah. As the *hachamim* explain from the words of the *Megilla*, they now fulfilled and accepted (*kimu vekiblu*) what they had accepted earlier.[112]

Understanding Sinai

At Sinai, the Jewish people unanimously declared, *Na'ase venishma*, "We will do and we will hear."[113] We were prepared to accept the Torah even before hearing what it demanded of us. The

---

111. *Esther* 5:13.

112. *Ibid.* 9:27.

113. *Shemot* 24:7.

hachamim say that even Hashem was surprised at hearing their words, which only angels had ever uttered until that moment. The other nations of the world had made their acceptance of the Torah conditional on first knowing what was in it. When they heard various commandments that went against their natural tendencies, they rejected the Torah. Only the Jewish nation was willing to accept the Torah on faith.

On the other hand, the *Gemara* tells us that Hashem lifted up Mount Sinai and held it over the Israelites' heads, threatening to bury them under it if they did not accept the Torah. Now, if a person is forced against his will to sell a possession, he can state before two witnesses that he is being coerced so that later he can reclaim in court what he sold. Here as well, by being forced to accept the Torah, it seems that the Jewish people were left with the possibility of later claiming they are not obligated to uphold it.

The contradiction is clear. On the one hand, the nation said, "We will do and we will hear"; on the other hand, Hashem held the mountain over their heads to force their acceptance. This situation, in which the nation's commitment to the Torah was made under duress, lasted for almost a thousand years, until the time of Mordechai and Esther.

The *Midrash Tanhuma*, however, explains that there really is no contradiction.[114] The Jewish people were willing to accept the Written Torah, and regarding this they said, "We will do and we will hear." They were not willing, though, to receive the Oral Torah. This is what Hashem forced them to accept. It is this Torah – the Oral Torah – that the Jewish people voluntarily accepted upon themselves in the days of Mordechai and Esther.

This requires further explanation, though, because there can be no

---

114. *Midrash Tanhuma, parashat Noah.*

Written Torah without the Oral Torah. For example, the Written Torah states only that *tefillin* must be bound to the hand and placed between the eyes; nothing more is said. From the words of the Written Torah alone, one could never know the literally hundreds of laws pertaining to *tefillin*. There are detailed laws concerning how the parchment is to be prepared and how the letters are to be written; there are laws concerning the preparation of the *batim* that enclose the parchments, how they should be placed on the body, and when the blessing is made. Therefore, it would be obligatory to accept both the Written and Oral Torah as a package deal. The Jewish people certainly knew and kept the Oral Torah from Sinai on. However, until the time of Mordechai and Esther, it was something they had been forced to accept.

Accepting the Written Torah is not nearly as weighty as commitment to the Oral Torah.[115] Studying *Humash* is not nearly as momumental an undertaking as the yoke of constant Torah study required by the Oral Torah. Initially, the Jewish people did not see the necessity for such a commitment. A rulebook with guidelines for daily life, complex though it might be, made sense, and this they agreed to learn and fulfill. But they did not understand the need for *yegia* and *amal*, the need to exert oneself and to be immersed in the study of Torah day and night all one's life.

To their credit, we can explain that the Jews of those generations preceding Mordechai and Esther did not feel any lack in their connection to Hashem. Their holiness, spirituality, and Divine service were all on a very high level. From the time they received the Torah at Sinai until they entered Eretz Yisrael, they were in the desert, an environment ideally suited to Torah study.[116] They had Moshe Rabbeinu, Aharon *Hakohen*, and the *Mishkan* (Tabernacle), and the

---

115. *Ibid.*
116. *Ibid. Beshalah* 20.

Divine Presence was with them at all times. They were guided by the pillar of fire by night and the clouds of glory by day. They had the Well of Miriam, they had manna, they saw constant miracles, and all their needs were taken care of. Throughout it all, they learned Torah directly from Moshe Rabbeinu, so they did not feel themselves lacking in their commitment to study Torah day and night.

When the nation entered Eretz Yisrael, they were elevated by its sanctity. The seven years of conquest were followed by seven years of apportioning the land. They had the prophets, the elders, and later, the kings. They had the *Bet HaMikdash*, they had the Divine Presence, and they witnessed great miracles. Their lives were so full of sanctity and purity that they did feel themselves lacking the toil and labor involved with learning the Oral Torah.

However, when the *Bet HaMikdash* was destroyed and the nation was driven into exile, having lost all their spirituality and miraculous assets, they realized that without the Oral Torah they had nothing. Living a life of toil in studying the Torah is what has kept the Jewish people alive to this very day. We no longer have prophecy, we do not have the *Bet HaMikdash*, and we do not have Eretz Yisrael. All we have is the "four cubits of *halachah*," of Torah study. And, in fact, that is all Hashem has left of this world.[117]

This was the realization of Purim, that the only thing that can keep the Jewish nation together is the Oral Torah. This is what saves us from assimilation and from being wiped off the world map by Amalek and all the non-Jewish philosophies that surround us today.

The war with Amalek changes form. Sometimes we are attacked physically by evildoers like Haman or Hitler, may their names be blotted out. Other times, the attack is spiritual and intellectual, as was the case with the Greeks. Both, however, have the same agenda,

---

117. *Berachot* 8a.

which is to uproot the holiness of the Jewish people. The only way to fight the evil impurity of Amalek is by accepting the yoke of Torah study, and this can only be done if a person perfects his character. Only one who is free of jealousy, hatred, and a competitive spirit, which causes rift and hatred among Jews, can truly accept upon himself the yoke of Torah.

The word *Amalek* is equal numerically to the word *safek* (doubt). Divisiveness and slackening in Torah brings doubts. Clarity is lost and questions of faith emerge. Perfecting character traits and eliminating feelings of jealousy, hatred, and a competitive spirit, bring a person clarity of vision, which is the essence of accepting the yoke of Torah.

Pesaḥ: Emunah and Bitaḥon

A s believing Jews, we live by our faith, our *emunah*. But what exactly do we – and should we – believe?

We believe there is a Creator of the world, and that He created the world for a purpose. We also believe that He continues to be involved with the world, that He is interested in it, knows everything that happens in it and has a hand in everything that happens in it. Nothing that takes place is a "coincidence" or a "chance occurrence," for there is no such thing as chance.

This belief in Hashem's ongoing, direct supervision – what we call *hashgahah pratit*, Divine providence – is unique to Judaism.[118] In previous eras, the non-Jewish world believed in a Creator but said the world meant nothing to Him. In their opinion, He looked down on the world from afar, as we would look down at an anthill. Hashem, they said, was above it all, *ram al kol goyim Hashem*[119] – so far above it all that He could not possibly lower Himself to be involved with the comings and goings of human beings. According to them, it was beneath Hashem to be involved in such things.

However, according to the Jewish outlook, Hashem's glory *is* in the higher worlds, as the verse continues, "Who is enthroned on high." But (and this is a big but), "He comes down into our world to see." Everything that happens in the world, that one person becomes rich and another poor, that So-and-so is healthy and another is sick,

---

118. *Orhot Hayyim* 1:26.
119. *Tehillim* 113:4. "Hashem is high above all nations, [His glory is above the heavens]."

is determined by Hashem. It is Hashem Who "raises the poor and uplifts the needy." He is the One running the whole show, down to the last detail. Realizing this is *emunah*.

The Exodus Is Proof that Hashem Runs the World

The first of the Ten Commandments states: "I am Hashem, your God, Who took you out of the land of Egypt, out of the house of slavery."[120] Rabbeinu Asher, known as the Rosh, wrote in *Orhot Hayyim* that believing only in the first part of the verse – that Hashem created the world – is not enough. A Jew must also believe in the continuation of the verse, that Hashem took us out of Egypt. Without this belief in *hashgahah pratit* – that Hashem is *actively* involved in the world – our belief is incomplete.

This explains why so much of our religion is based on the historical fact that we came out of Egypt. Otherwise, the emphasis would seem strange. Every *Kiddush* we make includes the words "in remembrance of the exodus from Egypt." A person could say, "It really happened, but that was a long time ago. True, we were slaves in Egypt, Hashem took us out, and we came to our land – but why talk about it now?" However, as the Rosh tells us, all the wondrous events of the Exodus – the fact that Hashem changed the course of nature, that He made miracles, that He brought ten plagues on the Egyptians and more – are proof of His direct involvement in the world.

In taking us out of the Egyptian slavery, Hashem made a clear statement: There is a purpose to creation, and that purpose is the

---

120. *Shemot* 20:1.

Jewish people, who are meant to keep the Torah – and I am involved in everything that takes place.

Every single thing that happens in our lives is *hashgahah pratit*. As our sages say, "A person doesn't bang his finger below without it being decreed from Above."[121]

Since the concept of *emunah* is rooted in the way Hashem took us out of the Egyptian exile, it is appropriate to explain here some of the basic aspects of Jewish *emunah*.

Direct Supervision
vs. General Supervision

All of the *Rishonim*, the Rambam, Ramban, and also many of the great *Aharonim*, including the kabbalists, such as the Ramhal, Rav Yosef Irgas the author of *Shomrei Emunim* – all, without exception, say that while *hashgahah pratit* applies to the Jewish people, other creations are governed by *hashgahah klalit*, a more general type of supervision.

However, some of the Hassidic masters disagree, saying that even a leaf's fall from a tree is *hashgahah pratit*, because nothing can happen in the world without Hashem's direct involvement.

The truth is that there is no contradiction, as the Rambam explains in *Morei Nevuchim*. There is *hashgahah* on everything created and everything that happens. What, then, is the difference between these two types of *hashgahah*?

If a cow in an African forest dies, one might call this an example of *hashgahah klalit*, because Hashem doesn't decide which cow will live

---

121. *Hulin* 7b.

and which cow will die. There are millions of cows in the world, and the decision made will be a general one about how many cows will live or die.

However, once the cow has an owner, it's not really a case of just cows dying. It's a case of Shimon's cow or Reuven's cow. Maybe Shimon owes a debt to Hashem, or maybe he has to be punished. If his cow died, it's because of *him*, because the cow was his, not because of a general situation regarding cows. So even though we are talking about an animal, because it has an owner, whatever happens to it is a result of *hashgahah pratit*.

Consider a huge anthill in an African jungle. Millions of ants are massed on a decomposing tree when suddenly an elephant runs rampant, charges into the forest and stomps on the anthill, killing a million ants. It is not *hashgahah pratit* that decided which ant was killed and which ant wasn't, but *hashgahah klalit*.

The *Rishonim* consider this an example of *hashgahah klalit* because the ants didn't belong to anyone; they were just there. What happened to any one particular ant, whether it lived or died, was decided by Hashem according to the rule of maintaining a balance in nature. Before we entered the Land of Israel, Hashem cast out all the wild animals that were living there. This was not done all at once, but in stages. Yes, we needed a safe place in which to live, but, at the same time, the balance of nature had to be maintained. This is part of *hashgahah klalit*.

The kabbalists tell us something beyond this. They say that sometimes, as a punishment, a soul can transmigrate and assume the form of a stone, water, or an animal. If there is a soul in a leaf or a cat, for example, then anything that happens to that leaf or cat, because it is part of the soul's *tikun*, is an act of *hashgahah pratit*. This is what is meant by those who said that whatever happens to even an animal or a leaf is Divinely ordained. Otherwise, an animal in the forest or a leaf in the jungle is ruled by *hashgahah klalit*.

Mazal vs. Hashgahah

How does *mazal* fit into the picture? The idea of astrology – that the position of the zodiac when a person is born creates a certain *mazal* for him – is accepted in the Jewish religion. But for a Jew, *mazal* is not the deciding factor. What really determines his future are his good deeds, his adherence to Torah, his study of Torah, and the *mitzvot* he does. Through the *mitzvot*, we have a direct connection to Hashem. True, the natural way for Hashem to relate to us would be according to our *mazal*. Everything operates within the confines of *mazal*, because we are in the physical world, which is run by these natural forces. But above and beyond that, Hashem runs the world, including nature.

For example, Avraham Avinu knew that the reason he didn't have children was because he was born with a certain *mazal*. However, when he said to Hashem, "You promised me children but I can't have children," Hashem replied, "What's the problem? I'm the One Who put the star there in the first place. Now I can change its place."[122]

In other words, because Hashem rules nature, we are never limited to our *mazal*. We can change our *mazal* completely for the good through our direct connection with Hashem by keeping Torah and *mitzvot*. By coming close to Hashem, we can be ruled directly by Him, without any connection to our *mazal*. Those who do not live according to the Torah will, of course, be completely ruled by their *mazal*, for good or for bad.

Bitahon – The Practical
Application of Belief

The application of our *emunah* is *bitahon*, trust. In every situation

---

122. *Shabbat* 156a.

we face, in every trial we encounter, we relate to events in the correct way by believing in Hashem, believing that He runs the world, and trusting that whatever He does is for our good. We rely on Him completely, knowing that only He can support, help, and save us in every situation. The following story about Rabbi Akiva has become a classic illustration of this.[123]

Rabbi Akiva was traveling from town to town and had with him a donkey, a lantern, and a rooster. Night fell. A strong wind blew out the lamp, the rooster was eaten by a cat, and the donkey was eaten by a lion. To each event, Rabbi Akiva's response was *kol d'avid Rahmanah l'tav*, "Whatever God does is for the best."

Later, a Roman army passed by, but was unaware of Rabbi Akiva's presence. If his light had remained lit, they would have seen it; if his rooster had been alive, they would have heard it crow; if his donkey hadn't been killed, its braying would have revealed his location.

The army continued past Rabbi Akiva to a nearby town where they killed all the inhabitants.

Rabbi Akiva was saved, and everything worked out for the best for him. For the person who trusts in Hashem and says *kol d'avid Rahmanah l'tav*, under all circumstances, everything happens for the best.

We would all love it if everything went one hundred percent according to our plans. And we are certain that what we want is what is good for us. Yet life, as we well know, is not like that. Hashem runs the world, and sometimes there are surprises, even unpleasant ones. We are given heavy burdens to carry and trials which we find difficult to face. These are really tests of our *bitahon*, to see how we apply our *emunah* by trusting in Hashem.

---

123. *Berachot* 60b.

How Does Hishtadlut Fit In?

Bitahon has many different levels. The greater a person is, the higher the level of trust Hashem expects of him. These levels are difficult to attain. For example, how would we expect a person to react if he were imprisoned on false charges? Would we expect him to say *"kol d'avid Rahmanah l'tav"* and leave it at that? More likely, he would hire a top lawyer and use his connections to gain his freedom.

During the time that Yosef was imprisoned by Pharaoh on false accusations, he met Pharaoh's wine steward and baker. After he did them the favor of interpreting their dreams, he said, "When you get out, please mention me to Pharaoh." Hashem punished him with another two years in jail for placing his trust in a human being.

But how can what Yosef did be wrong? Can a person just sit back and say, "Hashem, you know I believe in You. Now You take care of me. I'll send You all my bills, I'll tell You how much I need every month, and You just take care of me"? Why not? Didn't King David say, *"Hashlech al Hashem y'havecha v'Hu y'chalkelecha,"*[124] which literally means, throw your burdens on Hashem, the whole sackful, and tell Him, "You take care of everything." Doesn't this imply that a person can literally say, "I rely on Hashem to take care of me. I don't have to do anything"?

Yet we know that this approach is wrong, that a person must make a certain effort on his behalf, what we call *hishtadlut*. Each person has his own level of *hishtadlut* and has to serve Hashem by believing in Him and trusting in Him at that level. You can't take on a level that is beyond you. *Hishtadlut* has to be within the boundaries of what Hashem expects from you. Each person, according to his level of trust, has a different obligation as to making his personal efforts.

---

124. *Tehillim* 55:23: "Cast your burden upon God, and He will sustain you."

Take, for instance, the average businessman. He can't say, "Okay, for my *hishtadlut*, I'll go to the office two hours a day." He'd be making a big mistake, one that could very well destroy his business.

How can a person know what the right level of *hishtadlut* is for him? He should go by the norm for his situation. If businesses similar to his are open from nine to five, and he wants to come in an hour later and take off an hour earlier, maybe he can. He can add a little more time for learning, and spend a little more time with his family. He doesn't have to be a slave. As long as the pipeline is open, the *berachah* will come in.

Someone on a higher level may feel he can look for a business that won't take up too much of his time. He knows that the more people he has working for him or under him, the more time-consuming responsibilities he will have.

What about the person who thinks he can run a business from a computer at home? If he thinks he can do it that way and devote half a day to learning Torah – if that's his level – then Hashem will help him.

We have to serve Hashem according to our level of *bitahon*. We must fully trust Hashem and believe in Him on that level before we can take on more. For a person on Yosef's level, it was a mistake to think that any human being could help.

There Are No Guarantees

There's a lot of confusion about what *bitahon* really means. In Israel, people have a saying, *yehiyeh tov*, "It'll be good." Many people think this means that even if things don't seem good now, everything will turn out all right later. They think that having faith means believing things will *eventually* be good, and they feel that the story of Rabbi Akiva, where he said *"kol d'avid Rahmanah l'tav"* proves it. This is a mistake.

Rabbi Akiva accepted the light going out, he accepted his rooster and donkey dying *at the time that it happened*. His *"kol d'avid Rahmanah l'tav"* meant that at each stage, he accepted what happened as good. He was not saying, *"yehiyeh tov"* – it will be good at some future point. We think that good is what we feel we need and want, without always realizing that in Hashem's eyes it could be bad for us. In this case, it was easy to see that the outcome was good. Because all these things happened, his life was saved. But Rabbi Akiva was not counting on that. He was not waiting for the outcome before declaring that what happened was good. He accepted each event as good in and of itself.

As the Hazon Ish says in his book on the subject, there are no guarantees. We can never know what Hashem's plans are. *Bitahon* does not mean going through life thinking that no matter what's happening, it's eventually going to turn out okay according to our understanding of what "okay" is. True *bitahon* is trusting that whatever happens is for the good, because only Hashem really knows what our true good is.

Hashem knows each person and knows why he was brought into this world, what is expected of him, and what is best for him. When a person goes through a difficult time, he must realize that the suffering was sent to bring him to a higher level. It might bring him closer to religion, to a higher level of closeness to Hashem, or cause other important developments in his life.

Iyov's story teaches us this. Iyov was a righteous person with a high level of belief in Hashem. One day, the Satan said to Hashem, "Sure Iyov believes in You! You're very good to him. Let me take care of him for a while, let him suffer a little, and then we'll see if he's going to continue believing."

The suffering sent his way shook Iyov to the core. His wife and children died, he lost all of his money, he was afflicted with all sorts of diseases, and he began to have doubts. "Why is this happening to me?" he wondered. "I don't deserve this. I'm a good person, so why is all this happening to me?"

Four of Iyov's friends came to discuss the matter with him. They told him, "You must have transgressed. Hashem doesn't mete out punishment to a person unless he did something wrong."

Iyov argued with them. "No, I know I didn't do anything to deserve this. There must be some mistake."

Finally, one of the four, Elihu, said to Iyov, "The soul can descend to earth more than once. We believe in reincarnation, and it is certain that you are now suffering because of a previous existence."

Iyov was relieved. As long as his friends kept telling him, "You're suffering for bad things you did in this lifetime," he was upset, because he knew he hadn't done anything to deserve all the suffering that had befallen him. Once he understood that a person must sometimes pay back old debts, even those from a previous existence, he was able to cope with his situation. He could tell himself, "Hashem keeps accurate accounts. He knows what I did in a previous existence, and if He's collecting payment, it must be from an old debt."

This was the answer Iyov finally accepted, and it explains many things for us as well.

Even Strict Judgment Is Kindness

Only Hashem really knows what is good for us and what is expected of us. The verse says: *"Diminu Elokim hasdecha b'kerev heichalecha"* – "We imagined your lovingkindness, Elokim, from within Your sanctuary."[125] God's Name *Elokim* always denotes *middat hadin* – strict justice.[126] For instance, when Hashem metes out punishment according to the letter of the law, as a Judge, that's *middat hadin*. The word *diminu* is from the word *dimayon*, imagination. If, God forbid, a tragedy occurs, everyone says this is *middat hadin*, strict justice, the aspect of *Elokim*. But this verse is telling us, *diminu Elokim* – you only *imagine* that what happened is *middah hadin*. You only think that it's *middah hadin* because you don't see the whole picture. Really *hasdecha b'kerev heichalecha*, it is an expression of Your kindness from within Your sanctuary.

If we could see what is taking place from the vantage point of the higher heavens, if we could look down on the entire world and the whole six thousand years of existence, we would see that whatever happened was good. We would see that nothing could have been better for a person, and that going through whatever he did was his *tikun*, the complete fulfillment of his mission in this world.

We cannot know what is hidden from us. Only "from within Your sanctuary," only when we look at the map of existence from on high do we see "Your kindness," that everything is *hesed* from Hashem.

But we have to know what Hashem's *hesed* is. Like Rabbi Akiva, we have to know that, in fact, *kol d'avid Rahmanah l'tav*. We have to tell ourselves, "Everything that happens is for the best. I don't know why this is happening to me, but Hashem does. Maybe one day I'll find out."

Just before one of his prized students died, the Ramban, who felt the impending loss deeply, said to him, "Please return to me in a dream and tell me why you were afflicted with such punishment. I would like to know why you had to suffer so much in this world, and why you, who were so righteous and learned, had to die so young."

---

125. *Ibid.* 48:10.
126. *Midrash Rabbah, Bereshit* 33:3.

In time, the student appeared to his teacher in a dream and told him, "We are not really allowed to disclose the reasons for what took place. These secrets belong solely to Hashem. I can tell you only one thing: here, there are no questions."

From our limited vantage point, we have questions. From where we sit, we think winning the lottery is good and banging a finger isn't. But good is not what we decide it is. When you see the whole picture of how Hashem runs the world, you see that everything fits and that whatever happens is for the ultimate good. This is *kol d'avid Rahmanah l'tav*. Whatever happens was meant to be – because Hashem is running the world, and He is running it for our good.

Bitahon and Prayer

Having a high level of *bitahon* does not mean that a person doesn't have to pray to Hashem. We pray to Hashem that we should enjoy His goodness in a way we understand as good. One of the hassidic Rebbes used to say, *Hareinu Hashem hasdecha*,[127] "Hashem, we ask You for goodness, but not the deep, unfathomable goodness that only big rabbis or the kabbalists can see is good. Please give us goodness that even a housewife in the kitchen knows is good. Give us the simple, good things in life that we ask for, the goodness we can comprehend."

We ask Hashem to give us a good life, a profitable life, a successful life, a happy life, and a healthy life. We're allowed to ask Him for the good things. At the same time, we have to remember that He has the final say. He knows what to give and what not to give, when to hear our prayers and when to test us and perhaps put us in a situation we would prefer not to be in. All this is part of life and a test of how our *emunah* and *bitahon* hold up. It's all very well and good to learn about *emunah* and *bitahon*; it's putting them into practice that's difficult.

---

127. *Tehillim* 85:8. "Show us Your mercy, O God [and grant us Your salvation]."

Gaining Awareness of Hashgahah Pratit

Our sages say, "A person who assesses his behavior in this world merits Hashem's miracles."[128] A person who thinks about what happens to him and doesn't go through life assuming that it's all coincidence develops a close, personal relationship with Hashem.

We have to open our eyes to see how every moment of every day is guided from Above and how every person we meet is sent to us by Hashem. For instance, a man might travel to a foreign country and unexpectedly meet his intended wife. He thought he was making the trip for business purposes, but Hashem planned it otherwise.

A poor person stretching out his hand for help is also *hashgahah pratit*. The *Zohar* goes further and tells us that if a needy person asks you for help, it's not that he needs your help but that *you* need this opportunity to give. Hashem has plenty of ways of taking care of that needy individual, so if He sent him to you, it means you need a certain merit you can gain by helping him. We have to look at life from a totally different perspective to keep in mind that Hashem is running the world.

Sometimes you want to meet someone, and you don't meet him. That's *hashgahah*. Sometimes you want to meet someone, and you do meet him. That too is *hashgahah*. Everything is *hashgahah*, and you have to live this type of life, believing and trusting that Hashem runs the world.

People ask, "Where are the miracles?" Just pay attention to your own life. Open your eyes, and you'll see that life is literally a miraculous process. The opposite, taking things for granted, thinking everything is a coincidence, is a great sin. The Torah says, "If you go with Me *keri*"–

---

128. *Sotah* 5b.

if you treat everything that happens as a chance event – "I'll deal with you the same way."[129] This is a very serious punishment.

Picture a wife who trips and drops the expensive crystal vase she was carrying. Her husband shouts at her and insults her before finally saying, "Okay, let it be a *kaparah*." This kind of reaction, says the *Pele Yoetz*, loses the *kaparah*. The only way a loss can serve as atonement is if you accept it as Hashem's will the moment it happens and say, "*kol d'avid Rahmanah l'tav*." If your first reaction is one of disappointment and unhappiness with what happened, but then you think, "Okay, it's gone anyway, so let it be a *kaparah*," that's handling it the wrong way.

Bitahon Brings True Happiness

A Jew has to know that wherever he is, Hashem is right there with him.

There is no running away from Hashem. There's no such thing as thinking, "Who sees me? I'm in the privacy of my own home so I can do what I want and say what I want." No, Hashem is with you wherever you are. He knows not only what you are doing or saying; He knows what you are thinking and feeling. You may be able to put on a beautiful act and fool your family and friends, your boss, your coworkers and everyone else – but Hashem knows what is really inside. He sees it all.

A person arrives at this level of awareness through *emunah* and *bitahon*.

Everyone alive has sinned, and, because we have sinned, we have to suffer. Does suffering mean a person has to lose his money or health? No. The *Gemara* tells us that even putting your hand into your pocket to take out a dime and getting a quarter is a level of

---

129. *Vayikra* 26:23.

suffering. Because people are not aware of this, they go through life thinking that the little things that happen to them are meaningless, random events, and that there are no lessons to be learned from them. This is a major misunderstanding. Any type of suffering – even the minor snags – is just Hashem plucking your sleeve and saying, "Wake up and pay attention to Me."

If we train ourselves to reach this level of awareness of Hashem's presence, we become like a baby in his mother's arms, content at knowing that all our needs are taken care of. We accept even the occasional spanking, knowing it is for our own good. In this way, we feel the deep happiness that can be experienced only by a person living a life of *emunah* and *bitahon*.

Lag BaOmer

The days of the *omer*, between Pesah and Shavuot, are a time of mourning. During this period, we don't take haircuts, get married, or listen to music. We do this out of mourning for Rabbi Akiva's 24,000 students who died in a plague during this time period.

On Lag BaOmer, the thirty-third day of the *omer*, we don't say *Tahanun* and we are somewhat happy. According to the Rema, this is because on this day, the students stopped dying.

This sounds strange. If the plague stopped on this day, leaving some of Rabbi Akiva's students alive, it would be good reason for us to stop mourning. But all 24,000 of his students died. What is there to be happy about? They stopped dying, but there were none left.

The question has intrigued some of our greatest sages. The Pri Hadash was a great halachic authority and author of a commentary on the *Shulhan Aruch*, after which he is known. Though he hid the fact, he was also a kabbalist. He hints that the answer to the question is found in the writings of the Ari *z"l*, who says that on this day, Rabbi Akiva went to the south of Israel and ordained five new pupils who gave us the whole oral tradition that we have today: Rabbi Meir (Baal Haness), Rabbi Yehuda ben Illai, Rabbi Yosi, Rabbi Shimon bar Yohai, and Rabbi Elazar ben Shamoah.

With this, we can understand why our sages decreed the four weeks between Pesah and Lag BaOmer to be a time of mourning, which they did not do for any of the other tragic pogroms and sufferings of the Jewish people, besides the destruction of the Temple. If from five students we have the entire oral tradition, we can imagine how vast the Torah was before we lost those 24,000 students, and how tragic a loss their deaths caused. We can be sure that just as each of these five had their area of expertise, Rabbi Akiva had made each of the 24,000 who died an expert in one specific portion of Torah. What would our Torah be like today if we had the portions Rabbi Akiva taught them as well? Because our sages understood the scope of this loss, they decreed the days of the *omer* to be a time of fasting, sadness, and mourning.

All this serves to highlight the importance of loving our fellowman, a concept Rabbi Akiva himself called a "great rule in Torah." What motivated Rabbi Akiva to say this? When he saw that a lack of respect between his students caused all 24,000 of them to perish – along with all the Torah he had taught them – he taught that Torah must be learned and lived with happiness, peace, sincerity, and love between those who learn together.

It is mentioned in the *Zohar* that once, when Rabbi Shimon bar Yohai's students appeared before him happy and smiling, he told them, "The happiness and peace among you is the reason why the secrets of the Torah are being revealed on such a high level in our generation."[130] On the other hand, whenever there is hatred and controversy, the Torah cannot continue.

In order to grasp the idea that in addition to Rabbi Akiva's five disciples who gave us the Oral Torah we know today, there were once another 24,000 portions of Torah, we turn to *Menahot* 29b. There, we learn that when Moshe Rabbeinu went up to heaven to receive the Torah, "He saw the Holy One tying crowns to the letters." If you look at a *sefer Torah*, you will see that certain letters have three additional strokes on them, shaped like a crown, while other letters have one stroke on them. These are called *taggim*. The letters *shin*, *ayin*, *tet*, *nun*, *zayin*, *gimmel* and *tzadi* (remembered by the acronym

---

130. *Zohar* 2:190b.

sha'atnez getz) have three crowns on them. The letters *bet, dalet, kuf, het, yud* and *hay* (remembered by the acronym *bedek haya*) have one stroke on them. Moshe asked Hashem why He was doing that. Vowel marks and *ta'amei hamikra* are not written in the *sefer Torah*, but affect pronunciation when reading from it. Yet these crowns, called *taggim*, do not affect pronunciation at all. They are more like decorations on the top of certain letters. In answer, Hashem showed Moshe that there would come a day when a Torah scholar named Akiva would learn an endless number of *halachot* from each *tag*.

In addition, Rabbi Akiva learned from *gematriot, rashei tevot*, and *sofei tevot*. He could surely say *pshat, remez, derash*, and *sod* on everything. We can imagine the vast amount of Torah he taught his 24,000 students.

Since the transition between the 24,000 students Rabbi Akiva taught in his younger days and the five he ordained as rabbis afterward took place on Lag BaOmer, we rejoice on this day over the Torah that was saved, because whatever Rabbi Akiva taught those five students was transmitted to us.

Rabbi Shimon bar Yohai

Most people think of Lag BaOmer as the day of Rabbi Shimon bar Yohai's passing. It's called a *yom hillula* – a day of rejoicing – because when a *tzaddik* passes on, he takes with him a lifetime of holiness and goodness.

The Ari *z"l* calls Lag BaOmer "*yom simhato*" – "the day of his happiness," referring to Rabbi Shimon bar Yohai,[131] because on this day, Rabbi Shimon was ordained by Rabbi Akiva.

We have no authoritative source that Lag BaOmer is the date of

---

131. *Shaar HaKavanot* 87a/b.

Rabbi Shimon's death. However, there is a tradition that he passed away on this very day. The Ari *z"l* does not dispute this, but says the joyous celebration on this day is because it is the day on which Rabbi Shimon was ordained.

Both the Hida and the Ben Ish Hai say that Lag BaOmer is not only the day of Rabbi Shimon's happiness, but also of the other four rabbis ordained by Rabbi Akiva. The Ben Ish Hai says that those who live in Tiberius should go to the gravesites of Rabbi Akiva and Rabbi Meir. Those who live in Zefat and travel to Meron should stop on the way at the gravesite of Rabbi Yehuda bar Illai. We should visit all five, according to the Ben Ish Hai, because the happiness of the day belongs to all of them.

All five were already great sages at the time Rabbi Akiva ordained them, but it was on Lag BaOmer that he took them as his students, transmitted to them what he could, and continued learning with them.

The Zohar

Rashbi (an acronym for **R**abbi **Sh**imon **b**ar **Y**ohai) taught his students the secrets of the Torah, encapsulated later in the *Zohar*. Some years before his death, he taught the *Idra Rabba*, which is a very important text in which he reveals most of the secrets of the Torah. On the day of his passing, he transmitted the *Idra Zuta*, which is a small part of the *Zohar* (*parashat V'ethanan*), but the deepest part of it.

Idra means "circle." When they sat to learn, they sat in a circle around their teacher. When Rashbi had his full group of students, it was called the *Idra Rabba*, the Big Circle. By Lag BaOmer, the last day of his life, three of Rashbi's students had passed away, and he had a smaller group. The teachings he transmitted to them are called the *Idra Zuta*. After transmitting these final secrets of the Torah to seven select students, Rashbi left this world. At that moment, the other sages and students present with him in Meron heard a heavenly voice say, "Come take part in the happiness of Rabbi Shimon bar Yohai!"

This does not mean they burst out in song and dance. It does mean that the heavens rejoiced to receive his soul. The *Zohar* gives no date for Rashbi's passing nor does it say his passing should be commemorated *every* year. It just says that now, at his passing, join the celebration of the heavenly hosts.

The *Shulhan Aruch* says that when a *tzaddik* dies, it is a day of mourning.[132] The days that Moshe Rabbeinu, Shmuel, Aharon and his sons passed away are fast days, not times of rejoicing. How can the day Rashbi passed away be a time of happiness?

The Hatam Sofer explains this apparent contradiction. When a *tzaddik* dies, the heavens rejoice at such an elevated soul arising replete with Torah, *mitzvot*, and good deeds. Those of us remaining in this world are the ones who are unhappy.

Some people say the joyousness of the day is because Rashbi then revealed the *Idra Zuta*. If that were the reason, though, we could rejoice constantly, because Rashbi taught kabbalah and revealed Torah secrets every day of the year.

An Ancient Tradition

In *Shaar HaKavanot*, Rabbi Hayyim Vital finds authentic sources for all the different customs that take place at the Rashbi's tomb on Lag BaOmer. Among the proofs that Lag BaOmer is a day of rejoicing is the fact that the Ari *z"l* visited Meron from Egypt nine years before coming to settle in Eretz Yisrael with his family. The Ari was a young rabbi at the time, and in those days, the trip from Egypt

---

132. *Shulhan Aruch, siman* 125.

to Meron on donkeys and camels was arduous. He made the trip to cut his son's hair at the Rashbi's tomb on the boy's third birthday. Afterward, the Ari z"l made a feast and rejoiced.

Rabbi Hayyim Vital then says, "But I cannot bring that as a proof, because it happened nine years ago." Meaning to say, since the event took place nine years earlier, it may have been before the Ari z"l had experienced gilui Eliyahu – a revelation of the prophet Eliyahu, which gave all of his customs the stamp of authority.

"Last year though," Rabbi Hayyim Vital continues, "before I came from Damascus, he had just come from Egypt corresponding with the day of Lag BaOmer, and he participated in the celebration. Certainly, by then, he had gilui Eliyahu.... I wrote all this as proof that this custom has a basis and is custom."

Why did Rabbi Hayyim Vital go to so much trouble to prove that rejoicing on Lag BaOmer is correct?

There is a story that Rabbi Yosef Caro and his rabbinical court wanted to forbid Lag BaOmer celebrations in Meron. Apparently, in those days as well as ours, it was hard to maintain proper standards of behavior in such massive crowds. When the Ari heard about the move to stop the celebrations, he said, "Don't tamper with the Rashbi's celebration, because no good will come from it. I sanction it. If you are worried because 'all Jews are responsible for each other' – (this is especially true for a rabbinical court, which must try to ensure that there is modest, proper behavior in the area of its jurisdiction) – tell Maran [as Rabbi Yosef Caro was called] that on the day of Rashbi's celebration, everyone is responsible for himself. Those who act inappropriately will lose out, as always. But don't stop the celebration, because Rashbi is happy about it."

Rabbi Hayyim Vital took the trouble to write at length about Lag BaOmer to tell us that the custom is not one that began with the simple folk and then took on its own momentum. The opposite is true: Lag BaOmer celebrations began with the *gedolei Yisrael*, who saw it as a lofty event.

Mazal and Tikun

Hashem calculates the lives of the righteous precisely. There were righteous people who lived so correctly, so perfectly, that everything worked out to the point that they passed from this world on the same date as their birth.[133] In this instance, we have a tradition that Rabbi Shimon bar Yohai died on Lag BaOmer and that he received *semichah* on that day. It is obviously a significant date for him, so it might also have been the date of his birth.

A date can have significance. Our *mazal* is set according to the day we were born, although, as Jews, we can change this *mazal* through our actions. The Ari *z"l* taught people how to rectify their sins.[134] For every type of sin, he prescribed the appropriate way to correct the spiritual damage, whether through fasting or other deeds. One *tikun* mentioned is for a rabbi who wrote an amulet for a woman to ensure a faster birth. His sin was that he changed the child's *mazal*. Had the child been born when it should have, its *mazal* would have been different.

Why Only Rashbi?

We are still left with the question of why we celebrate the passing of Rabbi Shimon bar Yohai and no one else. We have other great *tzaddikim* who transmitted Torah, such as Rabbeinu Hakadosh, who wrote the *Mishnah*, Rabban Gamliel, Rabbi Meir Baal Haness and

---

133. *Sotah* 12b.
134. *Shaar Ruah Hakodesh.*

many others. None of them has the day of his passing commemorated in this way.

Over a century ago, the rabbis in Tiberius decided to make a day in honor of Rabbi Meir, who is buried there. After all, they reasoned, all the tourists go to Meron and make donations. Why shouldn't we do the same here?

They made a day for Rabbi Meir, a few days before Lag BaOmer, hoping to encourage people to stop off on their way to Meron. However, the idea never took hold. Rabbi Shimon bar Yohai's celebration is on a different level altogether.

Two hundred and fifty years ago, the students of the Baal Shem Tov and the Vilna Gaon started coming to Eretz Yisrael. Both these great rabbis encouraged their followers to come to Eretz Yisrael. At that time, most of the Jews living in Eretz Yisrael were Sephardim. The Chief Rabbi of Tiberius was Rabbi Hayyim Abulafia. Many great *hachamim* had yeshivot in the Galilee, and Tiberius and Zefat were centers of Jewish life. Yerushalayim at the time had barely a handful of scholars. When the Ashkenazi rabbis arrived from Europe, they also went up north.

In 1837, a major earthquake destroyed the Zefat community and leveled many homes in Tiberius. Many people died, including leading Torah sages. At the time, the Hatam Sofer was the venerated leader of European Jewry. In his eulogy of the departed rabbis, he makes a striking comment. "Why," asks the Hatam Sofer, "did Hashem bring this frightening punishment on all those who lived in the Galilee, in Tiberius, and Zefat? What did they do to deserve it?" You had great rabbis who gave up all their wealth and positions to go up to Eretz Yisrael; you had community leaders, judges and *roshe yeshivot* who gave up everything to live in Eretz Yisrael at great personal sacrifice, and all of a sudden, an earthquake destroyed everything and they died.

"In choosing to live in Zefat and Tiberius," said the Hatam Sofer, "they slighted the honor of Yerushalayim. Yerushalayim is *Ir HaKodesh*, the holy city. They were punished for insulting the holy city."

In addition, he asked why, in fact, they went up to Zefat in the first place instead of settling in Yerushalayim. The answer, he says, is because Rashbi and the Ari are buried there.

But that doesn't make sense either. Does Yerushalayim lack gravesites? Yerushalayim is filled with graves! Whenever they want to build and construction begins, they find graves – graves of prophets, kings, *Tannaim, Amoraim, Rishonim, Aharonim,* the holy city has them all. Kabbalists? Those too, and *halachic* authorities as well. Why would these rabbis leave all the graves of Yerushalayim in order to live near the graves of Rabbi Shimon bar Yohai and the Ari *z"l?*

The Secret Code

Rabbi Akiva taught all the sections of the Torah to his students. To Rabbi Shimon bar Yohai in particular, he revealed the secrets of the Torah. Rabbi Shimon bar Yohai in turn revealed these secrets only to his greatest students. At the time, there were hundreds of *Tannaim,* but he chose only a *minyan* of students to receive these secrets.

Rashbi states clearly that the form of teaching he revealed was unique. Although all the *Tannaim* knew kabbalah, this special form of understanding was very deep and was truly a Divine revelation. It was expounded in such a way and transmitted in such a hidden form that even if the other *Tannaim* had read a page of Rashbi's works, they wouldn't have understood what it meant.[135]

Rashbi's achievement in revealing the Torah's secrets and passing

---

135. Rabbi Hayyim Vital in his introduction to *Etz Hayyim*.

on his teachings to a group of students has great significance. The *Zohar* tells us that in the merit of learning the Torah's secrets, the Final Redemption will come. That is the reason why studying *Zohar* has such importance, especially in these generations when we are so close to the coming of *Mashiah*.

This doesn't mean you have to try to popularize kabbalah and turn it into a fad, God forbid. It means that the *hachamim* who are on the right level should learn kabbalah. By doing so, they will give the Jewish people the merit they need to deserve the redemption.

However, even though not everyone studies kabbalah, nowadays no one is cut off from the kabbalah, either. If you learn *halachah*, you can open the *Shulhan Aruch* and find the Magen Avraham, who brings down every single custom of the *Zohar* and quotes the opinion of the Ari z"l. If you are Sephardi, you are learning all the *minhagim* of the kabbalists when you study the Hida, the Ben Ish Hai, or the Kaf HaHayyim. We all live according to the *minhagim* of the kabbalists. Even if we are not necessarily kabbalists and don't learn the depths of the kabbalah, our *halachah* is based on the kabbalah.

The same is true in other areas of our lives. Our whole approach to life, our *hashkafa*, the *mussar* the Jewish people study today is all based on kabbalah. Whether it's the works of Ramhal, such as *Mesillat Yesharim* or *Derech Hashem*; the *Nefesh HaHayyim* by Rabbi Hayyim of Volozhin, the prime disciple of the Vilna Gaon, and other books of the *mussar* movement; or books by the hassidic masters, anyone who understands sees that even though they don't mention kabbalah, their content is based on the writings of the kabbalists. Almost every book you study is based on the teachings of the Ari.

Even if you say, "I'm only a layman. I don't know any kabbalah," you are living a life according to kabbalah. You may not learn *Zohar* or study the Ari, but the customs you follow come from the kabbalah, and the *mussar* you learn is according to kabbalah. The light of the kabbalah has come into our lives, and it's everywhere.

The development of Torah thought until and including our times comes primarily from the generation of the Ari z"l. Until then, the earlier Rabbis, including the Rambam, would explain the ideas behind the *mitzvot* by using philosophical concepts. Generally speaking, these ideas had their origin in Greek wisdom, but they could also be used to explain the Torah's concepts. However, many of the leading Torah sages, including the Vilna Gaon,[135a] spoke very strongly against the Rambam's use of philosophy to explain concepts of the Torah. They said that by connecting the Torah with philosophy and Aristotelian thought, one may open the Torah to attack, because when other philosophers come along and disprove Aristotle, they feel they are disproving the Torah as well, which, of course, is wrong, because the Divine wisdom of the Torah is infinitely above human comprehension.[135b]

In the era before the kabbalah was revealed, Torah scholars were very limited in how they could explain the depth of the reasoning behind the Torah. Once the kabbalah was revealed, it shed light on every single detail of Jewish life, no matter how small. Rabbi Hayyim Vital writes in his introduction to *Etz Hayyim*, the teachings of the holy Ari z"l, that according to the revealed Torah, we are very limited in our ability to understand the *ta'amei hamitzvot*, the reasons for each *mitzvah*. These reasons are only basic ideas of why we have a *mitzvah*, broad sketches that lack detail. For instance, you can say that when a man puts on *tefillin*, he should feel that he is subjugating all his physical and mental powers to Hashem. Fine, but why do the boxes have to be square? Why do you need to wrap the strap around your forearm seven times? Why are the letters written they way they are? Why are

---

135a. *Yoreh De'ah* 179:13.
135b. R' Tzadok HaKohen, *Sefer HaZichronot, mitzvoth* 1 and 3.

those particular verses from the Torah used? You have *halachot* upon *halachot*, thousands of points. What is the meaning behind them?

All these things have reasons. The philosophers can't give us those reasons, but kabbalah can. Those who know kabbalah know every reason for every aspect of Jewish life in detail.

Take shaking the *lulav*, for instance. According to the *Gemara*, we shake it up and down to push away evil winds and rains.[136] However, as Rabbi Hayyim Vital writes, this doesn't necessarily make a lot of sense.[137] But if you learn the deep meaning behind shaking the *lulav*, you understand every single movement. Extending the *lulav*, pulling it toward you, shaking it three times to the four corners of the earth, and up and down – every single action has a reason. We learn this in the kabbalah.

All the sages who came to Eretz Yisrael preferred this special connection to Rabbi Shimon bar Yohai, because they understood that his teachings were going to bring us to the Final Redemption. That is why they went to Zefat, and preferred it over Yerushalayim.

In every generation, only a few great rabbis had received the kabbalistic tradition. The *Geonim* certainly had it. The Ramban's teacher, Rabbi Ezriel, was in the first generation of *Rishonim* after the Geonim. In the first *Menorat HaMaor*, by Rabbi Yisrael ben Yosef Alnakawa, the author repeatedly quotes the *Midrash Yehi Ohr*. This is really the *Zohar*. Rabbi David Hanaggid, a grandson of the Rambam, also quotes the *Zohar* in his explanation to *Pirkei Avot*.

In those days, the *Zohar* was hidden from the world at large and known to individuals only, but about 600 years ago, the *Zohar* was revealed and kabbalah study flourished. However, until the Ari

---

136. *Sukkah* 37b.
137. See the introduction to the *Etz Hayyim*, p. 3b.

revealed the *Zohar*'s depths, even great Torah minds could not fully understand it. Even the Ramak, Rabbi Moshe Cordovero, who lived in the sixteenth century and was the Ari's teacher, was very limited in what he could understand of the *Zohar*'s depths. Though he wrote wonderful books explaining the *Zohar*, including his monumental *Pardes Rimonim* and the classic *Tomer Devorah*, he could still not explain the depths. This has to wait until the Ari revealed its inner secrets.

All the Torah giants – the Vilna Gaon, the hassidic masters, the Sephardi *hachamim*, even the Ramhal – would never deviate from the words of the Ari. The Ari was accepted by all of *Klal Yisrael* as the greatest authority on the *Zohar*.

The Ari first learned kabbalah from the books of his teacher, Rabbi Moshe Cordovero. Later, Eliyahu Hanavi revealed himself to the Ari and taught him the kabbalah, Torah secrets no human mind could have discovered.

In the Tzaddik's Merit

Rabbi Avraham Meyuhas, a great halachic authority who lived over three centuries ago in Yerushalayim, is known for his monumental compendium on *Etz Hayyim* titled *Deglei Ahavah*. Among other works, he wrote a book of responsa called *S'de Ha'aretz*, in which he asks the following question: Is someone who lives in Yerushalayim permitted to go visit a *tzaddik*'s grave in Meron, Zefat, or Tiberius?[138]

Going there, it would appear, doesn't make sense, Rabbi Meyuhas answers, because all prayer ascends to the heavens through the *Kotel*. If you pray anywhere else, your prayers still have to go

---

138. *S'de Ha'aretz*, part 3, *halachot Kiddushin*, *shayla* 11, p. 27a.

through the *Kotel*, so if you live in Yerushalayim, go to the *Kotel* and pray.

On the other hand, Rabbi Meyuhas notes, it is an ancient custom to pray at the graves of *tzaddikim*.

When we pray at a gravesite, the Rema explains in the *Shulhan Aruch*, we are not praying to the person buried there, God forbid.[139] That would be like idolatry. We pray to Hashem, and ask that the merit of the *tzaddik* buried there help our prayers ascend. But how can a person who passed away hundreds of years ago help us? The answer is that "the righteous are greater in their death than they are in their lives."[140] They know no rest, neither in this world nor in the next, but move higher and higher from one level to the next.

What part of a *tzaddik* ascends? His soul. The body remains buried in the grave. The kabbalists teach us that a tiny portion of the soul's spirituality remains in the bones until the revival of the dead. Keeping the *mitzvah* of *melaveh malka* on *motzaei Shabbat* strengthens this spiritual part of a person. It encourages part of the soul to remain with the bones until the resurrection. Then, since the body has maintained some spirituality, it will be rebuilt and be resurrected.

The *Zohar* explains that when a person passes away, the higher parts of the soul separate from the body immediately. Only the lower parts remain connected to the home in which the person lived. During each of the seven days of mourning, another portion of the soul goes from the home to the grave. Only on the seventh day, when the soul has fully entered the grave, do we set up a gravestone.

The soul remains at the grave until the flesh decomposes. Once it is decomposed, even that part of the soul goes to *Gan Eden*, leaving

---

139. *Shulhan Aruch, Orah Hayyim* 381:4, *Ba'er Heteiv* 17.
140. *Hulin* 7b.

only an aura of the soul on the bones. At certain times, such as *erev Rosh Hodesh*, the fifteenth of the Hebrew month, and on the *yahrtzeit*, a greater part of the soul comes down to the grave. That is why it is significant to visit a grave on the *yahrtzeit* or at these other times. In a sense, the departed person's spiritual presence is there at the grave. Furthermore, this presence is like a ladder, connected rung by rung to the highest worlds, like Yaakov's ladder. When we visit a *tzaddik*'s grave, study his Torah, and pray to Hashem, we become connected to him. The part of his soul that is still there is linked to all the higher worlds. For us, it becomes an elevator to take our prayers upward.

Rabbi Meyuhas concludes that since there is a custom to go to a *tzaddik*'s grave on the day of his *yahrtzeit*, someone living in Yerushalayim can leave the city and travel to Zefat to do so. However, he says, there are conditions that must be fulfilled. For instance, if by going you will miss praying in a *minyan*, don't go. If going means compromising on kashrut or coming to sin, don't go! It's not worth it. Stay in Yerushalayim and go to the *Kotel*.

We can see from this the importance of going to a *tzaddik*'s gravesite on his *yahrtzeit*, especially that of Rabbi Shimon bar Yohai on Lag BaOmer. However, we must plan our visit in such a way that only good and no bad will come of it.

Shavuot

The forty-nine days of *sefirat haomer* between Pesah and Shavuot are a time of preparation. The Maharal notes that during these days, we study one chapter of *Pirkei Avot* every Shabbat afternoon. This tradition stems from the idea that developing good character traits precedes the acquisition of Torah, as we discussed in chapter 1, above. Before a person can merit receiving the Torah, he must first keep *mitzvot* and perfect and refine his behavior. *Pirkei Avot* teaches us how to attain these traits. According to the Maharal, this is why *Pirkei Avot* has five chapters: to correspond to the five books of Moses. (The sixth chapter of *Pirkei Avot* is a *baraita*, a text that is not part of the *Mishnah*.)

Our sages say, "Anyone whose actions exceed his wisdom, his wisdom will endure."[141] Rabbeinu Yona explains that a person who fulfills the *mitzvot* even though he has not yet fathomed their reasons and deeper meanings will always seek more knowledge about how to improve his observance. He will also want to better understand what he does. On the other hand, when a person's wisdom exceeds his observance, he will eventually stop learning entirely, because his knowledge is merely abstract. It does not result in action. In fact, he may eventually stop observing, as well.

This is why our sages emphasize that one's actions should be greater than one's wisdom. This is really the secret, as our sages relate from the response of the Jewish people at Sinai, when they said, "*Na'ase venishma*."[142] When Hashem asked them if they wanted to

---

141. *Pirkei Avot* 3:9.
142. *Shemot* 24:7.

receive the Torah, they didn't ask what demands would be made of them. "Na'ase venishma," they replied. "We are willing to accept, and then we'll do what we've accepted, without question." We must always remain in this fresh, striving state in which we continue to fulfill *mitzvot* according to our understanding, yet remain eager to increase our wisdom and achieve a higher level of purity in actions and character. When we are in this mindset, we are always driven to learn more.

Another very important point for success in Torah is respect and unity, especially among those who learn together in a yeshivah. Even the Ari *z"l* told his students that the most important thing was for love and peace to dwell between them. Wherever there is honor and respect for one another, there is great blessing for success in learning. Torah cannot coexist with jealousy and hatred.

The main idea of *kabbalat haTorah* on Shavuot is that each and every one of us has a portion in Torah. In describing the presence of the nation at Sinai, Moshe Rabbeinu speaks of "those who are with us today and those who are not with us." Our sages explain this to refer to souls that were not embodied at that time. Even these souls came down from the heavens to Sinai, to receive a portion in the Torah. One of the prayers we say on Simhat Torah is: "Hashem, illuminate our eyes with Your Torah so that we will be able to bring out, discover, reveal, and publish to the world the *hiddushim* that relate to our soul." Even the most creative and prolific authors such as the Vilna Gaon and the Ben Ish Hai could not create and reveal the *hiddushim* that pertain to another Jew's soul.

Obviously, attaining one's unique portion demands a lot of toil in Torah. In secular studies, one merely reads; Torah study means toiling, literally. Only this can produce *hiddushim* in Torah.

Our sages wondered about the meaning of the verse, "If you go in (*telechu*) My decrees."[143] Does it mean to keep the *mitzvot*? This cannot be the whole meaning, because the verse continues, "and observe My commandments and perform them," which refers to keeping both the positive and negative *mitzvot*. What, then, is the meaning of "If you go in My decrees"?

The answer is that it means one must toil and labor in Torah. The word *telechu* means that one is so involved in Torah that he is continuously learning. When a person truly learns in depth, not one moment of his life lacks Torah. Even on a trip, his thoughts will be involved in learning. That is the sign: *telechu*.

Hashem prepared us for this hard work during our years as slaves in Egypt.

When you think about it, the Egyptian exile is difficult to understand. Why would Hashem choose us as His people and then throw us into the iron furnace of Egypt to live as slaves. It doesn't make sense.

There is a reason, though, and it is striking. Hashem chose us for a purpose: to serve Him, as the verses say: "You will serve Hashem on this mountain,[144] and, "I will take you out of the servitude of Egypt, and I will make you My servants."[145] The best preparation for becoming faithful servants of Hashem was to first learn the meaning of servitude.

Most of us barely tap our potential. Rare is the person who uses more than ten to fifteen percent of his mental or physical capabilities. We like to get a good night's sleep and eat three square meals a day. Home and work environments are adjusted for maximum comfort. Even when we learn Torah, we need the right seat in the right spot

---

143. *Vayikra* 26:3.
144. *Shemot* 3:12.
145. *Ibid.* 6:6.

with the right *shtender*. Under such conditions, is it any wonder we coast along with the bare minimum of effort?

The Jews who survived the Holocaust taught us much about human potential. In the camps, they proved that people could exist in conditions of forced labor without food, clothing, or family. Jews sent by Stalin to Siberia survived the harshest conditions for years. They worked eighteen hours a day on subsistence rations, and made it through frigid winters, where temperatures dropped to thirty degrees below zero, without winter clothing.

Hashem wants us to realize our true capacity for spiritual achievement. He put us in Egypt so that through enslavement to Pharaoh we would realize our potential. Then, He took us out and gave us the Torah, expecting us to put all of that revealed strength into our studies. Our sages learn this from the verse: "*Zot haTorah adam ki yamut b'ohel*,"[146] which literally means: "This is the law: when a man dies in a tent." That is, all who come into the tent and everything inside receive a degree of spiritual impurity for seven days. Our sages, however, derive a deeper lesson from the verse: "This is the Torah – a man must die in a tent." That is, one who wishes to master Torah must be ready to give up his life in the tent of Torah study, because "Torah only exists in a person who has killed himself over it."

Are our sages exaggerating to make a point? Absolutely not. On the contrary, they are teaching that we must immerse ourselves so completely in Torah study that even if we have to deny ourselves sleep or reduce our amenities, that is what Hashem wants from us. Our sages summed this up with a strong image: One must put such strength into learning that he "vomits up the milk he nursed from his mother."[147] This means that a person must toil to such an extent that

---

146. *Bamidbar* 19:14.
147. *Berachot* 63b.

he burns up not only yesterday's cholent or what he ate a month ago, but even what he took in from the moment of birth. All this must be given up for Torah.

In the *Haggada*, we say that even if Hashem had brought us to Mt. Sinai but did not give us the Torah, it would have been sufficient for us (*"dayeinu"*). This is hard to understand. Until this point, every line of the song makes sense. For instance, one verse says that if Hashem had killed the Egyptians without giving us their wealth, it would have been enough. Drowning the Egyptians who enslaved us was an end in itself. But arriving at Mt. Sinai was not an end in itself.

The explanation is this: If Hashem had brought us to Mt. Sinai, and said, "I am giving you the Torah, but I am not bringing it down for you. You will have to go up to the heavens and get it yourselves" – this too would have been enough for us. We would have built ladders and let nothing stand in our way of receiving the Torah. Torah is our life, so no matter what obstacles are placed in our way, no matter how hard it might be to reach, we will get to it.

Shavuot is not just a commemoration of the fact that three thousand years ago, Hashem gave us the Torah. Our sages say that every year, the Torah comes down anew on Shavuot. New revelations in the Torah, insights that pertain only to the souls alive in our generation, come into the world at this time. If we put in the amount of toil that Hashem expects from us, Hashem will light up our eyes to understand these *hiddushim*, reveal them and publicize them, and that will be our greatest merit in this world and the World–to–Come.

The 17th of Tammuz

On the 17th of Tammuz, we fast and begin a three-week period leading up to Tisha B'Av, the day we mourn the destruction of both the First and Second Temples. Both times, we were exiled from Eretz Yisrael, as well.

Regarding the exile following the destruction of the First Temple, the prophet Yirmiyahu asks: "Who is the wise man…or prophet who can explain why the land was destroyed…?" He asks, but does not have an answer. In the next verse, however, he receives the answer from Hashem: "Because they have forsaken My Torah."[148] Yet, if the destruction occurred because of a lack of Torah study, surely Yirmiyahu, and the other prophets and sages of that era would have known about it.

Rather, the problem was internal – not in *how much* they studied, but in *how* they studied. The *Gemara* explains that "forsaking My Torah" means that people did not say a blessing before learning.[149] The Ran, Rabbeinu Nissim of Gerona, Spain, one of the great *Rishonim*, explains that the Torah was not important enough in the people's eyes to warrant a blessing before they started learning. In other words, they had turned Torah study into a way of life. It became as automatic as brushing their teeth in the morning and putting on pajamas before going to sleep. Laying *tefillin*, putting on a *tallit*, praying, and learning Torah were all rote behaviors, and this was wrong. When they sat down to study Torah, they were not happy at doing Hashem's will, not excited at performing a *mitzvah*. This is what caused the destruction.

---

148. *Yirmiyahu* 9:11–12.
149. *Bava Metzia* 85b.

Other commentators say the First Temple was destroyed because the nation did not keep *shemittah*, the sabbatical year. *Shemittah* is the *mitzvah* to let the land of Eretz Yisrael lie fallow every seventh year. Plowing, planting, and other agricultural activities are prohibited during the seventh year, and any produce of that year is considered *hekfer*, ownerless, for anyone to enjoy. Anyone can come to a field, vineyard, or orchard and take whatever he needs to eat. The Babylonian exile between the First and Second Temples was seventy years long, one year for each *shemittah* year not kept.[150]

Was it lack of enthusiasm and appreciation for Torah study that brought about the destruction of the First Temple, or was it failure to observe *shemittah*?

Though some see these two answers as contradictory, they are actually one and the same. The purpose of the sabbatical year was to guarantee that even farmers, whose work is time-consuming and physically demanding, would be freed from their duties to devote themselves to Torah at least one year in every seven years.

Neglect of the Torah, diminished respect for Torah, and the wrong attitude toward keeping *mitzvot* caused the destruction of the First Temple and our exile from Eretz Yisrael.

The Second Temple

The Second Temple was destroyed for a different reason. No criticism is voiced about people not studying Torah or studying with the wrong attitude. Great, holy *Tannaim* lived at that time, and yeshivot filled with many students flourished. The problem was *sinat hinam*, baseless hatred. In addition, there was a pervasive, arrogant attitude of *kohi v'otzem yadi*, "My strength, and the might of my

---

150. Rashi on *Vayikra* 25:18.

hand" have brought me success.[151] People attributed their achievements to their own efforts and talents, forgetting that everything is from Hashem. This brought about the destruction of the Second Temple.

Obviously, these two reasons are connected, because a person will never know how to correct his bad character traits unless he learns Torah. *Pere adam yivaled*, "A man is born like an animal."[152] If a person doesn't work on himself and train himself to act properly, he will lose his temper easily, think only of himself and his desires, and never take other people into consideration. Perfecting our character until we attain the level of behavior the Torah expects from us requires self-awareness, which can only be gained through Torah study.

Talmud Torah k'neged kulam, "Torah study comes before everything else and outweighs everything else."[153] Even one word of Torah can outweigh all the six hundred and twelve other commandments. Talmud Torah is a *mitzvah* in and of itself, and it is also the key to the other *mitzvot*, because no *mitzvah* can be fulfilled without knowing the relevant *halachot*.

The Inner Sanctuary

It is hard for most of us to relate to the destruction of the *Bet HaMikdash*. We lack an appreciation of what it was and what it meant. Perhaps one who studies all of *seder Kodashim* might have a better idea of what we are missing. He would be familiar with the *korbanot*, how the different sacrifices and offerings were brought, the wonderful features of the *Bet HaMikdash*, the *klei hakodesh* and the

---

151. *Devarim* 8:17.
152. *Iyov* 11:12.
153. *Kiddushin* 39b.

laws of the priestly vestments, the order of the *avodah* and how the *kohanim* acted and behaved. But for those of us who lack this information, it all seems so distant and far off.

Furthermore, the destruction took place over two thousand years ago. Our sense of loss has diminished with time, as is human nature. In *halachah*, mourning over the destruction of the Temple is referred to as *aveilut yeshana*, an old loss. For this reason, the *halachah* is more lenient with the laws of mourning on Tisha B'Av than a regular, "fresh *aveilut*" for someone who died recently.

The *Zohar* talks about the exile of the *Shechinah*, the Divine Presence, which is now "lying in the dust." It describes how we must sit down on the floor and recite the *Tikun Hatzot* at midnight and strive to increase our *mitzvot* in order to raise the *Shechinah* from her low position. Even these concepts are foreign to us. We do not have a proper understanding of what the term *Shechinah* means, and what is meant by saying it "lies in the dust." How can it be dependent on us to lift the Divine Presence out of the dust? After all, the Holy One runs the whole world. In one second, He can change everything: He can send *Mashiah*, rebuild the *Bet HaMikdash*, and bring about all the wonderful things we are waiting for. Why would He need our help raising the *Shechinah* from the dust?

One way I find effective to help us connect with these ideas is to relate the *hurban* to ourselves. The prophet Yirmiyahu (7:4) refers to the Jewish people as "the sanctuary of Hashem." Every Jew is like a *Bet HaMikdash,* as the verse says, "They shall make for Me a *mikdash*, and I will dwell in them." The commentators note that it does not say I will dwell in *it*, but in *them*, inside each and every Jew. The Divine Presence comes into our homes, it rests inside each one of us, as we say in our *Yom Tov tefillah*, "Your great and holy Name You called upon us" – Your Name is inside us.

There are *midrashim* and other holy works that describe how each limb of a person corresponds to a different part of the *Bet HaMikdash*. This is a very lengthy topic, but we shall mention one example. Our sages say that during prayer, a person "directs his heart to the Holy of Holies." This indicates that the heart corresponds to the Holy of Holies. As we know, the heart rules the body. If you have a healthy heart, the whole body is healthy. Even the mind is ruled by the heart more than by anything else. Although the brain is the seat of the intellect, the heart is the seat of the emotions, and the bottom line is that a person operates according to how he feels.

This is why our sages teach us that the *yetzer hara* and the *yetzer hatov* reside in the heart. The evil inclination occupies the left side of the heart and the good inclination dwells in the right side. This is the arena where we fight our battles between good or bad. This is the most pivotal part of our spiritual existence, and it therefore corresponds to the *Kodesh Hakodashim* of each Jew's private *Bet HaMikdash*.

So, if we want to get a feeling about the *hurban*, we can think about ourselves. How much *Shechinah* is there in our personal *Bet HaMikdash*? To what extent are we lacking spiritual perfection? How often do we get angry, speak badly about people, or act incorrectly? These actions cause the *Shechinah* to leave us and that is our private *hurban Bet HaMikdash*. As our sages say, *kol dor shelo nivneh Bet HaMikdash beyamav ke'ilu neherav beyamav*, "every generation in whose times the *Bet HaMikdash* is not built is considered as if it was destroyed in its time."[154] How are we to understand this? The *Bet HaMikdash* was destroyed nearly two thousand years ago. How is it considered as if it were destroyed again? The answer is that we are talking about this personal *Bet HaMikdash* that exists today as a representation of the higher *Bet HaMikdash*, and by doing something wrong, a person can drive away the *Shechinah* in a renewed *hurban Bet HaMikdash*.

---

154. *Talmud Yerushalmi, Yoma* 1:1.

Rabbi Hayyim of Volozhin writes something quite frightening. He says that a Jew who allows a lustful thought or image to enter his mind causes a greater desecration than that of Nevuchadnetzar and Titus. They defiled only the physical *Bet HaMikdash* of this lowly world, a *mikdash* built of wood and stone, while the Jewish people, whose souls are connected to the higher worlds, have the power to destroy the spiritual *Bet HaMikdash* high above in the spiritual worlds. As our sages say, "The spiritual, higher *Bet HaMikdash* corresponds to the physical lower *Bet HaMikdash*."[155]

So, while Titus and Nevuchadnetzar did disgraceful and vulgar deeds and committed terrible, destructive acts, they affected only the lower *Bet HaMikdash* of sticks and stones. But if a Jew, God forbid, allows an evil thought to enter his mind and lets his heart be consumed with the fire of the *yetzer hara*, he is setting fire to the higher *Bet HaMikdash*. This is a literal destruction of the *Bet HaMikdash* in our days.

Now, having understood our personal *"hurban,"* we can fully understand that by studying Torah we can "rebuild" ourselves and bring perfection to the whole world.

Hochmah, Bina, and Da'at

The *Shemoneh Esre* is made up of three sections. In the first three blessings, we praise Hashem. In the following thirteen, we make our requests. Some requests are personal, while others are for *Klal Yisrael*, for the coming of *Mashiah*, or for the building of the *Bet HaMikdash*. At the end, we say three blessings thanking Hashem for all the good He does for us and for answering our prayers.

In the middle thirteen blessings, the first thing we ask Hashem is to

---

155. *Tanchuma Vayikra* 7.

bestow us with all facets of human intelligence: *hochmah, bina,* and *da'at.* We are asking for the most important thing in the world – the wisdom of the Torah. This is what differentiates us from the gentiles, from animals, and from all other elements of creation. Without this, a human being would be no different than an animal. Animals enjoy eating, and we enjoy eating, too. They enjoy splashing in water, and we enjoy splashing in water, too. We're basically the same. What makes us different? Torah. Therefore, the first request we make concerns our intelligence, which is what sets us apart from the animal world. Being created in God's image means that we have been given a spark of the Divine intellect, and this is what distinguishes us from all other creations. We have the capacity to understand the abstract and the spiritual. The more a person studies and sanctifies his life, the deeper his insight will be and the more intense his spirituality.

The human brain is divided into three parts. Each occupies one of the skull's three sockets, located on the right, on the left, and at the back of the head, at the nape of the neck. The kabbalists teach us that the right brain is *hochmah,* wisdom; the left is *bina,* insight gained through comparison; and the central brain at the back is *da'at,* wisdom and insight in perfect balance. Each part of the brain has a specific function. The *hochmah*-wisdom part of the brain can absorb tremendous knowledge, like a computer. Using the *bina*-insight part of the brain, we compare points of wisdom, define differences and similarities, and gain deeper understanding. *Da'at,* at the center, is the balance point. *Da'at Torah* is the ability to weigh differing opinions to determine the true *halachah.*

There are four volumes of the *Shulhan Aruch,* but every *halachic* authority must know the fifth as well. The fifth volume is common sense, which we all know is not that common at all. *Da'at Torah* is knowing how to apply the wisdom of Torah. It means saying the right thing to the right person at the right time. A *halachic* authority must take into consideration the person asking the question as well as his particular circumstances. Each community has different conditions, different problems, and different customs, so rendering a decision requires not only great wisdom, but also the ability to translate this wisdom into the realm of correct action.

Our *hachamim* tell us that a stinking carcass is better than a Torah scholar without *da'at*. He may have a lot of *hochmah;* he may even know the entire Torah in depth. But if his practical application is incorrect, all his wisdom is worthless.

Learning how to apply Torah practically comes only from being in the company of great rabbis. What is learned from their every action cannot be learned from books.

The purpose of studying Torah is to repent and to do good deeds. The Torah must change us. We must feel that the Torah is uplifting us and changing our way of thought and behavior, making us more considerate, more accommodating, and more thoughtful of others.

We forget that we are surrounded by opportunities to do *mitzvot*. People tend to divide their lives into two separate worlds, the holy and the mundane. There's the world of the synagogue, where you don *tallit* and *tefillin* and pray, and then there's the jungle out there, where you work. But that's not that way it is. By saying a kind word to someone you meet on the way to work, you are fulfilling the *mitzvah* of *gemilut hassadim*. Providing financial help is one type of *hesed*, but the possibilities are endless. You can give someone a good idea, you can give them a business contact or an investment tip. *Hesed* can be a word of encouragement or a smile. People don't realize that Torah and *mitzvot* encompass our entire lives.

Changing Our Order of Priorities

When Yaakov Avinu brought his family down to Egypt, he sent Yehuda ahead of everyone else. Rashi brings the words of our sages who say Yehuda was sent to establish a place of learning.[156] Yaakov made sure that by the time his family arrived, a yeshivah would already be established with rabbinical authorities to decide *halachic* issues. A community without Torah leadership, without spiritual guidance, without Torah classes and lectures has no value and will eventually disappear. Yaakov Avinu taught us that the first thing any community needs is the "four cubits" of *halachah*. Begin with Torah. Set up the yeshivah, the Talmud Torah, the synagogue, and the *mikveh* first. Above all, make sure you have Torah centers, places where people come to study and grow in Torah.

Today's generation cannot transmit Torah to the next generation in the same way as did previous generations. It is no longer enough to tell a child, "This is the way we do things because this is the way we've always done things, and this is the way you're going to do things, too." Maybe the outside world had fewer temptations back then, or maybe children have changed, but one thing is certain: this approach will no longer work. If we want our children to follow in our tradition, we ourselves will have to develop and grow, to be able to show them that there are answers and explanations to every question that can be asked.

Recently, a prominent individual asked me a scientific question about the creation of the world. When I answered him fully, he was shocked. "Rabbis know this as well?" he said, astonished. We have to know what to answer a non-believer.[157]

In the old days, a Jew could point to the world outside and say to

---

156. *Bereshit Rabbah* 46:28.
157. *Pirkei Avot* 2:14.

his children, "Do you see all those people out there? Thank God, we're better than they are." Today, that's not saying much. Today's outside world is one where morality and ethical values are at new lows. Drugs, corruption, and degenerate lifestyles are all par for the course. Saying we're better than they are is like going to a zoo and saying, "You see all these animals? We're better than they are." It's no longer enough just to be better than what is out there; we have to demand more from ourselves. Today, the middle of the road is very dangerous. In order to end up in the middle, you have to be a little bit to the right. That way, when you are pushed and pulled, you will at least remain in the middle.

Everything – our home, our future, our children, our happiness, and the continuation of our communities – depends on our setting aside time for Torah study. We have to make the time. You don't have to be a slave to your job or business. You don't have to be the first one at the office in the morning and the last to leave at night. No one should make the mistake of thinking those extra hours are going to bring in more money, because that is one hundred percent incorrect. Work whatever is the accepted norm for the job, but not more. Use the morning and evening hours before and after work to learn Torah. As long as your pipeline is open, blessing and success can flow from Above.

This is not to say one should neglect his business. Our *hachamim* tell us that if a person hires workers and doesn't pay careful attention to what they are doing, he will surely lose his money. But within the framework of living your life, there is a lot of time that can be allocated or reallocated to Torah study. Beyond family and job concerns, we have to ask ourselves why we are here in this world and what is expected of us.

The Ben Ish Hai says most people reverse the true order of priorities: They give ninety percent of their attention to their business, and most of what's left to their family. Beyond that, they go to *shul*, pray, and listen to a Torah lecture here and there. When they pass on to the next world, though, all that is left behind. A person's family accompanies him only as far as the grave, and his wealth not even that far. The only things he takes with him are Torah, *mitzvot*, and good deeds. What he considered trivial during his lifetime was really his biggest investment. Even the best financial investment on earth cannot match the returns on spiritual activities, which pay out dividends forever.

On a trip to Panama, I met a prominent member of the community who put this ideal into practice. He wanted to make progress in his own learning, and he wanted his children to get the right Torah education as well. He did not let the lack of facilities in his location stop him. Following a tradition practiced by Jews everywhere throughout the ages, he hired a rabbi to live with the family. He pays the rabbi a substantial salary, equivalent to that given to the executives who work for him in his business. In exchange, the rabbi teaches him. On the way to work, he and the rabbi study together. At home, the rabbi teaches his children, and the rabbi's wife teaches his wife. The extended family and friends also study with the rabbi and rebbetzin.

I told this businessman that he had rejuvenated an old Halebi custom. In Haleb (Aleppo), Syria, even working men were very learned. They knew the entire *Tanach* by heart, and were fluent in *Mishnah* and *Gemara*, which they studied daily. Some businessmen were Torah scholars of great stature, *hachamim* who authored serious books on Torah topics. Every workingman took into his home at least one *hacham* and his family, and sometimes two or three, to form a private *kollel*. The *hacham* studied with the father, taught the children, and answered *halachic* questions on the spot.

It was possible then, and it's possible now. We need to connect to a place of Torah, and spend our time with Torah scholars.

Even if study does not come easily, just keeping company with *hachamim* will help a person grow in Torah. If you apply yourself in Torah, you will succeed. A person should never feel, "I didn't learn when I was young. Now I'd like to learn, but I can hardly read. What can I do?" Previously, he may not have had the opportunity or he may not have taken his studies seriously enough, but now he can make a start. Our guiding principle is that "one who wants to purify himself is helped to do so."[158] If you want to improve yourself and you put in the effort, Hashem will help you. "Make an opening the size of the eye of a needle," Hashem tells us, "and I will open up the gates of a banquet hall."[159] You just have to make that tiny effort. Start and you will see the blessing and success.

When a person toils in Torah, the Torah toils for him. "He toils in this place, and his Torah toils for him in a different place."[160] Every Torah scholar will verify that this is true. Sometimes, you find a certain *Gemara* difficult. You work on it, you break your head over it, and finally, you understand whatever you can. Because you toiled over this *sugya*, when you go to learn another part of the *Gemara*, you find the discussion literally opens itself up before you. You look in the commentators and are amazed to discover that your line of reasoning is identical to that of the Rashba. What happened? The Torah revealed itself to you. You have a personal relationship with Torah. As the *Gemara* says, *Yagata umatzata, ta'amin*, "You toiled and found, believe it."[161] Notice that it does not say, "You toiled, and you were successful." You don't necessarily get what you toiled for. *Yagata umatzata* – you toiled, and you found. When Torah is revealed to you and you understand, it's a discovery.

In the business world, this happens all the time. You can channel

---

158. *Yoma* 38:2.
159. *Midrash Rabbah* on *Shir Hashirim* 5:2.
160. *Sanhedrin* 99b.
161. *Megillah* 6b.

your efforts in one direction, but the money comes in from another angle entirely, one you never dreamed of. If you toil in Torah, you are going to get back big dividends. Success is guaranteed. All you need to do is try.

Because Torah is the most important thing in life, our first request in the *Shemoneh Esre* is that we be given full mental powers – the best computer in the world – to use for learning Torah. Torah is the only thing that can build our minds so that we think in the right way, act in the right way, do *mitzvot* in the right way, pray for the right things, know how to pray, and know what we're doing in this world.

The 17th of Tammuz, when our sadness over the Temple's destruction is greatest and our prayers to see it rebuilt more intense, is a good time to make, or renew, a commitment to dedicate ourselves to Torah. By learning Torah, we are in fact doing the utmost we can for our Creator Whose home in this world has been destroyed. Think of it: the Divine Presence is without a home. It's a frightening thought. It leads us to ask ourselves what we can do to remedy the situation.

The answer is as stated by our sages. From the day the Holy Temple was destroyed, nothing is left for Hashem in this world except four cubits of *halachah*.[162] Someone who sits down to study Torah is actually preparing his small corner of the world to be a home for Hashem. Eventually, all these little corners will cover the whole world, thus building the third *Bet HaMikdash* – the ultimate home of Hashem in this world.

---

162. *Berachot* 8:1.

Hanukat Habayit

W hat is the idea behind the custom of making a *hanukat habayit*, a dedication of a new home?

After Moshe Rabbeinu built the *Mishkan*, there was a week of dedication in which sacrifices were offered. This was called *hanukat hamizbe'ah*, "dedication of the altar." That is the reason for translating *hanuka* as "dedication." On the other hand, there is a similar word which seems to imply just the opposite. "*L'hanech*" means to educate, as King Solomon said, "Educate (*hanoch*) a child according to his way,"[163] which means to bring out the good in the child's character and develop it. The verse continues, "Even when he grows old he will not abandon it," meaning that because this goodness was inherent in the child, it will remain with him when he matures.

These two connotations of the word *hanukah* seem diametrically opposed. The first implies dedicating something new, while the second refers to bringing out something that already exists. However, there is no real conflict, for *hinuch* combines both meanings, both the initial establishment of a value system by which to live, as well as the ongoing implementation of this system.

Our sages tell us that all beginnings are difficult.[164] This is because "Sin crouches at the door (*petah*)."[165] The word *petah* can mean more than door. It also implies a beginning. The evil inclination

---

163. *Mishle* 22:6.
164. *Yalkut Shimoni* 276.
165. *Bereshit* 4:7.

always tries to get hold of us right at the start of any endeavor. When a person moves into a new home, it looks for ways to worm its way in and set up shop. In the beginning, the evil inclination crouches down, looking for an opening to sneak in. Later, it will stand up straight and try to take over.

The curse given to the serpent in *Gan Eden* is that "he will crush your head, and you will crush his heel."[166] The simple meaning is that in order to kill a snake, you must crush its head, but beware that the snake does not bite your ankle. When I was a child, my grandmother told me a story about a person who saw a snake and cut it into pieces, but didn't smash its head. In the morning, when the man went to put on his slippers, the serpent bit him, and he died. My grandmother was teaching me that to get rid of the evil inclination, you have to crush its head.

Rav Hayyim Vital explains this with an interesting twist.[167] When does the serpent, the evil inclination, make his greatest effort to interfere? At the head or beginning. Whenever there is a beginning, anything fresh or new, the evil inclination looks for a way to slink inside. However, if a person takes control of the situation from the outset and refuses entry to his home and his life, then he can completely uproot the evil inclination. If he doesn't stop him in the beginning, however, then, as Hashem tells the serpent, "*you will crush his heel*" – the serpent will get a person in the end.

Every beginning sets a pattern on which the future is based. Take buying a home, for instance. For many people, buying a home means keeping up with the Joneses. A bigger home or a more beautiful home adds to a person's sense of prestige. But that's not the true value of a home. Commencing life in a home begins a pattern, and

---

166. *Ibid.* 3:15.
167. *Derech Hayyim*, beginning. See also Rabbeinu Bahya on this verse.

this beginning is what will determine the continuation – and ultimately, the end.

I often point out to couples before their marriage that the way they start their lives together will set a pattern for the rest of their lives. If they resolve from the outset to be decent and well-mannered, never to insult or hurt their partner, then such standards will remain with them, God willing. On the other hand, if they are not careful in the beginning, they can become accustomed to improper modes of behavior that are very hard to uproot later. The real battle is at the beginning, which is why our sages say that when a person buys a new home he must make a *hanukat habayit*, to dedicate his home and set it on the right track.

How does one make a *hanukat habayit*? You invite family, friends, and rabbis, and you dedicate your home to Torah, with words of Torah, blessings, and good intentions of how you plan to live your life in that home. Once this is done, everything follows as it should.

The Malbim illustrates the power of intent by describing three weddings. At each wedding, a *hatan* gives the *kallah* a ring. At each wedding, distinguished rabbis say the *sheva berachot*. Each wedding has a *ketubah* (marriage contract), wine, guests, and all the rest. However, one of these weddings is not really a wedding but a business deal, and another wedding is just a party. Only the third wedding is a real wedding.

It all depends on the intentions of the people involved, says the Malbim. The first *hatan* has in mind that he is marrying the daughter of Mr. So-and-so, who is very rich. "As his son-in-law," he thinks to himself, "I will be taken into the family business." In other words, this *hatan* is making a business deal out of his wedding, despite the *sheva berachot*, the ring, the wine, and the rest.

The second *hatan* chose a very attractive girl, because, basically, he wants to have a good time. Of course, he does so with the rabbi, the *berachot*, the ring, and the *ketubah*, but ultimately, he's going to a party, that's all.

The last couple understands that marriage is a responsibility. It's building a family. Each checks out the other person and his or her family, character and behavior before marrying with the proper intentions. This time, the *sheva berachot* are real *sheva berachot*, the *ketubah* is a real *ketubah*, and the ring is a real ring. In all three cases, the external actions were the same, but intent is the determining factor to what really takes place.

Declaring Our Intent

When the Jewish people entered Eretz Yisrael and conquered the seven nations, they took possession of the latter's homes. At this period in history, we had a unique *mitzvah*. The *mitzvah* applied when signs of a spiritual affliction called *tzara'at*, which was like a fungus or plague, appeared on the walls of a home. The residents would call a *kohen*, who would scrutinize the affected area and put the house in quarantine. A week later, the *kohen* would return to reexamine the home. If the infection was still there, the walls of the house were dismantled, and the infected stones were broken and taken outside the town, far from where people lived.

The sages asked why this strange disease and its purification process took place only then and not in later generations. The Talmud answers that before the Canaanites abandoned their homes, they hid gold and silver within the walls. Hashem wanted us to discover these treasures, which this *mitzvah* of purification enabled us to do, when we eventually broke down the infected walls.

The *Zohar* presents another interpretation. Why do we say the *l'shem yihud* prayer before doing *mitzvot*? "For the sake of the union of the Holy One and His *Shechinah*, I am hereby ready and prepared to fulfill the *mitzvah*..." The *Zohar* explains that by stating our pure intentions before actually doing a *mitzvah*, we bring holiness into whatever we do.[168] As an example, the *Zohar* mentions the construction of the *Mishkan*. People donating items would say, "This is in honor of the *Mishkan*, in the honor of Hashem." Women who wove fabrics, and craftsman working on gold and silver would say, "This is for the sake of Heaven, for the *Mishkan*." By saying that, the items were imbued with tremendous sanctity.

The *Zohar* goes on to point out that the forces of impurity, meaning the occult and evil, work the same way. When idolaters of previous eras built a temple, they would say, "This is in honor of-_____," mentioning the names of their gods. Just saying those names brought great impurity upon those buildings. The *Zohar* tells us that the Canaanites would mention the names of their gods when they built their homes, causing their homes to be filled with evil spirits or evil forces. The diseases that beset these homes gave an opportunity to throw those parts away, to bring new materials, and to purify the homes from the evil influences of those forces.

The *Zohar* finds proof for this in the fact that the infected stones could not be reused. If the purpose of dismantling the walls was, as stated in the *Gemara*, solely to find treasure, why not put the old stones back once the treasure was discovered? It seems clear that the stones themselves were impure and infected with evil.

The *Zohar* says this idea lies behind the custom of *hanukat habayit*. *Hanukat habayit* means bringing *kedushah*, sanctity, into your home. When dedicating a new home, the *Zohar* instructs us to say, "This home is a home for the *Shechinah*, the Divine Presence, a home for *mitzvot*. It is a home for *tzedakah*. It's a home for *hachamim*, for *shiurim*, for *berachot*, for raising children properly and for all the wonderful things we want in a Jewish home." By saying

---

168. *Zohar* 3:7a.

this, we begin a life in the new home of purity on the right foot, in the way of the Torah. These words remove any evil influence that was ever in the home, purifying it and allowing the Divine Presence to enter. A home founded on such a holy base will never be a place of sin.

Dedicate Your Marriage

A verse dealing with the *Mishkan* provides an important insight into how the Divine Presence enters a Jewish home. *V'asu li Mikdash veshachanti betocham*, "They [the Jewish people] shall make for Me a Tabernacle, and I shall dwell in them."[169] Our sages point out that grammatically, the sentence should have read, "and I shall dwell in *it*." They derived from the unusual wording that the *Mishkan* was to serve as a power plant generating spirituality. Just as the energy generated by a power plant is meant not to remain in the power plant but to be distributed to individual homes, so, too, the spiritual energy generated by the *Mishkan* was not meant to stay within it, but to reach *them*, the Jewish people, to dwell in their homes.

When a husband and wife merit it, the *Shechinah* dwells with them. "Man," in Hebrew, is *ish*, spelled *aleph-yud-shin*; "woman" is *isha*, spelled *aleph-shin-hey*. Both man and woman share two letters, the *aleph* and *shin*. Each has one unique letter as well: the man has a *yud*, and the woman, a *hey*. Our sages explain that the *yud*, because of its small size, symbolizes the World–to–Come, because very few actually merit it. The *hey* symbolizes this world. Like this world, it has two openings, one to go down, for those who don't improve their behavior, and a little hole between the leg and the roof through which one can go up to *Gan Eden*. There is always an opening through *teshuvah*.

These two letters hint at the differing responsibilities of each

---

169. *Shemot* 25:8.

partner in a marriage. Matters relating to the next world, the spiritual world, should be decided by the husband. For example, if a husband knows of a better school for the children, one more insulated from undesirable influences and with a stronger spiritual program, his wife should defer to his judgment on the matter. The home is the wife's department, and her husband should not interfere, for instance, in her choice of interior decoration. Anything connected to worldly matters should be decided by her. Like a well-run business, marriage will run more smoothly with clearly defined areas of responsibility.

Together, the husband's *yud* and the wife's *hey* form one of Hashem's Names. When husband and wife join together as a team, these letters join together as well, bringing the Divine Presence into the home. However, in marriages without sanctity and mutual respect, unity is also missing. The letters stand alone, unlinked, and the Divine Presence is absent. Instead, the *aleph* and *shin* of both husband and wife remain, forming the word *esh* – fire. This is a fate we do not wish on anyone.

The ultimate aim of a Jewish home is *shalom bayit*, peace between husband and wife. The extent of marital harmony determines the atmosphere of a home. Once a week, the woman of the house has a special *mitzvah* to light the Shabbat candles. This brings *shalom bayit* into the home. So essential is this *mitzvah*, that even if the money to buy oil and wicks must be begged, it must be done. Although there are many customs regarding how many candles to light, the primary obligation is to light two. They represent the commandment of *shamor v'zachor*, keeping the Sabbath and remembering it. Mainly, though, the two candles represent husband and wife, who bring light into the home through their elevated behavior. When there is mutual love and respect between parents, children grow up surrounded by warmth and goodness. They witness daily the small acts of kindness each parent does for the other. This is a healthy atmosphere, one the children will wish to recreate when they become adults.

Bilaam's Strategy Revisited

We can learn from Bilaam's curses – which Hashem changed into blessings – what Bilaam actually intended on destroying. What did Bilaam see that impressed him? Jewish homes. He saw the modesty practiced in the homes, the purity, and the fact that the doors of one home didn't face the other. He could not hold back his tongue from praise: "How good are your tents, Yaakov, your dwelling places, Yisrael!"[170] How wonderfully holy are your homes and your synagogues, your yeshivot, your schools!

When Hashem brought the flood to the world, He told Noah to prepare a huge ark and to bring his family and all living creatures into it so as to preserve what Hashem had created. As we know, all living beings inside the ark survived the flood.

Today, our ship is tossed by stormy seas. Wherever we live, we are surrounded by evil. Waves crash against us, and winds roar, trying to tear our sails. The streets outside, the mass media, non-Jewish culture – all these forces crash against us hoping to capsize our ark. Modesty has disappeared along with common human decency, and human conduct is far from what Hashem intended. In this turbulence, only a strong ship will survive. What is our Noah's ark? Our home. Now more than ever, every Jew's home must be his castle, a fortress to protect him.

Living among non-Jews brings with it the danger of assimilation. Without strong links to their heritage, Jewish youth marry out and disappear, lost to the Jewish nation. Statistics show that millions more than those killed by Hitler are being destroyed by assimilation.

Today we can understand what the founding rabbis of America's Syrian community achieved by forbidding – unconditionally – the acceptance of proselytes into their community. This was a truly great

---

170. *Bamidbar* 24:5.

thing for them, because they feared that conversion could be misused. Any gentile wanting to marry a Jewish boy or girl would say, "Sure I'm willing to convert," and then they would go to a reform or conservative rabbi, who performs an un-*halachic* ceremony and says, "You're Jewish." That's it. That's the end of the Jewish people, *halilah*. Children of such "marriages" will not be Jewish, and the community would be destroyed. Therefore, "Who is wise? One who foresees the inevitable."[171] The rabbis who instigated and formulated this *takanah* almost a hundred years ago foresaw what could be, and they protected the community. *Baruch Hashem*, the community, the synagogues, the yeshivot, the schools, and specially these homes are protected from the misuse of lenient, improper conversions.

Once, a rabbi from Israel visited America for the first time. When asked what his impression of America was, he replied, "America is just like the generation of the flood and the generation in which Hashem scattered the nations over the globe. Down on the streets, people behave like animals, and when I look up, the buildings I see are just like the Tower of Babel." Who will be protected? Those who maintain a Jewish home based on Torah and *mitzvot*. Shabbat, family purity, kosher food, daily prayer and study, Torah education for their children – these are what protect a Jewish home and give it a future. Such a home will remain Jewish forever.

This is why Bilaam set his evil eye precisely on the Jewish home, because he knew that if he could somehow infiltrate it and bring immorality into that home, the Jewish nation would be finished. He knew, though, how fortified the homes were, and so devised a scheme to break through their defenses.[172] Bilaam advised Balak, the Moabite king, to set up stalls selling products at reduced prices. When

---

171. *Tamid* 32a.
172. *Bamidbar Rabbah* 20:22.

a Jew went to shop, he found an old lady sitting in a beautiful, tastefully decorated booth.

"We have unbelievable items here at rock-bottom prices. Inside are even bigger bargains, almost free of charge," she would say.

Curious, a man would go inside the booth where a young Moabite woman sat waiting to entice him. At the point of sin, he would be seduced to worship their idol, Baal Peor. Through this evil plan, Bilaam brought the Jewish people to both immorality and idolatry, for which they were severely punished. Twenty-four thousand people died,[173] and this number reflects only those who tried to fight Pinhas. Many more thousands perished because of this sin.

Bilaam saw no chance of attacking the Jewish people in their homes. His strategy was to lure the husband away from his wife by attracting him into a store. I am sure many did not go shopping and others did but ran away when they realized it was a trap. What I wonder is, how much would Bilaam have paid to be able to bring television or the Internet into a Jewish home? What would it have been worth to him as a business investment?

It is a safe guess that Bilaam would have given billions to install such a device in a Jewish home. Mass media is filled with the three cardinal sins of idolatry, immorality, and murder. The biggest hero is the one who kills more people and acts more immorally. To this day, commercial advertising plies its wares using Bilaam's ploy. After all, a close-up of a watch on the wrist of a rabbi will not pull in shoppers.

And these things are installed in our homes! A religious man will not bring a television into his home, but he thinks to himself, "There's no harm in a computer." After all, today the computer knows all of *Shas* and more. It knows the *Shulhan Aruch*, the *Zohar*, and kabbalah. It's like having a chief rabbi in your home. You press a

---

173. *Bamidbar* 25:9.

button, and you have instant access to the entire Talmud. Fantastic. But there's another button, and when you press it you're in Paris or who knows where. Bilaam would have given anything to have this ability to contaminate Jewish homes.

Some people willingly bring these despicable items into their home. They think they serve some educational purpose for their children. But instead of studying, children are wasting their time with Mickey Mouse, Superman, Batman, and whoever else. Beyond the time wasted from their studies, constantly viewing evil people and their deeds does tremendous harm. It is possible to watch two children playing and see, by their movements and gestures, which one has a television at home.

When Bilaam saw the beauty of the Jewish home, he made a plan to catch us outside. Today, they're catching us inside as well. How much more do we have to strengthen our homes so that the Divine Presence will be with us!

Ki ha'adam etz hasadeh, "a man is a tree of the field."[174] The different parts of a tree – roots, truck, branches, twigs, leaves, and fruit – find their parallel in man. The roots of a tree seek nourishment. In man, the roots that nourish us are our predecessors and ancestors who were righteous and learned in Torah. We must remain connected with their lives, or we will wither and fail to grow in the right direction. The trunk symbolizes our spiritual leaders, such as the rabbi of the community or the head of the household; the branches represent the educators and spiritual instructors; the twigs and leaves are those who work for the benefit of the community in education and *hesed*. The fruits of our tree are the children. They are the future of the community and contain within them the seeds of future trees.

The fruit are beautiful. Each one has a different shape, color, smell,

---

174. *Devarim* 20:19.

and taste. They are truly the hope of the future. Yet, unfortunately, if we are not careful, a worm can penetrate the beautiful fruit and cause it to rot within. The worms come from outside, from television, video, images and books of the non-Jewish world.

Let us be strong to protect our children from Bilaam's evil plans even in our day.

A Strong Home Protects the Children

Our sages tell us that a home in which one does not constantly hear words of Torah could one day, God forbid, be destroyed. It lacks the merit to withstand the dangers of the outside world. Someday, the walls will crumble, and the outside world is going to come in – in full force. Sometimes, people wake up too late. I know many people who, although they belong to good, respectable families, have children who are not religious. Years ago, I told the parents, "Take care, or your children will go astray." "Impossible," they replied. Their children were going to the best schools. They weren't religious schools, but still, the parents were certain their children would turn out well-educated, well-behaved, and cultured. They would be good people, moral and ethical in all ways, even if not religious. Instead, their children turned to drugs, left the country, married non-Jews, and were destroyed. These parents lost their children. Their families have been wiped off the Jewish map for all eternity. All this starts at home, because more of a child's education takes place in the home than in school or in the synagogue.

When Rav Alfandari, one of the great rabbis, was asked who his main teacher was, he replied, "My mother, because what I learned from her, no rabbi could ever teach me." This echoes King Solomon's teaching that education starts when the child is still an infant.[175] The

---

175. *Mishle* 22:6.

sages reiterated this when they said that one who learns when he is young is compared to new paper being written on for the first time.[176] Impressions are strong and clear. For this reason, whatever a child absorbs in his home is a matter of utmost importance. Is he absorbing nonsense, or is he absorbing *kedushah, taharah*, and the presence of the *hachamim*?

Of course, children are children and need to play. However, their toys and games must be checked carefully. A father once came to me for advice. Among other things, he mentioned a certain children's game in his home. It involved pushing buttons, with the goal being that a drug peddler could escape the police. A child who plays this game learns that there is something called drugs, that they are illegal, and that the person who sells them can run away from the police. All these concepts become integrated into his way of thinking. This is truly dangerous. A parent has to check for harmful undertones in every single book his child reads and every single game he plays.

Our sages say that one should make his home a meeting place for *hachamim*.[177] There are several commentaries on this statement that have particular relevance to our subject. First, anyone who can organize a class and invite rabbis to speak in his home should certainly do so. Whenever rabbis need to hold a meeting, offer your home. "Would you like to use my home? We'll set up a nice table. The rabbis can be comfortable and discuss whatever they have to." The point, of course, is for the host to humble himself before the rabbis, sit at their feet and eagerly drink in their words, not that he should brag about his open house and the important guests he hosts.

Another sage says that having an open house does not mean

---

176. *Pirkei Avot* 4:20.
177. *Ibid.* 1:5.

inviting important guests, such as rabbis. Rather, it means welcoming poor people into your home, which rarely brings the host any honor.[178] In fact, the guests may not even be so easy to tolerate. Still, just as Avraham Avinu accepted all people, we, too, should be kind to even the most pitiable individuals. Avraham Avinu's tent was open on all four sides so that no matter from which direction a guest came, he was welcome. It should make no difference who the guest is, a celebrity or a poor wayfarer. Maybe his presence won't be much to brag about. No one will say, "You know who was at his house? President So-and-so! Chief Rabbi So-and-so!" It may not bring honor, but having this type of open house is the right thing to do.

The sages add, "And let the poor be members of your household."[179] In addition to the straightforward meaning noted above, we can give a novel interpretation to this statement as well: It costs a lot of money to be able to offer guests all they need. With guests, one may be lavish. However, one should not be lavish concerning one's own family. Bring them up with a more low-key style of living. Let the poor be the members of your *own* household. Raise your children to enjoy a simple lifestyle, and don't let them get used to luxuries, which always pose a danger.

Do It Right at the Beginning

This leads again to the idea of *hanukat habayit*, of starting out on the right foot. As soon as you come to the new home, start with words of Torah, blessings, and *mitzvot*. In *Bereshit*, Noah teaches us how crucial beginnings are. After the flood, immediately upon leaving the ark, it states *"Vayahel Noah ish ha'adama."*[180] This can be translated

---

178. *Ibid.*
179. *Ibid.*
180. *Bereshit* 9:20.

as "Noah began as a man of the land." The first thing Noah did was to plant a vineyard. Our sages point out, though, that "*vayahel*" is also related to the word *hulin*, in which case it would mean, *to make profane*. What did Noah, the man of the land, make profane? He planted a vineyard. And the outcome was that he made wine, became drunk, exposed himself, and disgraced his Divine image. This drunken behavior brought curse and destruction into the world. By planting a vineyard, Noah profaned the beginning. He could have planted wheat, barley, fruit, or other things that would have brought bounty to the world. Instead, he brought curse into the world.

Moreover, the sages say that what took place was miraculous. On the very day that Noah planted the vineyard, it bore fruit that ripened that very day. The wine he made also fermented that same day. It had a strong, delicious taste, and he drank and became drunk – all on that very first day after leaving the ark. Why did this miracle take place?

The Maggid of Dubno explained this with a parable. He said that once a Jew who was struggling hard to make a living heard that a very great rabbi had come to town, and decided to get a blessing from him. He waited in line quite some time until he finally stood before the rabbi with his request. The rabbi told him, "I bless you that the first business you involve yourself in will see tremendous success, a hundred thousand times your investment. So be careful to do a good thing, so that the blessing will rest upon a good thing."

By the time the man arrived home, it was very late at night, and his wife was waiting for him.

"Where were you?" she said.

"I went to a rabbi to get a blessing," he replied.

"What do you mean you went to a rabbi?" exclaimed his wife. "At two in the morning you went to a rabbi? I don't believe you! I want to know where you were."

"Please, I'm very tired now," he said. "Let's go to sleep now, and we'll discuss it tomorrow."

"No!"

"Don't make an issue of it, please."

"I want to know now! Tell me where you went. What did you do?"

The two began shouting at each other, and the blessing the man had received went into this argument. That's how they lived, unhappily ever after.

The Maggid of Dubno explains that at every beginning, blessings flow into the world. After the flood, when Noah stepped out of the ark, it was a new world, a new beginning of exceptional magnitude. Hashem had once again prepared tremendous blessings, this time for the new world Noah now had the opportunity to dedicate. His actions would set the pattern for the entire world. How did Noah start this new life? He planted a vineyard, made wine and became drunk. What is usually a long process miraculously took place in only one day due to Hashem's blessing.

The blessing was wasted. Noah profaned it. Had he built a yeshivah, the world would be filled with thousands of yeshivot. Had that couple gone to sleep peacefully and started a business the next morning, the blessing would have gone into the business instead of arguments.

This is the idea of *hanukat habayit*. *Hanukat habayit* means that Hashem gives a special blessing to a new home being established, and He wants this blessing to be used for good things. Therefore, invite rabbis, invite family and friends to wish you success, happiness and health, and dedicate your home with words of Torah. These things must be declared verbally. In donating for the *Bet HaMikdash*, people had to say, "This is for the *parohet*," and so on. So, too, it is good to declare, "My home will be a dwelling place for the

Shechinah." Until the Bet HaMikdash is built, the Shechinah will remain in exile. Nonetheless, every Jewish home can be a resting place for the Shechinah.

If we use the blessing that comes with a new beginning properly, it will continue, giving us financial success, parenting success, and a life filled with satisfaction. If we make a Torah-true Jewish home, the Shechinah will be with us. Of such a home, it can be said, "How good are your tents, Yaakov, your dwelling places, Yisrael!"[181]

---

181. Bamidbar 24:5.

The Power of Prayer

Most people have a very limited view of prayer. They think it means reciting a set formula three times a day at *Shaharit*, *Minhah* and *Maariv*. The wording in your *siddur* may follow *nusah Ashkenaz*, *nusah Sefard* or that of the Ari, and you have to pay attention to pronunciation, but other than that, you are reciting the same unchanging text as everyone else. Not feeling a personal connection, many people fall into a rote repetition of the prayers. Our sages tell us, though, that prayer without feeling is like a body without a soul.

Real prayer comes from the heart.

Many people think prayer means asking Hashem to give us what we think we need. This is inaccurate, because: (1) Hashem knows what is good for us even if we don't ask; and (2) only Hashem knows what we deserve. Anyone can say, "Hashem, I would love a Rolls-Royce, and, if You don't mind, throw in a palace, too." The list could go on and on. But Hashem may feel I don't deserve what I'm asking for, or that it would be dangerous for me to have it. Saying to Hashem, "I want this, so please give it to me" and expecting to receive what was asked for, is not praying.

The Ari *z"l* explains that when a person feels he lacks something, prayer gives him the opportunity to reinforce his belief in Hashem by asking Him for what he lacks.[182] When we turn to Hashem in prayer, we make a powerful statement of His Omnipotence. We demonstrate our conviction that no one else can

---

182. Introduction to *Shaar Hamitzvot*.

give us what we need, for everything is in His hands. We put all our belief and trust in Him.

When troubles arise, whether financial, health-related or any other type, people tend to look for easy solutions. "Maybe," they say, "there's some sort of *segulah* (mystical practice) or *kameya* (amulet) that will help." Maybe the *mezuzah* can be blamed or a fault found in the *ketubah*. Maybe it's *ayin hara* (the evil eye). It's as if they are saying, "Let the problem be anything but me."

The truth is, though, that the difficulties that beset us are just Hashem gently tugging on our sleeve and saying, "Come closer. I want to talk to you." Hashem is waiting for us to relate to Him. He is waiting for us to say, "Hashem, please help me." Running away from Him in search of instant solutions that don't exist misses the whole point.

When Moshe Rabbeinu told Pharaoh to let the Jewish people leave Egypt, Pharaoh responded with even harsher decrees. Moshe returned to Hashem and asked, "Why have You done evil to this nation? Why did You send me?" Hashem rebuked him. "Avraham, Yitzhak and Yaakov never doubted Me, yet you complain that I have done evil!"

Most people think Moshe was rebuked for complaining that his mission to Pharaoh only made things worse. We know, though, that the Egyptian bondage was like a smelting pot: the hotter it gets, the faster the gold melts. When gold melts, pure gold rises to the surface and impurities sink to the bottom. Pharaoh's evil decrees helped speed up the purification process the nation had to undergo, allowing the Jewish people to leave Egypt earlier than they would have otherwise.

Some *hachamim* explain the passage differently. They say that what angered Hashem was not the first question but the second: "Why did You send me?" The implication was, "I failed. Pharaoh did not let the Jewish people leave. If so, why did You send me in the first place?" What point was there to Moshe's mission if it ended in failure? The truth is, though, that when a person is sent on a mission by Hashem, his personal success or failure is not an issue. We must be willing to serve as Hashem's agents no matter what the outcome. More important to Hashem than our success is our willingness to try.

The same holds true for prayer. Whether we pray once, twice or a hundred times, if the prayer is not answered, we are still fulfilling our duty to the fullest by turning to Hashem in our time of need. Nothing more is expected of us; the rest is up to Him. If He wants to give us what we prayed for, fine – we will be happy to receive it. But if not, we have already done a wonderful thing and have fulfilled our duty to turn only to Hashem in our hour of need.

Are Your Prayers in Place?

There's another important point concerning prayer. It is not enough simply to call out and pray. We must first make sure to take all the necessary steps so that Hashem can give us what we are asking for.

"Whoever fixes a place for his prayer will be helped by the God of Avraham."[183] When such a person passes on, it will be said about him, "He was a humble person, a very pious person, a student of Avraham Avinu."[184] It seems remarkable that such a simple action – fixing a place for prayer – can reap us the reward of being considered students of Avraham Avinu and gaining Hashem's help. Although it is a mitzvah to pray daily in the same seat in the same synagogue, Hashem is everywhere and hears our prayers wherever we are. There must be more to this promise than that.

---

183. *Berachot* 6b.
184. *Ibid.*

Some explain fixing a place for prayer with the following analogy: A poor man walks into a bank and says, "I'd like to start a business, and I need a ten million dollar loan." If the manager wants to be nice, instead of showing him the door immediately, he asks, "Do you have any collateral? Do you have a cosigner or any way to guarantee the loan?" If the poor man has no grounds to make his request, he'll be sent away empty-handed. Were a well-known multi-millionaire to walk into the bank and ask for the same loan, he would get it on the spot.

The difference between the poor man and the rich man is this: The poor man's request was *out of place*. In light of the wealthy man's circumstances, his asking for a loan was *in place*. Before we pray, we have to know if we have made a place for our requests by preparing ourselves. If we haven't done all we can, which is up to us, how can we expect Hashem to do what we ask of Him?

The Hafetz Hayyim says we are often like the fellow who routinely asks Hashem in the morning prayers to "light up our eyes with Your Torah." When Hashem hears this prayer, He immediately instructs the angels to take huge barrels of Torah and wait for the man to open a *Gemara*. The minute he does, they are to shower him with Torah. But the man never opens that *Gemara*, and the barrels just wait. If he does his share, if he opens a *Gemara* and tries to learn, Hashem will light up his eyes with Torah. If you really try, Hashem helps. But if you don't make the effort, what's the use of your prayer?

The same is true in all that we do. We have to be like the rich man. By the time he makes his request, he has already done all he can. His own efforts have created a place for Hashem's blessings.

Even a Sharp Sword

Hashem loves our prayers. Avraham, Yitzhak, and Yaakov were all childless until they prayed, because Hashem wanted to hear their prayers. We have to pray for everything – and prayer doesn't necessarily mean taking a *siddur*, standing in front of the *aron hakodesh* and waiting for the next *minyan*. Prayer is thinking, feeling, or, even better, saying aloud every step of the way, "I hope Hashem will help me in this." That is praying.

One misstep can result in a fall and serious injury, or a soft landing. It's all a matter of *hashgahah pratit*. If we set out to a destination and actually reach it, we have to thank Hashem. It can be done in our heart and mind, but we must feel it, because the fact is, some set out on the same path and never arrive. Whether it's a transcontinental flight or crossing the street, there are plenty of people who never make it to the other side.

Before making a long trip, we are obligated to say *tefillat haderech* (the prayer for a journey); after returning, *birkat hagomel* (the blessing of thanksgiving). Yet statistics show that more people die each year crossing the street than they do flying, and double that amount die from accidental falls. This should impress on us the importance of praying for Hashem's help before any venture.

Before a business deal, say, "Hashem, please help me make the right decisions and bring me success." If you are successful, say, "Thank You Hashem for making me successful." We have to get used to this way of relating to all that happens to us.

Our sages tell us that even if a sharp sword is at a person's throat, he should not despair of Hashem's mercy.[185] At the time of the infamous Damascus blood libel in 1840, Rabbi Yaakov Antebi was chief rabbi of Damascus. Local Christians accused the Jews of killing an elderly Italian monk to use his blood for Pesah wine. The Muslim ruler leapt at the chance to persecute the Jews. He arrested and tortured innocent Jewish victims to extract a confession before

---

185. *Berachot* 10a.

deciding it would be even better to get the rabbi to admit to the crime. For the next six months, he had Rabbi Antebi subjected to daily torture. As Rabbi Antebi describes in his books, not one inch of his body went unscathed. Despite his suffering, he did not utter a single word, for he knew that anything he said would be twisted by his captors into an admission and used as an excuse for a pogrom.

At one point, the Muslim ruler brought in the executioner. The man put the blunt edge of his sword against Rabbi Antebi's throat and asked him, "Do you confess?"

"No," said Rabbi Antebi.

The executioner turned the sword around and put the sharp edge against the prisoner's throat.

At that, Rabbi Antebi began jumping for joy and singing.

"Are you crazy?" they asked him.

"No," said Rabbi Antebi. "I just finally understood what our sages meant when they said 'even a *sharp* sword.' It means don't ever lose hope, not only when they first put the sword's blunt edge against your throat, but even when they turn the sword around and place its sharp edge against your throat."

As is known, the rabbi and the whole community were eventually saved in a miraculous way.

No matter how desperate the circumstances, a person has to open up his heart and pray to Hashem. We can never know when a prayer is going to be answered. If a prayer is not answered immediately, it is wrong to assume this is because Hashem didn't hear the prayer. He hears our prayers, but at the same time, He knows what is best. He knows how much suffering we have to go through, and sometimes we need this suffering to atone for our sins. But each prayer makes an impression. More, each prayer expresses our belief in Hashem and brings us one step closer to the redemption. There are no limits to prayer.

Five Hundred and Fifteen Prayers

When Moshe Rabbeinu sought permission to enter Eretz Yisrael, he prayed five hundred and fifteen separate prayers. Each prayer was different, and could be compared, roughly, to an argument. Each prayer put forward a new line of reasoning to convince Hashem to allow him entry into the Holy Land. The Ramhal wrote a book about this, *Taktu Tefillot*, in which he brings five hundred and fifteen possible versions of Moshe Rabbeinu's prayer.

Like Moshe Rabbeinu, when we pray, we need to say what we feel at the moment. How are we going to pose our request to Hashem? What are our reasons for our asking? Do we deserve what we are asking for? Have we prepared ourselves to receive what we are asking for? Is our request in place? We have to give Hashem a chance to answer our prayers.

When a teenager asks for a car, his father first considers whether having a car would be good for him. He might decide that, at the moment, it isn't a good idea for the boy to have a car. He may feel that having a car will not be of benefit to his son at this time in his life. Hashem considers our requests like a loving father. He wants only what is good for us. Because we do not see the whole picture, we cannot possibly know what is really good for us. Our prayers are a statement of belief and trust: belief that Hashem alone can grant us our heart's desires, and trust that only He knows what is best for us.

Nothing in life should be taken for granted. The privilege of bringing children into the world is considered part of nature by many people. Yet how many tears are shed and how many prayers are said just to find the right marriage partner? And once that step has been taken, how many people suffer years of childlessness? Becoming a parent is far from automatic. Every baby born is one of the greatest miracles we can imagine, and we have to appreciate this. The *Hovot HaLevavot* enumerates in detail fetal development and the impact of even a small flaw on the process. Even when a child is born completely healthy, there are no guarantees. Beyond physical health, parents need hundreds of miracles daily to raise children in the proper way according to the Torah.

A friend of mine was married for many years without being blessed with children. After years of treatments under many doctors, he became such an expert in the field that, through his guidance, literally thousands of people have had children. I will never forget what happened on one of my visits to his home. At the time, his wife was almost fifty years old. Despite the fact that both husband and wife are quiet people, just as I was leaving the house, his wife screamed out to me, "Rabbi Hillel, save us! We have no time left. Do something!" It was a cry of desperation I will never forget.

This couple was miraculously blessed with twins. Someone who has not gone through what they went through cannot imagine their gratitude. All the more appreciative must be those of us who did not suffer years of waiting before becoming parents.

Some people make the mistake of thinking they are in charge of deciding when to have children. "We're waiting a few years," they say, as if they, and not the Creator, control such matters. Later, they are filled with regret.

Our prayers do not stop once a child is born. If anything, they intensify. A child's soul is a precious gift, and each child is filled with unbelievable potential. Parents realize their responsibility and pray for *siyatta diShemaya* every step of the way.

My father-in-law, Rabbi Yitzhak Ohana, a close disciple and

assistant to Rabbi Baruch Toledano in Morocco, told me the following story.

"Rabbi Toledano had many children, dozens of grandchildren and many more great-children, and each was a *talmid hacham* or married to a *talmid hacham*. I once asked him how he merited this. He told me, 'Today, people think it's automatic, but they don't know.'

"However, I *do* know," my father-in-law continued. "I used to be with Rabbi Toledano at midnight. He would get up, recite *Tikun Hatzot*, and then, for over an hour, he would pray for his children, grandchildren and great-grandchildren, each one individually. One needed a good study partner, another a good yeshivah, another good friends, another health, another good eyesight and so on. He would pray for *every* single child, crying for hours.

"Now he answered my question by asking, with raised eyebrows, 'Do you think good children come just like that?'"

Parents pray for their children's success in Torah studies, and pray they will have the right rebbe. Many times a rebbe blames a student's poor performance on the boy, yet when the boy switches to a different rebbe, he rises to the top of the class. This happens because the previous rebbe did not develop a relationship with his student.

A good yeshivah is important, too. Good teachers, good friends, a good environment – all are important. However, we cannot achieve anything on our own. We need Hashem's help. Prayer accesses the higher sources of blessing to bring them down on us. The more heartfelt the prayer, the greater its power, as we see in another true story about Rabbi Toledano.

During the Second World War, Morocco called up its reserves. Roads and trains were full of soldiers, making it a very dangerous time for any citizen, let alone a Jew, to travel. Despite the danger, when Rabbi Toledano heard of a village that lacked a Talmud Torah, he decided to go there at once and establish one, for no city is allowed to be without a Talmud Torah.

He asked my father-in-law, Rabbi Ohana, to travel with him. Miraculously, they survived the train journey, standing the entire way surrounded by hostile soldiers who would have thought nothing of pushing them off the open train. It was a journey of true self-sacrifice because they literally endangered their lives.

When they arrived, they were greeted by the community's dignitaries, escorted to the synagogue, and invited to speak.

Rabbi Toledano launched into a fiery speech about the necessity of a Talmud Torah. The people listened and then discussed it among themselves. Finally, one of the representatives spoke on behalf of the group.

"There is no doubt that we need a Talmud Torah, and we take it upon ourselves to establish one at the first opportunity. Now, though, we are in the middle of a war. Money is scarce. We hope that when things calm down, we will be able to do it."

Rabbi Toledano began screaming and crying like a child whose candy had just been taken away. He beat his chest, saying, "*Ani rasha!* I am an evildoer!"

The people were shocked. "Stop!" they pleaded, but Rabbi Toledano would not stop. The people were terrified. What had they done? "Rabbi, please tell us what's wrong."

"I am to blame," answered Rabbi Toledano. "Our *hachamim* tell us that words spoken from the heart enter the heart. If my words didn't penetrate your hearts, that means I am evil, for my words did not come from my heart. If I really believed in what I was telling you – that you have to establish a Talmud Torah – it would have gone into your hearts. If it didn't, I am to blame," he said, launching again into a wailing cry and striking himself.

"No, Rabbi," the people said, "you are not to blame. Tomorrow we're going to build a Talmud Torah."

We only see a person's exterior, but Hashem sees into our hearts. When we pray to Hashem, He knows how much heart is behind what we're saying. This is the main point when praying: to have our heart and mind intensely feel our need and really want Hashem to help.

Imagine having a hotline to a high-ranking government official. Realize, then, that you have that kind of a direct access to Hashem, the Creator and Ruler of the world. He is right there in front of you, listening to your prayers. Each prayer is collected and recorded, because each prayer is precious.

Each of your prayers has an effect. It may have an effect now on the world in general, it may affect other people, and it may eventually affect you yourself.

Shabbat: The Central Light

T he reward for keeping Shabbat – both in this world and even more so in the World–to–Come– is beyond our imagination.

Our sages teach us that

– the *mitzvah* of Shabbat outweighs all the other *mitzvot* of the Torah.[186]

– if the Jewish people keep two consecutive Shabbatot, *Mashiah* will come and take them out of *galut*.[187]

– anyone who honors the Sabbath with three *seudot* (meals that include bread) will be saved from three difficult situations: (1) *Hevlei Mashiah*, the suffering preceding *Mashiah's* arrival; (2) punishment in *Gehinom*; and (3) the war of Gog and Magog – the world war foretold for the time of *Mashiah*;[188]

– anyone who enjoys Shabbat, physically, emotionally, and spiritually, will be given unlimited reward and all his heart's desires;[189]

– if a person sinned even to the point of worshiping idols, he will be forgiven if he keeps Shabbat.[190]

One aspect of Shabbat that makes it such a pivotal *mitzvah* is its link to belief in Hashem. In the first of the Ten Commandments,

---

186. *Shemot Rabbah* 25:12.
187. *Shabbat* 118b.
188. *Ibid.* 118a.
189. *Ibid.* 118b.
190. *Ibid.*

Hashem tells us, "I am the L-rd, your God, Who has taken you out of Egypt." Wouldn't the first half of the sentence be enough as far as our belief in Hashem is concerned? What significance is there in mentioning that He took us out of Egypt?

The answer is that Jewish belief in Hashem is unique. We believe that Hashem is not only the Creator of the world, but that He continues to run it. The first time in history that this was openly revealed was when Hashem took us out of Egypt. We were a people enslaved. Without direct, ongoing Divine supervision of the world, we might have stayed there, continuing to suffer. Instead, Hashem not only took us out of Egypt, but He changed nature to do so. Each of the ten plagues He brought on the Egyptians occurred only because the natural function of an object or being was changed. Concerning this Hashem said, "Why did I do it? To teach My people that I, Who created nature, control it. Though I gave the universe a set order of operation called 'nature,' I have not relinquished control. When I want to, I can change any facet of creation, including these fixed patterns."

The first word in the Torah is *Bereshit*, "In the beginning." Our sages teach us that this means *bishvil reshit*, "for the sake of *reshit*." Now, since both the Jewish people and the Torah are called elsewhere *reshit*, we learn that Hashem created the world for the express purpose of giving the Torah to the Jewish people.[191] Bringing the Jewish people out of Egypt to receive the Torah was a major step in bringing the world to its ultimate purpose, a goal desired by Hashem.

Pharaoh's attitude, as revealed in his dialogue with Yosef, typifies gentile belief. When Pharaoh called Yosef from the dungeon and asked him to interpret his dream, Yosef said, "That is beyond me. *Elokim* (God) will answer regarding Pharaoh's well-being."[192] Pharaoh accepted this reply. Yet when Moshe and Aharon went to

---

191. *Ibid.* 88a.
192. *Bereshit* 41:16.

Pharaoh with Hashem's command to let the Jewish people leave Egypt, Pharaoh replied, "Who is Hashem that I should listen to His voice to send out the Jews? I don't know Hashem."[193] Was Pharaoh an atheist or wasn't he?

The answer is that Pharaoh believed in the forces of nature, alluded to by the Name *Elokim*. The *gematria* of *Elokim* is eighty-six, the same as the *gematria* of the Hebrew word for nature, *hateva*. Pharaoh believed that Hashem created the world and the natural forces that run the world. He had no problem accepting Yosef's answer and went on to tell him his dream.

But when Moshe came, he used the *Yud-Kay-Vav-Kay* Name, which symbolizes God's rulership and perpetual involvement in running the world. Pharaoh vehemently rejected this concept when he said, "I don't know Hashem." He was, in effect, saying, "I've never heard of such a thing! You're bringing me a new religious concept. We believe there is a Creator, but we don't believe He runs the world."

On Shabbat, we declare our staunch belief in this basic tenet of Judaism. The words of *Kiddush* bring together these two concepts when we say that Shabbat is a "remembrance of the act of creation" *and* a "remembrance of the Exodus from Egypt."

Divine creation differs from that of human beings. When a carpenter makes a table or a builder constructs a home, those objects exist independently of their creators. If the carpenter or builder dies, their works continue to exist. Hashem, though, created the world in such a way that if He were not continuously connected to it, if He did not continuously imbue the world with the force of existence, it would revert to *tohu vevohu*, complete nothingness, and would cease to exist.

---

193. *Shemot* 5:2.

After creating the world stage by stage in six days, Hashem created on the seventh day a special entity called *menuhah*, rest.

Resting on Shabbat is a creation of its own.

Physical vs. Spiritual

To get full value out of Shabbat in terms of benefits and enjoyment, we need to understand what resting on Shabbat really means. Some people think it means working hard six days of the week and taking it easy on the seventh. Asked to explain Shabbat in brief, they might say, "As long as you don't work, you're observing the Sabbath." Taken to an extreme, a person might think, "No problem. I'll lounge around in pajamas all day. That's rest, isn't it?" Would he be keeping Shabbat? Far from it.

Whenever the Torah speaks about Shabbat, the phrase "*Shabbat laHashem*" appears. Shabbat is a day for God. During the other six days of the week, people are obviously involved in the physical world. Motivated by positive goals and good intentions, they earn a living, raise their children, and run good Jewish homes. With the right attitude, the workweek is elevated to a higher level. Even so, during those six days, we are involved in the physical world. On Shabbat, our involvement is with the spiritual world. During the six workdays, we're active in the marketplace; on Shabbat, we spend time with our family. Shabbat is a day for looking into the depths of our soul, for taking stock of the spiritual side of our lives.

The physical and spiritual components of a person are locked in an ongoing battle for supremacy. When one dominates, the other submits. If you build up your spiritual side, your physical side will lose its power over you. Conversely, if you empower the physical side and make it the most important thing in your life, your spiritual side will be neglected.

Hashem wants a balance. For six days of the week, we're out there earning a living. These days can also be filled with many wonderful spiritual activities such as prayer, *mitzvot*, and giving charity, but they are basically days of physical action. On Shabbat, everything stops. The physical side is put on hold, allowing the spiritual side to soar to its highest levels. This is the idea of resting on Shabbat. We stop our involvement in the physical world to immerse ourselves in the spiritual world.

For example, due to business pressures, many people do not have much time to study Torah. During the workweek, they do their best to fulfill the *mitzvah* of toiling in Torah day and night by setting fixed times for study morning and evening. On Shabbat, though, when such a person is freed from his business obligations, he is expected to be more involved in Torah study and in developing the spiritual side of his life.

Many people are confused about what it means to observe the Sabbath. The intricate laws of Sabbath observance seem daunting. They wonder if Hashem really cares about people abiding by all the exacting *halachic* details. Take, for instance, the *halachah* of *borer*, "selecting." On Shabbat, we are not allowed to move aside food we don't want in order to choose the food we do want. An example of this would be pulling a fish bone out of a piece of fish. Instead, we should eat the fish, leaving the bone. The laws of *muktzeh*, what we are allowed to touch and move, are another area of Shabbat observance covered in detail by the *Shulhan Aruch*, as is carrying from one domain to another. Some people find such laws hard to understand. They wonder, "If I go outside carrying a handkerchief in an area that has no *eruv*, how will that disturb my rest? What does carrying a handkerchief have to do with work?" But if there is no *eruv* and a person carries a handkerchief outside his house, he is desecrating the Sabbath.

Some people look at Shabbat as a day full of restrictions. You can't turn on a light, you can't talk on the phone, and you can't drive. It sounds like a day of suffering. "How is it possible," someone once asked me, "that on Shabbat I can carry an armchair up and down the stairs for twenty-four hours straight and that's allowed, but if I just flip a switch, which takes no effort at all, it's considered desecrating Shabbat. It doesn't make sense!"

Once the principle of Shabbat is understood, though, everything falls into place. Shabbat is a day that commemorates Hashem's creating the world in six days. In those six days, He brought into existence all the forces in the world. On the seventh day, He stopped creating; He rested. We commemorate this by stopping our creative work, too.

Work is defined as transforming an object into something else. For example, flipping a light switch activates an electrical process. Energy is generated and transmitted through wires until it turns into light. This is a creative process, and, as such, is forbidden. Carrying something is not a creative process, but bringing it from one domain to another changes its status. Change of status, as defined by Torah law, is a creative act. Bringing an object from a private home to the street, which is a public domain, effects a change in the object's status. This is not allowed because on Shabbat, everything must rest; where it was, it should remain. Moving an object, no matter how heavy, within the same domain, such as up and down the stairs of a private home, though, does not change the object's status, no matter how strenuous the task. Therefore, it is permitted.

Saying Hashem rested does not mean He grew tired from creating the world and needed a break. The concept of "being tired" does not apply to Hashem, Who keeps the whole world going. Though He created the world with ten utterances, He could have done it with only one. Just as the six days of creation did not tire Him, so He did not need Shabbat to rest. The word used for Hashem's resting on Shabbat is *vayenafash*, which, as Rashi explains, always indicates the spiritual dimension.[194] It can be explained as follows: just as Hashem created Adam's physical body first and then blew into it the spirit of life, so He created the physical aspect of the universe first, during the six days of creation, and only afterward, on Shabbat, did He blow into it spiritually. In this context, *vayenafash* can mean, "He blew in the spirituality" on Shabbat. For this reason, Shabbat remains a day that enables us to connect with spirituality.

Source of Blessing

For some people, life is a vicious cycle. If you ask someone, "Why do you work?" he'll say, "I have to earn a living if I want to eat." "Why do you eat?" "I have to eat, or I won't have the strength to work." What's the point?

There's a well-known tale about a man who was exiled to Siberia, where he was kept in solitary confinement. As part of his punishment, he had to spend his day turning a massive wheel that was attached to his cell wall. As the prisoner turned the wheel, he often wondered what was attached to it on the other side of the wall. He imagined all sorts of useful purposes for his forced labor. "Perhaps it is grinding wheat in a flour mill, or drawing water from a well to irrigate the fields," he would muse.

After many years, he was released and allowed to leave the room. At that moment, he said to his captors, "After all my hard work, I'd like to know what I achieved these past ten years. What's the wheel attached to?" When the guard said, "Nothing. You were just turning a wheel," the man passed away on the spot. His whole life and all his suffering had been meaningless.

We ask ourselves the same question: What am I doing here? Those

---

194. *Ibid.* 31:17.

who eat to work and work to eat are just turning that wheel around. The true purpose of life is to realize that there is a Creator and then to move closer to Him. Because the physical world pulls us away from the spiritual, Hashem gave us one day out of seven when we can free our minds from the distractions of investments, real estate, business, the stock market, and all the rest. At least on one day of the week, we can clearly see our life's purpose. Shabbat then becomes the day when we delve into the resources of our true life, our spiritual life. This, in turn, illuminates our lives for the whole week.

Some people think they honor and can enjoy Shabbat thanks to what they earn during the week. This is a misconception. The truth is that we are successful during the week because we keep Shabbat.

Shabbat is the source of all blessing. The sages teach us that the days of the week are not arranged one after another, but are like the *menorah* in the Temple. Shabbat is the center of the week, with three days preceding it and three days following it. So, too, the *menorah* had one central branch, with three branches on the right and three on the left. When it was lit, the three flames on the right and the three on the left leaned toward the central flame. We wonder why the central light was the one that remained lit. What is the significance of the central light, and why do all the lights on the right and the left have to point toward the central light?

The answer to this question lies in understanding the *menorah's* connection to Shabbat. To us, it seems that when a person closes his business and rests on Shabbat, he's losing money. People in the retail trade say you can make as much as ten times the profit on Saturday as during the rest of the week. The Torah tells us just the opposite. Any success we experience during the six days of the week is part of the blessing that comes down on Shabbat. The one day of the week that seems to be unproductive as far as earning an income is concerned is actually the one day of the week that brings all blessing and bounty into your life. The flow of blessing spills over into the other days of the week and is acquired through hard work. But the source of that blessing is Shabbat, as it says, "*vayevarech Elokim et yom hashvi'i vayekadesh oto*" – "And God blessed the seventh day and sanctified it."[195]

That was the idea of the seven lights of the *menorah*. The central light, where the miracle took place, symbolizes Shabbat. The first three days of the week – Wednesday, Thursday, and Friday – lead up to Shabbat. The three days after Shabbat – Sunday, Monday, and Tuesday – bring blessing into the week. The central point of our life is Shabbat. The workday week is not supporting Shabbat; Shabbat gives life to all the other days.

Uplifting the Physical

The kabbalists tell us that Hashem created not only this lowly, physical world but also untold other worlds.[196] The physical world we live in is the last and lowest part of creation; there exist spiritual worlds above and beyond ours. There is the world of the angels, and above that, many other worlds about which we have no idea but which the kabbalah discusses. Basically, we speak of four levels of creation. One world is the *Olam HaAsiyah*, which is this lowly, physical world. Above this is the *Olam HaYetzirah*, which is mainly the world of the angels who praise Hashem. Then there is the *Olam HaBeriyah*, a higher world that could be called the "World of the Throne." Above this, at the highest level, is *Olam HaAtzilut*, which you might say is like a king sitting on a throne. All these terms are only figurative. These are spiritual worlds, completely abstract, with no form or substance.

The week parallels this formation, and we are meant to ascend

195. *Bereshit* 2:3.
196. *Shir Hashirim* 6:8, Zohar.

from level to level, serving Hashem on each day according to its level. For example, Wednesday corresponds to *Olam HaAsiyah*, the lowest world. Thursday is *Olam HaYetzirah*, a higher world. Friday is *Olam HaBeriyah*, a yet higher world, and Shabbat is *Olam HaAtzilut*, the highest world. Descending from Shabbat, Sunday corresponds to *Olam HaBeriyah*, Monday to *Olam HaYetzirah* and Tuesday to *Olam HaAsiyah*. In fact, the kabbalists even tell us what we should do on each day. Tuesdays and Wednesdays are when you could be working to earn your living. They are also the days when you should do *mitzvot* that depend on walking, like visiting the sick or collecting money for charity, because Tuesdays and Wednesdays are the *Olam HaAsiyah* (the world of doing). Monday and Thursday correspond to the *Olam HaYetzirah*, which is the level of Torah. These are days when you should add an extra class or do a little more learning. That's why we read from the Torah during prayers on Mondays and Thursdays. Friday and Sunday, which are closest to Shabbat, correspond to *Olam HaBeriyah*. These are days for deep introspection and scrutiny of our deeds, days of *mussar*, and an ideal time to work on ourselves and come close to Hashem. Shabbat is the pinnacle, the central light in the *menorah*, the main day of the week toward which all the other days point.

This is also a timetable for how we should prepare for Shabbat, because Shabbat is not just a day you fall into all of a sudden, sometime on Friday afternoon. In the Hebrew calendar, there is no Sunday, Monday, or Tuesday. The days are named by their relationship to Shabbat: *yom rishon l'Shabbat Kodesh, yom sheni l'Shabbat Kodesh*, the first day toward Shabbat, the second day toward Shabbat and so on. The whole week is a countdown to Shabbat.

Our Shabbat is what we make of it. The more we invest in it, the more we benefit. The more we treasure it, the more we will enjoy it. An honest look at our lives will show us how immersed in materialism we are and the extent to which we neglect our souls.

Is man nothing more than an animal? The question has already been asked, and the answer is no. We are a unique creation in the universe. True, we do have a physical aspect of our existence that is similar to an animal's. But the spiritual part of us far surpasses anything animals possess. Animals have natural instincts that serve them well, but they are limited. They can never develop a thought, or rise above their existence in spiritual searching.

When we say that man was created in the image of God, we refer to the spiritual image. We have a soul and an intellect that place us on a high level. Shabbat is the opportunity to bring out the best in ourselves, to involve ourselves with our spiritual aspect, which is the most important aspect of our being.

If only people realized what they could achieve on Shabbat! One of the traditional songs sung around the Shabbat table is "*Yom Zeh Le'Yisrael Ora Vesimhah.*" *Ora vesimhah* means "light and happiness." This day is a day of light and happiness for the Jewish people. On Shabbat, you can come so close to Hashem that spiritually, you'll be in a world of light. By comparison, the six days of the week are like a world of darkness. And by enjoying Shabbat, you can experience and bring forth into your life deep happiness.

On Shabbat, every Jew has a *neshamah yeterah*, a higher soul. On this day, our souls are elevated to a much higher spiritual level. The *Gemara* asks how this extra spirituality is expressed, and answers: through more eating and greater enjoyment. It seems like a contradiction. If the *neshamah yeterah* brings heightened spirituality, why should this find expression in the physical realm? It's the exact opposite of what we would think.

The explanation is that when we are on a higher spiritual level, we now have the power to literally uplift the physical to a much higher plane than we can on weekdays. Only when we are on a higher spiritual level can we uplift the mundane activities of eating and drinking to the level of serving Hashem. Our table becomes like an altar where sacrifices were offered to Hashem.

On Shabbat, there is a special *mitzvah* of *oneg*, which means to enjoy. On *Yom Tov*, we have the *mitzvah* of *simhah*, but not of *oneg*. *Simhah*, being happy, is a spiritual feeling that does not necessarily have anything to do with the body. *Oneg*, on the other hand, is physical. Only Shabbat is on a level high enough to uplift even physical pleasures to a pinnacle of spiritual involvement and enjoyment.

Rearranging the letters in the word *oneg* creates the word *nega*, affliction. If a person is a glutton and overeats during the week, it will harm him physically and spiritually. But on Shabbat, *nega* is transformed to *oneg*. Overeating on Shabbat is transformed from gluttony to permissible pleasure, because eating is uplifted to a higher plane. Other *mitzvot* involving physical enjoyment are similarly elevated on Shabbat.

The Ben Sorer u'Moreh

The workweek not only distracts us from satisfying our spiritual needs, it also steals us from our families. This neglect of our spouses and children is harmful, because they need our attention. Shabbat gives us time to devote to our families, time to understand each child and his needs. Most people don't give enough time to their marriages. Shabbat is the perfect opportunity to enjoy being together, to eat, drink, sing, and exchange ideas.

The Shabbat table is also the perfect opportunity for a person to express Torah thoughts to his children. We all send our children to Jewish schools where Torah is taught, and every normal parent is constantly encouraging – sometimes even pushing – his children to learn more. But the best way to educate your children to learn is through example, because to a child, actions speak louder than words. If children see their father come home from work, pick up a newspaper, or drop off to sleep on the couch, they see that his relationship to Torah is not very strong. This is the meaning of *Veshinantam levanecha vedibarta bam*, "Teach them thoroughly to your children, and speak of them."[197] If you want to thoroughly teach your children Torah, speak words of Torah! If they see you learning and speaking Torah every spare minute, they will learn from you to respect Torah, and they will also learn from you to study Torah as well.

This point is brought out in an interesting interpretation of the verses that speak of the *ben sorer u'moreh*, the rebellious son.[198] The rebellious son is a glutton who wants to satisfy all his lusts and desires. Eventually, the evil path he is on will lead him to acts of theft and murder. Despite warnings, he refuses to change his ways. A youth determined by the *bet din* to be a *ben sorer u'moreh* is sentenced to death.

The *Gemara* informs us that there never was and never will be such a case. However, many lessons are learned from studying this hypothetical situation. One in particular applies to our discussion here.

We wonder how the rebellious son became such an evil child. The clue lies in the verse, *"Einenu shomea b'kol aviv uv'kol imo"* – "He never heard the voice of his father or the voice of his mother."[199] This is interpreted as meaning that the son never heard his father praying or studying. He never heard his father's voice as the voice of Yaakov, raised in prayer and Torah study, nor did he ever hear his mother's voice saying *Tehillim* or praying when she lit the Shabbat candles.

---

197. *Devarim* 6:7.
198. *Ibid.* 21:18–21.
199. *Ibid.*

Had he heard his parents' involvement with Torah, he would have wanted to be like them. Because he grew up in a house where he never heard his father's Torah or his mother's prayers, he went astray and became an evildoer.

Shabbat is a great opportunity for parents. It's unbelievable how much wisdom a father can give over to his family on Shabbat. Doing so requires preparation. A parent may not know Hebrew and may not be able to talk knowledgeably about the *parashah*. However, with the hundreds and even thousands of English-language books now available, everyone can find Torah ideas to impart to children on Shabbat.

The Shabbat table should be a pleasurable experience for the whole family, not a time of tension. One of Eretz Yisrael's greatest *roshe yeshivot*, an outstanding giant in Torah with thousands and thousands of students, was once asked why his son did not become a great Torah scholar while the son of his neighbor, a simple man, did. The Rosh Yeshivah said if he had sung songs at his Shabbat table and related to his family as his neighbor had done, his son would have become a Torah scholar, too.

The power of a parent's influence by personal example is not limited to his children's younger years. The mother of an assimilated family in the States once called me. She was desperate to save her daughter from intermarriage. One son had already married a non-Jew, two daughters were already involved with Christianity, and even though the third son was still young, he too was headed in the same direction. The parents sent one of their daughters to Israel hoping to save her, but they didn't realize that the missionaries work in Israel even more effectively than in America. Finally, the mother called me.

"Rabbi, please save our daughter."

I agreed to try, and she sent her daughter over. The girl arrived with another woman who seemed strange. While I was speaking to the girl, the woman said not a word, but only stared at me fixedly. I asked the girl, "Who is she?"

In the end, I found out that she was a missionary. They would not let the girl out of their clutches. They were brainwashing her and intimidating her. I invited the girl to come to our home for Shabbat, but the missionaries wouldn't let her. They claimed the Jews would brainwash her.

In the end, the girl became a *ba'alat teshuvah*, and today she is married to a rabbi.

Then we worked on the second daughter, and she too came back. The younger son is today a rabbi. They have reared families that anyone would be proud of.

How did this amazing turnabout take place? Because of the mother. When this woman originally called me about her daughter, she was not religious. Her home was not a kosher home, and she did not observe the Sabbath. When she called and asked me to save her daughter, I asked, "What do you want me to save her from?"

"What do you mean?" she said. "She's becoming a Christian!"

"Did your children ever see you show any respect for Judaism at home?" I asked.

"No, I must admit that they did not."

"Then what do you want from them?" I asked. "I should tell them not to become Christians when you showed them no respect for your own religion?"

At that moment, she made a decision. "I'll change," she said. And she did. She changed from one extreme to the other. She took it upon herself to have a kosher home and to observe all the *mitzvot*. Because of this, we could change a whole family. When she passed away, she was truly an *em habanim smehah*, "a joyous mother of children," with three children heading the best families you can imagine.

If our homes are empty of the light and beauty of Shabbat, our children are going to miss out. Many children are not with their father when he sets out to pray in the early *minyan* and catches the train into the city. By the time he comes home from work, they're already asleep. On Shabbat, though, a father can sit with his family at the Shabbat table for two or three hours discussing interesting topics. It doesn't necessarily have to be learning. He can give over stories, open up interesting topics for discussion, and talk about inspiring personal experiences. A parent's own life experiences can imbue his children with faith, and teach them to trust Hashem always. They will realize what a wonderful thing Shabbat can be, that it is, in fact, *orah vesimhah*, light and happiness. It strengthens and enriches the family, and this blessing is felt throughout the whole week.

Without taking the trouble to prepare for Shabbat, nothing will come of it. The *Gemara* relates that throughout the week, the great sage Shammai would look for special things, a tasty fruit, or a special cut of meat, and buy it, saying, "This is for Shabbat." His thoughts were always on how to better honor the Sabbath, from the moment one Shabbat ended until the next.

One way we honor Shabbat is by wearing special clothes set aside for that day alone. The *mitzvah* is to change every single garment especially for Shabbat. Most people are particular that one's exterior garment – a suit, for example – should be especially for Shabbat, while it is enough that all other garments be clean and fresh. But some opinions go so far as to say that every item from head to toe should be specially designated for Shabbat. Our sages also say you shouldn't walk on Shabbat the same way you walk on a weekday. On a weekday, you charge about, running here, jogging there. But on Shabbat, you walk like a king. You're at ease, so you walk differently. They also say that the way you speak on Shabbat should be different, too.

Shabbat encompasses everything, the way you dress, the way you walk, and the way you talk. Everything about it should be unique. People buy flowers, have special dishes, silverware, and glassware – everything possible to beautify their Shabbat table. In short, Shabbat is something we have to invest in. When we do, the profits we can reap are inestimable. We must not look at Shabbat as a day of limitations – this is forbidden and that is forbidden – but instead focus on *menuhah*, rest as we described it: spiritual elevation and enjoyment.

The Seventh Year

Just as six days are followed by a seventh, Shabbat, so too are the years arranged in a cycle of six years followed by a seventh. The seventh year is called *shemittah*, the Sabbatical year, when one lets his field lie fallow. During that year, everything that grows is *hefker*, ownerless; it cannot be bought or sold like private property, and anyone who needs can take it.

Not working on the Sabbatical year is not meant to be an end in itself. Just as Shabbat is the source of spirituality for the six days of the week, so is the Sabbatical year the source of spirituality for the six years between one *shemittah* and the next. This concept has found a place in the secular world of higher education where professors are given a Sabbatical year for rest, renewal of energies, and extended research. During our Sabbatical year, as Jews, we are supposed to detach ourselves from our fields and businesses to devote ourselves to spiritual pursuits. At least once in seven years, we need to recharge our spiritual batteries.

Shabbat is a chance to step back and take a look at the master-piece we are creating – our own life. It's a time to step back from manipulating Hashem's creation and simply enjoy it. It's an opportunity to remember and appreciate what a wonderful world we live in, and to let the inspiration draw us closer to our Creator. On Shabbat, we transcend the animalistic forces within us to reach a higher, spiritual level. Standing at the pinnacle of the week on Shabbat, we gain a panoramic view of the rest of the days of our lives.

By honoring Shabbat and keeping it as it should be kept, we bring light and blessing into every day of the week. May Hashem bless us that we keep Shabbat correctly, with all its details, that we never transgress Shabbat, and may the Shabbat bring us blessing throughout our lives.

Making Time for Torah

O ne of the mainstays of the life of a Torah Jew is the times he sets aside for learning Torah. This is referred to by our sages as *keviut itim laTorah*, fixing times for Torah study, as the *Shulhan Aruch* writes: "A person should fix a time for learning."[200] The simple meaning of the word *keviut* implies that a person should have a fixed amount of time that he studies each day. The Tur describes this time as *kavua vetakua*, fixed and firm.[201] This means that the actual time of day should also be kept the same, rather than just a casual commitment to study one hour or more sometime during the day.

Many commentators, including the Hida, give the word *keviut* an interesting twist. They say that it can also mean to steal, as we find in the verse, *hayikba adam Elokim*, "Can man steal from God!"[202] This indicates that sometimes a person must "steal" time from his working hours to be able to learn. We hear nowadays of people who take off time from their business to attend a *shiur* in the middle of the day. This type of learning has tremendous value. Our sages tell us, *lefum tza'ara agra*, "The reward is commensurate with the difficulty encountered."[203] There is nothing harder for a person than to tear himself away from his desk, leave his office, turn off his cell phone, and turn his back on everything that's going on in the world.

---

200. *Shulhan Aruch, Orah Hayyim* 155.
201. *Ibid.*
202. *Malachi* 3:8.
203. *Pirkei Avot* 5:22.

Today's business world is fast paced. People are glued to the charts like never before, because the market fluctuates every single minute. It is not like in the old days when you worked during the day and slept at night. Now you can have the whole world in the palm of your hand. If you own a big company, you have to be connected twenty-four hours a day.

Yet we know that what really keeps the world going is Torah study. "If not for My covenant [of Torah study] day and night, I would not maintain the laws of Heaven and Earth."[204] Rabbi Hayyim Volozhin in *Nefesh HaHayyim* explains that if there would be one second when no one in the world was studying Torah, the world would be destroyed. What keeps the world alive and ticking is people learning Torah. This means that anyone who takes time off to learn Torah has a share in sustaining the world.

Timeless Torah

The holy Shelah, whose name is an acronym based on the title of his pivotal work, **Shnei Luhot Habrit** ("The Two Tablets of the Covenant"), points out an amazing contradiction in the words of our sages on this topic. On the one hand, the *Gemara* states that the first question a person is asked in the World–to–Come is, "Did you set aside times for Torah study?"[205] If he can answer yes, he gets an entrance pass and is welcomed into *Olam Haba*.

(By the way, the next question is, *nasata venatata be'emunah*, "Were you honest in your business dealings?" It is not enough just to spend time learning Torah. The Torah obligates you to be a good person, to deal honestly with everyone. That is all part of the deal – learning Torah and being honest.)

---

204. *Yirmiyahu* 33:25.
205. *Shabbat* 31a.

In any case, we see from this that *keviut itim laTorah* is of primary importance and a source of great merit in the World-to-Come. Yet, we find another statement of our sages that seems to say the exact opposite. The Midrash on *Sefer Shmuel* (chap. 1) comments on the verse, "*'et la'asot laHashem heferu Toratecha'*[206] – *kol ha'oseh Torato itim mefer brit.*" "'It is a time to do for Hashem, they have annulled Your Torah' – Whoever makes times for his Torah study has violated the covenant." Apparently, having set times for learning Torah is not a good thing at all. How can we understand this blatant contradiction?

The holy Shelah resolves these contradictory statements by noting that *Klal Yisrael* has two levels of people involved in Torah study. There are *shelomei emunei Yisrael*, the general Jewish public, who fulfill the great *mitzvah* of *nasata venatata be'emunah*. These are people who earn their living honestly and are not dependent on others for their support. Our sages say, "He who lives by the toil of his hands is greater than the *yarei Shamayim*, the God-fearing person."[207] To be a workingman and earn one's living honestly is a very high achievement. When such people take time out of their busy schedules for regular Torah study, they guarantee themselves entry to the World–to–Come. Some can manage more time, some less, but as long as they have the right intention – to find favor in the eyes of Hashem by studying His Torah – they will be rewarded.

On the other hand, there are the *hachmei Yisrael*, the yeshivah students, those studying in *kollel* who devote their lives to Torah study. These people cannot say, "I set aside time for learning." It would be wrong for someone who is being supported so that he can devote his life to Torah to say, "We learn until nine o'clock, and then

---

206. *Tehillim* 119:126.
207. *Berachot* 8a.

we are done for the day." Their obligation is to toil in Torah *yomam valaylah*, day and night,[208] non-stop, as long as they can.

The Hazon Ish showed us what this meant. The scope of his writings is unbelievable. They cover the entire *Shas* in depth, even the more difficult, less studied tractates. He would continue learning for as long as his strength allowed. He would gauge how much energy he had left and leave himself just enough strength to walk across the room from his table to his bed. When he miscalculated, his family would find him asleep on the floor.

Occasionally, when the Hazon Ish quotes an earlier work, he writes, "It is not available to me right now." The comment seems strange since he rarely traveled, and he studied and wrote in his study surrounded by bookcases full of *sefarim*. Those close to him explain that when he wrote that, he meant he did not have the strength to get up and take the book off the shelf!

This is an example of someone who completely fulfilled the obligation to toil in Torah day and night. A *talmid hacham* cannot say, "I work from nine until six; then I have free time." There is no such thing as free time for someone on the level of a *talmid hacham*. We expect a very high level from someone who devotes his life to Torah. He should constantly have his mind occupied with Torah thoughts.

The *Gemara* tells us about a sage who was asked, "What is the secret of your long life?" The answer was, "I never walked four cubits without learning Torah." That means that even as he walked in the street, his mind was occupied with his learning. No matter what he was involved in, he was continuously thinking over what he had learned.

For the public, learning Torah day and night means setting aside

---

208. *Yehoshua* 1:8.

times for Torah study morning and evening. But when a rabbi, who is supposed to be learning all the time, says, "I learn so many hours by day and a short time by night," he is destroying Torah.

Some but Not All

Two of the greatest Talmudic sages, Rabbi Shimon bar Yohai and Rabbi Yishmael, actually argued over this point.[209] Rabbi Shimon bar Yohai points out an apparent contradiction: on the one hand, we are told, "*v'hagita bo yomam valaylah,*" "you must study Torah day and night";[210] on the other hand, we say in the *Shema* that if we keep the *mitzvot*, Hashem will bless us with bountiful produce and "you will gather in your grain."[211] "If a person ploughs his fields in the winter," asks Rabbi Shimon bar Yohai, "and sows seeds in the spring, and harvests his crop in the summer, and then threshes it and winnows it in the fall, when is he going to have time to learn Torah?" How is he going to fulfill the verse "*vehagita bo yomam valaylah*" if he is occupied the entire year with his work?

We know that Rabbi Shimon bar Yohai is always very strict in his interpretation, so when the verse says "*yomam valaylah,*" it means day and night, literally. The question is, how are you supposed to support yourself and your family? Certainly he must offer us a practical solution as well. He answers that Hashem will take care of righteous people, and their work will be done by others. There will be a rich brother or uncle, or someone else who will take care of their needs. Hashem has many ways.

Rabbi Yishmael disagrees. He advocates "*hanheg bahem minhag derech eretz,*" "act according to what is normal in the world," which

---

209. *Berachot* 35b.
210. *Yehoshua* 1:8.
211. *Devarim* 11:14.

is the approach of "*yafeh Torah im derech eretz,*"[212] "Torah is beautiful when combined with making a living." In other words, get a job and set aside times for learning Torah.

The *Gemara* concludes this discussion with an observation of Abaye that many followed the way of Rabbi Yishmael and were successful, while many tried the approach of Rabbi Shimon bar Yohai and were unsuccessful.

Rabbi Hayyim of Volozhin understands from this that although many failed at Rabbi Shimon bar Yohai's approach, some were successful; otherwise, we would be told that they *all* failed. Certain exceptional individuals succeeded.

In other words, Rabbi Shimon bar Yohai and Rabbi Yishmael are talking about two categories that exist within the Jewish people. For the exceptional cases, we have the ruling of Rashbi that they can rely on their sustenance being taken care of by others. However, this is not the rule for the majority. They have to adopt the policy of Rabbi Yishmael: *hanheg bahem minhag derech eretz,* you have to take your job seriously and earn a living, yet at the same time you have to set aside time for Torah study.

The Holy and the Holy of Holies

The *Mishkan* had to be built by all of *Klal Yisrael*, which is why everyone contributed to its construction. Being thus built, it represents the two basic segments of the Jewish people mentioned above: those who fix a time to learn, since they are also occupied with earning a living, and those who learn day and night. These two groups are symbolized by the *Kodesh* (Holy) and the *Kodesh Hakodashim* (Holy of Holies).

---

212. *Pirkei Avot* 2:2.

Both the *Mishkan* and the *Bet HaMikdash* were divided into two parts. There was the *Kodesh Hakodashim*, the inner sanctum, and the *Kodesh*, or the *Hechal*, the outer chamber. The *Kodesh Hakodashim* contained the *Aron*, the holy Ark, with the *keruvim*, the two cherubic forms on its cover. Into the *Aron* were placed the *luhot habrit*, the tablets engraved with the Ten Commandments, and the broken remains of the first tablets. A jar of manna, as a reminder of what we ate in the desert, was also kept in the *Kodesh Hakodashim*.

The *parohet* was a curtain that divided between the *Kodesh Hakodashim* and the *Kodesh*. In the *Kodesh*, the *menorah* was on the left side; on the right side was the *shulhan hapanim*, the table that held twelve loaves of bread and a few other items.

Light always symbolizes Torah, so we understand that the *menorah* represents the light of Torah. Why, though, was there another symbol of Torah, the Ark, in the *Kodesh Hakodashim*? Are there two levels of Torah?

The answer is yes. The *Kodesh* represents the general public whose Torah study is set within defined limits. They have a time to work and a time to learn. For this reason, the *Kodesh* contained the *menorah* on one side and the *shulhan hapanim* on the other. The *shulhan* with its twelve loaves of bread represents success in *parnassah*, earning a living. Someone who is in the *Kodesh* is in the middle, between the *shulhan hapanim* and the *menorah*. When he is learning, he is connected to the *menorah*, which represents Torah. When he is working, he is connected to the *shulhan hapanim*.

Our sages hinted to this when they said, *harotzeh lehahkim, yadrim; harotzeh leha'ashir yatzpin,* "let he who wants wisdom turn to the south; let he who wants wealth turn to the north."[213] Though we

---

213. *Baba Batra* 25b.

should face Yerushalayim when we pray, if a person feels he is lacking wisdom, he can turn slightly to the south to draw wisdom from the *menorah* which stood on the south side of the *Hechal.* Someone who feels a need to pray for *parnassah* can turn slightly toward the north, corresponding to the *shulhan,* which was on the north side.

This applies to someone who is in the middle. He sets aside some of his time for work and some of his time for Torah. When he needs *parnassah,* he turns to the *shulhan,* and when he needs wisdom, he turns to the *menorah.* The time factor is indicated by the twelve loaves on the *shulhan,* which correspond to the twelve months of the year, and the seven branches of the *menorah,* which represent the seven days of the week. These units of time are in the *Kodesh* because they represent the working Jew who is *kove'a itim laTorah,* and apportions his time between working and learning, *echad hamarbeh ve'ehad hamam'it,* "some more and some less, according to their time constraints."[214] A workingman can say, "It's a quarter to two, the *shiur* is over. I have to get back to work." There is a time limit.

But there is another form of Torah study, which is symbolized by the Ark in the *Kodesh Hakodashim.* This represents the *hachamim* who fulfill the *mitzvah* of *vehagita bo yomam valaylah,* "learning day and night." There are no time limits here. There is no seven-branched *menorah* or twelve loaves here, because the *talmid hacham's* obligation is to learn Torah without time limits.

Guaranteed Income

We mentioned that the jar of manna was also placed in the *Kodesh Hakodashim.* What was it doing there? Our *hachamim*

214. *Berachot* 5b.

taught, *lo nitnah Torah ela le'ochlei man,* "The Torah was given only to those who ate manna."[215] The ideal Torah learning opportunity in history was when the Jewish people were in the desert and Hashem supplied them with a daily portion of manna. There were no problems of earning a living in the desert. There were no stores, nothing to buy, no factories, no orders, and no telephones or fax machines. They were surrounded by the clouds of glory that leveled out the hills and paved firm roads for them. The clouds laundered and ironed their clothes and repaired their shoes. All their needs were taken care of. You woke up in the morning and found the manna outside your tent. You gathered it in and found the exact amount you needed for yourself and your family.

Our sages tell us there was never such an ideal learning situation. We had the best teacher in all history – Moshe Rabbeinu. We had Aharon and his sons, Yehoshua bin Nun, and the other elders. The *Shechinah* was with us, and we were studying Torah at this highest level day and night without any worries.

This is why the manna was kept in the Holy of Holies, to remind us that those who devote themselves to Torah study day and night will be taken care of just as Hashem took care of the Jewish people in the desert. The yeshivot and Torah scholars will all be taken care of in a miraculous way. This is the message of the jar of manna placed next to the Ark, the Torah, in the *Kodesh Hakodashim.*

Whenever the topic of the *kollelim* comes up, people like to quote the opinion of the Rambam as stated in *hilchot Talmud Torah* and in his commentary on *Pirkei Avot.* When explaining the *Mishnah, al ta'aseha kardom lahpor bo,* "Do not make the Torah a spade with which to dig,"[216] the Rambam writes that a person must not say, "I am going to learn, and I will have other people support me." He

---

215. *Midrash Tanhuma Beshalah* 20.
216. *Pirkei Avot* 4:7.

describes the ideal situation of a businessman who works three hours a day and studies nine hours a day. He speaks very strongly against those who make a living from their Torah and are supported by others. As we know, the Rambam was a world-renowned medical expert and royal physician to the sultan of Egypt. He lived by his principles and supported himself.

However, almost all of the *Rishonim* of his era and following generations disagree with his opinion in a very forceful way, and this is the way the *Shulhan Aruch* rules, against the Rambam's view. They argue that if we were to follow the opinion of the Rambam, we would have no rabbanim, no *hachamim*, no *halachic* authorities, and no educators. Everyone would be so occupied with making a living, they would have no time to learn.

In earlier eras, a person's needs were few. All he asked for was food, clothing, and a roof over his head. Nowadays, that doesn't satisfy us. Everyone wants all the luxuries and amenities of modern life plus a few million in the bank. If a person has less than that, he keeps on working. I have a good friend who tells me that he is very worried. He has seven children, and he hasn't yet put away ten million dollars for each child, so he can't sleep at night.

Therefore, the rabbanim say that in our day and age, more than ever, if we don't have those who are going to devote their lives to Torah, even if they have to be supported, there will be no Torah. Though it is generally thought that the Rambam disagrees with this idea, in my opinion, the Rambam also accepts this approach.

At the end of *hilchot Shemittah Veyovel* (13:13), the Rambam discusses the unique status of tribe of Levi. Of the twelve tribes, the tribe of Levi was the only one not given a portion in the Land of Israel. Even during the Egypt bondage, the Levites studied, and this was to remain their task in the Holy Land, where they were supported by tithes. They are Hashem's army, the Rambam writes, and He therefore takes care of their needs.

The Rambam continues with a very interesting idea that seems to be his own *hiddush*, for no source is given for it. He writes:

> Not only the tribe of Levi alone [have this guarantee from Hashem], but every single person from whichever country he comes, whose heart prompts him and whose intellect gives him understanding to separate himself [from worldly matters] to stand before Hashem, to serve Him and to worship Him; to know Hashem [through studying His Torah], and he goes on the straight path as Hashem made him and throws off the yoke of many worries [of earning a living] that people seek, he is sanctified to be the Holy of Holies, and Hashem will be his portion and his lot forever and ever, and He will give him in this world that which is sufficient for his needs, as He gave to the kohanim and the levi'im.

This person is not a *kohen* or a *levi*; he is just a simple *yisrael*. Wherever he comes from, Hashem will take care of his needs. The Rambam concludes, "King David said, 'Hashem is the gift of my portion and my cup; You will support my lot.'"[217] These words of the Rambam seem to be a complete contradiction to his opinion about not using the Torah as a spade.

The resolution to these apparent contradictions is the principle we have developed above. A workingman who sets aside time for learning Torah cannot say, "I'll learn a few more hours, and people will support me to make up the difference." But a person who gives up all other opportunities in life and instead of aspiring to become a millionaire devotes himself entirely to Torah study will be helped by Hashem. He doesn't demand that anyone support

---

217. *Tehillim* 16:5.

him. He doesn't throw himself on the community. He decides to sit down and learn, and Hashem will help him. How? We don't know how. Hashem has many ways. The jar of manna in the *Kodesh Hakodashim* reminds us that Hashem will take care of those few select people who themselves become, as the Rambam says, *Kodesh Hakodashim*.

So we see that the Rambam makes the distinction between the *hachamim* and the *bnei Torah* who represent the *Kodesh Hakodashim* and the rest of the Jewish people when they study Torah within their time limits.

The Irremovable Support

There is one more point that needs clarification. The Ark had four golden rings, two on each side through which the *badim*, the rods, were inserted so that the Ark could be carried whenever necessary. The Torah commands that the rods must remain in the rings at all times, even when the Ark was stationary. This seems strange. If the rods must always be together with the Ark, then why have rings? Why couldn't the rods be permanently attached to the Ark? And since they have rings, why not take them out when not carrying the Ark?

To understand this we have to realize that these rods represent the *tomchei Torah*, the supporters of Torah. Here we have the person who is in the *kodesh*. He learns and works. He sets fixed times for learning Torah and he is *neheneh miyegia kapav*, he enjoys the toil of his hands, which, as we mentioned before, makes him greater than the *yarei shamayim*. Hashem has great affection for him. But if he also supports Torah learning – if he is one of the *tomchei Torah* – then he also has a place in the *Kodesh Hakodashim*. He is part of the yeshivot, of the *hachamim*; he is an indispensable part of the Ark that holds the Torah. The Ark cannot move without him. Nevertheless, he has to realize that although it appeared that the Levites were carrying the Ark, in reality, *ha'aron noseh et nosav*, "The Ark carries its bearers."[218]

While it is true that *im ein kemah, ein Torah*, "Without flour there is no Torah,"[219] still, *im ein Torah ein kemah*, without the merit Torah brings, there would not be any blessing in the world.

This is the symbiotic relationship between Yissachar and Zevulun. This is the connection between the rabbanim and the working people who support Torah. Without their generous support, the yeshivot could not continue, but without the Torah study, the supporters would not see a blessing in their endeavors.

We have gained an understanding of how the *Mishkan* and *Bet HaMikdash* are composed of the two parts of the Jewish people, those who learn constantly, and those who are *kove'a itim laTorah*. Any weakening of Torah study, both private learning and supporting Torah study, is a *hurban habayit*, a destruction of the holy structure. The rods must remain at the sides of the Ark; Yissachar and Zevulun must remain connected. The *Kodesh* must lead into the *Kodesh Hakodashim*. The two parts of the Jewish people must appreciate each other. When they join into a partnership, this represents the *binyan Bet HaMikdash*, the building of the Holy Temple.

As we say at the end of our daily *Shemoneh Esre*, "May it be His will that the Temple be rebuilt speedily in our times, and place our portion in Your Torah."

---

218. *Sotah* 35a.
219. *Pirkei Avot* 3:21.

Understanding Kabbalah

What Is Kabbalah?

The Rambam in his major work, *Mishneh Torah*, incorporated all that a Jew needs to know in order to perform the 613 *mitzvot* of the Torah. At the beginning of this work, he discusses the fundamentals of Jewish faith and talks about the most sublime topics, such as the heavenly worlds and levels of prophecy. Yet it is well known that he did not base his ideas on the principles of kabbalah. It appears that he had not been introduced to the teachings of the kabbalists, although the *Migdal Oz* (Rabbi Shem Tov ben Abraham Ibn Gaon), one of the *Rishonim* who explained the Rambam, writes that toward the end of his life, the Rambam discovered the wisdom of kabbalah.[220] Rabbi Moshe Hayyim Luzzatto, best known as the Ramhal, and Rabbi Yosef Irgas, author of the *Shomer Emunim*, both great kabbalists who lived some 350 years ago, write that toward the end of his days, the Rambam received the kabbalistic tradition and regretted many of things he had already written according to philosophic concepts.

In those days, the kabbalah was transmitted from one rabbi of the generation to a chosen student; it was not in the public domain. The Rambam's grandson, and the Ramban, did receive the kabbalistic tradition, and many of the great *Rishonim* hint vaguely at kabbalistic concepts in their writings, although they would not speak openly about this. In fact, the Talmud, we now know, definitely alludes to many kabbalistic concepts, although subtly, as explained and proved by many later authorities.

---

220. *Halachot Yesodei HaTorah* 81, *halachah* 10.

Kabbalah – Receiving

The word *kabbalah* means "receiving." It is a wisdom that cannot be learned on one's own but must be received from a teacher as part of the tradition. The reason for this is that the kabbalists used a secret terminology whose words must not be taken literally. In their secret code, every word means something other than it appears on the surface.

As human beings, our minds can mainly grasp that which we can sense with physical faculties. We are familiar with tangible things in the physical world. It is difficult to clearly understand abstract concepts and impossible to grasp purely spiritual ones. We all believe that we have within our bodies a soul. It's part of us, but do we have any concept of what it is? If we can't understand our own soul, how much more so do we lack the words to describe higher spiritual worlds. It goes without saying that we have no way of understanding the Creator Himself. The Torah tells us, *ki lo r'item kol temunah*, "For you did not see any form of likeness."[221] Hashem has no form whatsoever. He is a completely abstract Being, totally removed from anything physical, which we cannot understand in any way.

We don't have the words with which to discuss such topics (even in the Hebrew language, how much more so in a foreign tongue). That is why the kabbalists have a special terminology. Though the words relate to the physical world we know, they refer only to spiritual concepts and are meaningful only in that context. Those who have the key to this code and study kabbalah texts accordingly, understand their deeper meaning and are not in danger of misinterpreting what is being said. However, without receiving the tradition, one cannot approach works of kabbalah, because they will certainly be interpreted out of context, resulting in consequences verging on heresy.

We read the *Humash* from "*Bereshit*" to "*Le'einei kol Yisrael*" and

---

221. *Devarim* 4:15.

all the words appertain to the physical world. Yet the kabbalists have a completely different dictionary, and they see these words in a spiritual context. This dictionary was hidden and handed down as a secret code from teacher to student. Anyone who tries to read the words of kabbalah without this key will be shocked by what he is reading. He will find statements attributing to the Creator physical terms, parts of the human body, so to speak. Even the Rambam, they say, when he first came across a work on kabbalah, wrote strongly against it, calling it idolatry and heresy.

Knowing Hashem

The Ari *z"l* is of the opinion that studying the wisdom of kabbalah is included in the *mitzvah* to study Torah. Moshe Rabbeinu says, "*Veyadata hayom vahashevota el levavecha...*," "You shall know today and take to heart that Hashem, He is God in heaven above and on earth below – there is no other."[222]

There are two parts to this verse: knowing and internalizing. *Veyadata hayom*, knowing that Hashem is the only power in the world is something that everyone understands. We all said *Na'ase venishma* at Sinai, and we all believe in Hashem and in His Torah. This is part of our faith, which has been passed down through the generations.

Our grandmothers never studied the *Zohar* or the *Etz Hayyim*, yet they were willing to be burned at the stake for their faith. Hundreds of thousands of Jewish women and children died for their beliefs without ever having learned kabbalah. This is *Veyadata hayom*. They just knew it as an undisputable fact. They had *emunah peshutah*, simple faith.

Then there is the second stage: *vahashevota el levavecha*,

---

222. *Ibid.* 4:39.

internalizing, bringing into your heart and mind this knowledge that Hashem exists. In earlier times, before the kabbalah was revealed, this level was reached through philosophy. The first section of *Hovot Halevavot, Shaar Hayihud*, is devoted to proving the existence of Hashem, His Oneness, and all the other fundamentals of our faith through logical arguments, using the philosophical approach.

A Secret Language

The kabbalists have a different approach. Their method is the way that was given to Moshe on Mount Sinai. For many generations, it was never revealed publicly. As part of the Oral Law, it was not to be written down. Originally, even the *Mishnah* and the *Gemara* were transmitted orally and not transcribed. However, Rabbeinu Hakadosh, Rabbi Yehuda Hanasi, who lived many years after the destruction of the Second Temple, permitted the writing of the *Mishnah*. He based himself on the verse, "*Et la'asot laHashem, heferu Toratecha*," "A time has come to do for Hashem, they transgress your Torah."[223] Rabbi Yehuda read the verse backwards, however: "We will have to transgress the Torah's prohibition of writing down the Oral Law, because the time has come to do for Hashem." When he saw that the Oral Law was in danger of being forgotten, he permitted transcribing parts of it, beginning first with the *Mishnah*, followed by the *Gemara* and the rest of the revealed Torah. However, revealing the *Zohar* was not permitted. Although it was written down, it was transcribed in a secret code so that no one unsuitable would understand it.

Rabbi Hayyim Vital writes in his introduction to *Etz Hayyim* that when Rabbi Shimon bar Yohai revealed the secrets of the *Zohar*, he had ten pupils. These were all great *Tannaim* who were worthy of hearing these teachings. When he revealed the *Idra Rabba*, there

---

223. *Berachot* 54a.

were ten. Later, when he taught the *Idra Zuta*, there were only seven, because three has passed away. In the beginning of the *Idra Zuta*, he said, "Rabbi Elazar may teach; Rabbi Abba may write down. The rest may revise what they heard, but the others may not teach others or write anything down." Rabbi Hayyim Vital asks why only Rabbi Abba was chosen to write, and explains that only Rabbi Abba knew how to write in the secret code so that the text would be incomprehensible to people outside the circle, even other *Tannaim*.

This means that great *Tannaim*, authors of the *Mishnah* whose rulings form the basis of our *halachah*, were not able to understand the words of the *Zohar*. Only seven people were able to understand it. Yet nowadays, any youngster who can hardly read Hebrew studies kabbalah and thinks he understands the *Zohar*. Of course, without knowing the secret code, he can't understand anything.

Worse, if one takes these concepts literally, one is, God forbid, saying words of complete *kefirah*, blasphemy. For example, if one would give a literal interpretation to what the Ari says in the first chapter of *Etz Hayyim*, he would be a heretic. Heaven protect us from those people who think that since they can translate Hebrew well, they have understood the words of the Ari.

Our great rabbi and teacher, the Ben Ish Hai, wrote a responsa in his *sefer, Rav Pa'alim*, about a man who translated into Arabic books of kabbalah, including the *Shomer Emunim* of Rabbi Yosef Irgas as well as *Shir Hashirim* from the *Tanach*. I have seen these books, and they are rare collectors' items. He wrote a linear translation, with the Arabic translation written in Hebrew characters above each word of the Hebrew text. The Ben Ish Hai put a ban on the man and on studying all three works, even *Shir Hashirim*. He wrote that one may translate only those parts of Torah that have a literal meaning.

For example, the *Humash*, the five books of Moses, can and should be taken literally, even though we know every word can be read with great depth and explained according to kabbalah. When children are taught *"Bereshit bara Elokim,"* "In the beginning, God created," every word is translated for them in a literal sense. In fact, someone who denies the literal meaning of the events in the Torah, saying, for example, that *Gan Eden* didn't really exist but is only a concept, is also called an *apikorus.*

Every word in the Torah was transmitted by Hashem to Moshe and has a literal meaning. This symbolic simple meaning is called the *pshat.* If we delve deeper, we find a meaning, called *remez,* followed by allegorical interpretations or *derash,* and then the hidden meaning, *sod.*

Wherever there is *pshat,* as with the *Humash,* the text can be translated, because the translation corresponds to the literal meaning. But where there is no literal meaning, the text may not be translated. *Shir Hashirim* by Shlomo Hamelech has no literal meaning. On the surface, it appears to be a love song. To understand this in a literal sense and think that it is a description of the relationship between a man and his beloved is heresy. *Shir Hashirim* can only be understood on deeper levels, either as explained by the *Midrash,* which says it describes the relationship between the Jewish people and God, or according to kabbalah; it may not be translated literally. That is why our rabbis said *Shir Hashirim* in the Holy of Holies. This is what the *Hacham* Yosef Hayyim ruled for us.

For this reason, in my opinion, people who translate parts of the kabbalah into English are doing the wrong thing. The kabbalah cannot be translated. One might be able to translate some vague ideas, the *mussar* of the *Zohar* or the *Midrashim,* but the kabbalistic abstract concepts should not be translated.

Hashem's Omnipresence

Kabbalah, in essence, comes to clarify and deepen our belief in

God. The first of the Ten Commandments directs us to believe that the world has a Creator and that He is One. We affirm this belief every time we say the *Shema*.

We must believe that not only did Hashem create the world, but that His sovereignty and direct supervision is ongoing and constant. Others may acknowledge that God created the world, but say He has no further interest in what happens here on earth. Human beings are too insignificant and the details of their lives too minor for Hashem's consideration or involvement. We, though, believe that everything that takes place in this world, every word spoken and every action taken, is willed by Hashem. All is done with His consent and with His guidance, and not a single event is coincidence. We call this Divine providence, *hashgahah pratis*. Everything, even sinning, is done only with Hashem's *hashgahah*.

(The "Ramak," Rabbi Moshe Cordovero, in his work *Tomer Devora*, enumerates the Divine attributes and explains how we must emulate them. He writes that Hashem is referred to as a *"Melech Aluv,"* a king who bears insults [*aluv* comes from the word *elbon*, an insult]. The Ramak explains that this is like a mother who is feeding a sick child. While she gives him the food that is keeping him alive, he kicks her. In the same way, every time a Jew sins, Hashem is, at that very moment, giving him the life and energy to rebel against Him. This is the extent of Hashem's mercy and *hashgahah* over us.)

Understanding Creation

In addition to clarifying our belief that Hashem created the world and runs it according to His will, kabbalah gives us an understanding of what it means when we say God is One. This very deep concept is one of the fundamentals of kabbalah.

The kabbalah also gives us an insight into the concept of creation. If you ask a child, "Where is Hashem?" he will answer, "He is everywhere in the world." Our sages, however, teach us a deeper understanding. One of the names we use to refer to Hashem is *Hamakom*, the Place. Our sages explain this to mean that Hashem does not dwell in the world, but that He created a place for the world within Him: *Hu Mekomo shel olam*, "He is the Place of the world."[224] Before Hashem created the word ex nihilo, *yesh me'ayin*, there was no place for the world, because Hashem was everywhere, His existence unending in space, time, and power. First Hashem had to create a place for the world. Then He created the world from nothingness to fill that space.

The kabbalah also discusses the different levels of creation. There are numerous worlds above worlds, each more wondrous and spiritual than the one before. The entire cosmos, to whose ends no satellite can traverse and no telescope can see, represents no more than *tahtit Olam HaAsiyah*, the lowest level of the lowest of the four worlds mentioned by kabbalah.

Through these worlds, Hashem runs our world. In it, He placed the human being, the pinnacle of creation, and "breathed into his nostrils the soul of life."[225] The *Zohar* states, "One who blows, blows from within Himself," so to speak. The Jewish soul is described as being a *helek Eloka mima'al,* "a part of God Himself." It is very difficult to grasp such a concept, but these are the words of our teachers.

The human soul is Divine, "hewn out from under the Throne of Glory."[226] This wonderful creation which we call man is really a spiritual creation. The body is merely a garment, tailor-made to fit the soul. Rabbi Hayyim Vital in his work *Shaarei Kedushah* brings support for this idea from a Torah verse concerning the *shemen hamishha*, the sacred oil used for anointing the *Mishkan* and other

---

224. *Bereshit Rabbah* 68:9.
225. *Bereshit* 2:7.
226. *Zohar* 3:29b.

anointments. The Torah writes *al basar adam lo yisah*, "It may not be used to anoint the flesh of a man."[227] This implies that the real man is not his flesh, but the soul that resides within the body. The body is merely an outer garment for the essential man, who is the soul within.

We all know the custom not to name a baby boy until his *brit milah*. For eight days, he is nameless. If the *brit* is delayed, the naming is also delayed. The moment the child is circumcised, he is given a name. The reason for this is that the name is given to the soul, not to the body. Until the foreskin is cut off, the baby has only a *nefesh habehamit*, the physical life force we share in common with the animals. The spiritual soul doesn't enter until the *brit* is performed and the forces of evil are separated from him together with the foreskin. Only after the soul enters the child can we give him a Jewish name; before that, he is just a piece of flesh.

The kabbalah teaches us the purpose of man and what he is supposed to achieve in this world. We learn that each *mitzvah* has the power to bring about a separate *tikun*, perfecting the universe and the higher spiritual worlds in a unique way. The same is true of our prayers. We all recite the same words, yet we know that every word builds spiritual worlds and brings *tikun* to the higher worlds, bringing them to perfection. The *Zohar* teaches that there is nothing greater than learning Torah, for every word of Torah learning creates a new world.

Rabbi Hayyim Volozhin writes that only the lowermost part of the soul, what might be called the sole of the soul, enters the body; the full soul is still connected to the higher worlds.[228] The actions of a human being affect and relate to the higher worlds, because part of his soul is still there. Yaakov Avinu dreamt of a "ladder firmly planted on earth, but whose head reaches the heavens."[229] The lowest part of

---

227. *Shemot* 30:32.

228. *Nefesh HaHayyim, shaar* 1, Chapter 5 בהגהה.

229. *Bereshit* 28:12.

our soul is firmly planted on earth inside the body; the rest of our soul soars upward and reaches the highest heavens.

This is the wonderful wisdom of the kabbalah. It gives us an understanding into the hidden meaning of every word in the Torah, the meaning of the *mitzvot* and their effect on the universe. It enables us to appreciate the purpose of creation, the reasons for man's existence and the scope of his duties here in this world. The kabbalah teaches us all this and more.

The Secret Wisdom

The wisdom of the kabbalah is referred to as *hochmat hanistar* or *hochmat hasod*, the hidden or secret wisdom. There are two reasons for this. The first is that the topics under discussion are matters that are hidden from human perception. When we learn the *Mishnah* about the types of damages inflicted by a *shor* or the *bor*, we know exactly what each is: an ox and a pit. These are tangible objects that exist in our world. But when we discuss kabbalistic ideas, we are talking about abstract concepts that are completely spiritual and beyond our grasp.

The earliest work on kabbalah is *Sefer Yetzirah* written by Avraham Avinu. It describes the *sefirot*, the emanations of the Creator, so to speak, and refers to them as, "*Eser sefirot blima.*" The Rayvad, one of the great *Rishonim*, explains in his commentary to *Sefer Yetzirah* that *blima* means "without substance," or *bli ma*; that is, something we can never fathom or understand. The only way we can discuss these topics is through the secret code of the *hachamim* mentioned above, through which they give us some way of relating to these spiritual concepts. And there is a condition. "The heavenly *hayyot* in the vision of Yehezkel ran forward and returned."[230] The

---

230. *Yehezkel* 1:14.

hachamim explain this to mean that when you think about any kabbalistic idea, you may contemplate it for a moment, but then you must immediately retreat. The reason for this is because a human being has two parts to his intellect: *sechel hamufshat*, abstract thought, and *sechel hamedameh*, comparative thinking. A person can momentarily grasp an abstract idea using *sechel hamufshat*, but his mind will immediately switch to *sechel hamedameh* and try to compare the abstract concept to something tangible. We are forbidden to do this with spiritual concepts. For this reason, it is very dangerous for a layman to dabble in kabbalah, since he may profane the sublime spiritual concepts by clothing them in physical and bodily connotations.

Take, for example, the concept of a soul. For a moment, one might grasp the spiritual aspect of what it is, but he may not dwell on the topic for too long. Otherwise, his mind will try to give form to the concept, and he will find himself imagining it to be a type of light or some sort of vapor. If you are discussing the Creator and seeking to understand a spiritual concept used to describe Hashem and His higher worlds, by dwelling on the thought, your mind will try to form a picture of something tangible with which to compare it. That would be *avodah zarah*. The Torah warns, "Cursed is the man who makes a graven or molten image…and places it in secret."[231] The *Zohar* explains this to mean someone who tries to give a physical form to the secret spiritual concepts of the kabbalah that apply to the Creator.

Of course, the Torah does use physical terms when talking about Hashem. Verses mention "the eyes of Hashem" and "the feet of Hashem." The reason for this is that since we are human beings, we can only understand physical terms. But should a person take these metaphors literally, even for a split second, he would be guilty of idolatry. We may not attribute any physicality to Hashem.

---

231. *Devarim* 27:16.

This requirement is even greater when studying the *Idra Rabba*, the *Idra Zuta*, and the other kabbalistic writings that symbolize the higher worlds and Divine concepts in physical terms, comparing them to the human body. This is why I repeatedly stress the dangers of unqualified people trying to study kabbalah. Someone not on a level to understand the secret code that the kabbalists use is committing a great sin by reading their words, because it is certain he will misinterpret them.

The Concealed Wisdom

One reason why the kabbalah is called *hochmat hanistar*, concealed wisdom, is because it is wisdom hidden from human conception, as explained above. However, a second reason is that the *hachamim* warn us that this wisdom must be kept hidden. One is not allowed to reveal it publicly. The Hida writes that he cries and mourns over the fact that so many works of kabbalah were printed in his times, because these sublime spiritual and holy ideas are not to be made public.

Many people mistakenly quote Rabbi Hayyim Vital who, in the introduction to *Etz Hayyim*, praises the study of kabbalah and encourages it. He writes that it is because people are not studying the kabbalah that *Mashiah* has not come yet. But they don't read what he is saying carefully enough. He is not talking to laymen or new *baalei teshuvah*. He is not talking to women and children. He mentions many times in his introduction that he is speaking specifically to the great *hachamim* of his time. They are the ones who should be learning the secrets of the kabbalah.

To quote part of his introduction, "A person should not say, 'I will go and learn kabbalah,' before he has studied Torah, *Mishnah*, and Talmud, because our sages have taught us that a person cannot study the kabbalah before he has filled himself with *basar veyayin*, the main course of meat and wine." Only then can he be *metayel bepardes*, "stroll in the orchard" of the hidden part of the Torah. Only after eating the main course can you bring in the dessert. In the same way, only after a person has learned *Shas* and *poskim* can he study the kabbalah.

In fact, the entire wisdom of kabbalah is built on an understanding of the revealed Torah. Only a person who understands the full depth of the *Gemara* will be able to appreciate the depth of kabbalah. If he has not studied *Gemara* in depth, he will make mistakes in his studies which touch on *ikrei emunah*, the fundamentals of our faith. So a person might think he is doing a great *mitzvah* by studying kabbalah, when in fact he is interpreting what he is learning in a manner that is *kefira gemura*, utter heresy. It will not help if he repeatedly states, "I sincerely, with all my heart, believe and know that I don't understand." This is not a satisfactory answer. Kabbalah is meant to be understood, and understood correctly. The only one who can do this is a person who has developed himself and his knowledge in the way our *hachamim* wanted. He must first study the *Torat haniglah*, the revealed Torah, become well versed in *Mishnah* and *Gemara*, and keep the *mitzvot* properly. Rabbi Hayyim Vital swears in God's Name, at the beginning of his *sefer*, that if a person studies his *Etz Hayyim* after keeping these conditions, he guarantees him a long and healthy life. However, someone who jumps to the kabbalah without fulfilling the proper conditions, endangers his life, God forbid.

The *Zohar* writes on the verse, "*Lishmor et derech etz hahayyim*,"[232] "to guard the way to the tree of life," that Hashem placed angels with circling swords on the path to the *etz hahayyim*. This refers to the secrets of the Torah. This study is not to be made available at every street corner, inviting all and sundry elements to

---

232. *Bereshit* 3:24.

come and learn kabbalah. It is the most holy study, which every one of us must strive to be worthy of attaining. But the only way is to start from the beginning and build oneself up. There is no jumping up the rungs of this ladder. If a person jumps, he will find that he has nothing to hold onto and has no place on which to stand.

Deliberately Unclear

We can get an idea of just how difficult the study of kabbalah is by comparing it to the Talmud written by Ravina and Rav Ashi. In their generation, the *Gemara* was like the *Kitzur Shulhan Aruch* or the Ben Ish Hai to us. Ravina and Rav Ashi did not try to conceal anything. They wrote as clearly as they could. Their purpose was to give the Jewish people a clear text that would teach them the laws of the Torah and explain exactly what the Torah wants from us. They were not trying to hide anything.

Nevertheless, we see just how hard it is to learn a page of *Gemara*. We break our teeth over even the simple meaning of the words, and strain our mind over every concept. And then we would like to understand Rashi's commentary. We find ourselves pondering why Rashi explained it this way and not some other way. We want to understand every word and nuance. Then we have to understand why Rashi differs from *Tosafot* and why *Tosafot* argues with Rashi. We know that wherever they disagree, there is a good reason for it, based on their different ways of understanding the *Gemara*. We consider what questions can be raised on the way *Tosafot* learned, and we seek to understand what made Rashi learn the way he did. We can be sure that when Rashi studied the *Gemara*, he had six or seven other ways of explaining it. What made him choose just this way? He must have had proof that this is the correct way. The same is true for *Tosafot*. Then we find that the Ritva has a different approach, and the Rif and the Rambam have their interpretations.

And then the *Aharonim* give their interpretations. There are no end to clarifications and points to ponder.

We have to study all this to be able to arrive at a conclusion and say, "This is the *halachah*." Who can do that? Maybe one in a million can be called a *ba'al halachah*, a master of *halachah*. This is not just someone who can open a Ben Ish Hai and read the *halachah*, but someone who understands how the Ben Ish Hai arrived at that conclusion. He would have to be someone who understood the Talmud and all the different opinions of the *Rishonim*. Then he would need to understand how the Bet Yosef brings down the various opinions and finally wrote the *halachah* in the *Shulhan Aruch*. Then there are the various *Aharonim* who discuss the *Shulhan Aruch* and often disagree with each other. It is an unbelievable task to finally arrive at a definitive *halachic* ruling. However, all this is the most basic thing that our sages and teachers come to teach us. They tried to make it easy for us, so that we should know what to do. Nevertheless, perhaps one in a million can understand.

How does this compare to the study of kabbalah, which is a spiritual topic? Our *hachamim* tell us that when teaching the revealed parts of the Torah, the 613 *mitzvot*, you should choose students who are *tocho keboro*, "whose insides are like their outsides." When a person is honest and sincere, not someone who says one thing and does another, you can teach him Torah.

But when it is a question of teaching someone kabbalah, there are many conditions a student must fulfill. His conduct must be exemplary, beyond the *halachic* requirements that bind every Jew. Rav Eliyahu Mani explains the reason for this in his book *Kisei Eliyahu*. He connects these requirements with the point we made before. In this area of wisdom, we have to understand everything in an abstract form. Yet, we are faced with a contradiction, because we use human, physical terms to discuss these topics. When an ordinary person hears the word "hand," he pictures a hand. When he hears about the head, he pictures a head. To him, hair means hair, and a beard makes him think of a beard. Since he is closer to his body than to his soul, he takes these ideas in a physical sense. This is called *hagshamah* and is forbidden. This is why people who have not worked on perfecting themselves for many years may not learn kabbalah. If they do, they are doing something very wrong.

But when the kabbalists use these words, they are referring to abstract concepts. The head is not a head, the beard is not a beard, and the hair is not hair. When a person keeps all the stringencies of a true kabbalist, he purifies himself to the point that his brain is only minimally influenced by his physical side. He will be able to understand these abstract concepts without attributing them to their physical counterparts.

The Ramhal, in his book *Hoker U'Mekkubal*, tries to define the kabbalah in one sentence. He says the kabbalah comes to teach us about how Hashem is One, how He created the world and the purpose of creation. The central concept is *Yihud Hashem*, the Oneness of Hashem. Those who are superficial in studying the kabbalah misunderstand its true deep meaning and arrive at exactly the opposite conclusion. The Rivash, one of the great *Rishonim*, writes in one of his responsa concerning those who study kabbalah that "the Christians believe in three, and the kabbalists believe in ten." God forbid. The Rivash understood the kabbalah, but saw that superficial people in his generation who were dabbling in kabbalah misunderstood and misinterpreted the kabbalah, and he was very afraid of their attempts to learn it. He wanted to make them aware of what they were doing. The bottom line being that the ultimate purpose of the kabbalah is to teach that Hashem is One.

This is the difference between studying *Gemara* and learning kabbalah. If a person makes a mistake in understanding the *Gemara*, no great harm will result (unless he is a rabbi or a *halachic* authority whose mistake leads to an incorrect ruling; about this, our sages say that careless misinterpretation can lead to willful transgression[233]). But if he tries to learn kabbalah and misunderstands it, he is, God forbid, making mistakes in the fundamentals of our faith, which is the most serious offense one can make. That is heresy and blasphemy.

The bottom line is that studying Talmud and *halachah* is certainly not easy, and yet the topics are physical and comprehensible. How much harder is it to learn kabbalah, whose topics are abstract and spiritual. Moreover, the sages who taught the kabbalah revealed a few inches of its secrets, but hid miles more, quite often deliberately writing the opposite of what is meant in order to hide the truth from people who are not supposed to know it. They relied on the fact that the right person will understand it anyway. Unquestionably, this special study is meant only for the chosen few and not for the masses.

What Is a Kabbalist?

Today, people have a distorted perception of what a kabbalist is. Most people think of him as someone who dispenses magic charms and amulets, gives out blessings for wealth and success, and acts in strange, mystical ways. People often ask me, "How can you be a kabbalist when you're so normal?" As one person at a lecture whispered to another, "He even has all his teeth!" They are looking for something strange, odd, or crazy. "If he makes odd movements with his hand, he must be a kabbalist."

The whole purpose of kabbalah is to teach us that Hashem is One, that He created the world and continues to rule it, that He is close to us and guides us. If a person has a problem, whether one of finances, ill health or any other, what response does Hashem expect from us?

---

233. *Pirkei Avot* 4:13.

Our *hachamim* say that when suffering comes to a person, he should examine his deeds. Maybe he is doing something wrong. Maybe he is not learning enough Torah or giving enough charity. Nowhere does it tell us that when suffering comes upon us we should run to a kabbalist. In this day of instant everything, people want instant solutions to their problems, so they look for a kabbalist. After all, he's got something for everything. If someone has no money, he'll give him an amulet. If someone comes looking for a cure, he'll make him a *tikun* and give him a *berachah*.

We have to change our way of thinking. Why does Hashem bring problems? It's His way of saying to us, "I miss you. I'd like you to talk to Me a little bit. Open your heart to Me. Say something. Pray to Me! I am the One Who is giving you this problem."

Sarah, Rivka, and Rahel were barren because Hashem wanted them to pray to Him.[234] Hashem longs for our prayers. In order to hear them, He sometimes pricks us a little bit. When this happens, we should say to ourselves, "I must be doing something wrong. Let me check my actions." Then, we should turn to Hashem and say, "Please, Hashem, help me. I've done what is up to me."

If it has been decided that a person should lose his money, suffer illness or worse, no matter what the decree is, you can change it – but not by going to a kabbalist or by getting an amulet. Nowhere in the entire *Gemara* does it advise such a thing. *Teshuvah, tefillah,* and *tzedakah* nullify an evil decree. First, you have to repent. You have to search your actions for flaws. Do your homework, and see what's wrong. Then, you have to give charity. This atones for a person's sins. Then you have to entreat Hashem to accept your *teshuvah* and *tzedakah*, and ask Him to hear your prayers.

Instead, everyone's looking for someone to give him a friendly slap

---

234. *Midrash Rabbah* on *Shir Hashirim* 2:14.

on the back and say, "You're okay, Charlie. All you need is this little piece of paper. Wear it around your neck, and everything will be just fine." This is missing the point. This approach has nothing to do with the way of our Torah whatsoever.

The sages credit Chizkiyahu, King of Yehuda, with several positive acts, among them concealing *Sefer Refuot*, the Book of Healing. This was not a medical textbook, but a spiritual sourcebook that gave the cure for every illness. Chizkiyahu saw that people were turning away from Hashem. When a person took ill, instead of doing *teshuvah* and praying to Hashem, he instead looked for a cure in the book. So Chizkiyahu buried the book forever.

The situation parallels our own. People often tell me, "Rabbi, you're the first person who told us that it's also up to us. We never knew that before. We never knew we had to change. We never realized Hashem is speaking to us."

Kabbalah comes to teach us that Hashem is One, and that He rules the world, but would-be kabbalists are trying to teach that we don't need Him at all. They'll solve all our problems. According to them, there's a new slot machine called kabbalah. You just put the money in, things start moving, and everything becomes okay.

Believe me, this is not kabbalah. Nowhere in the *Etz Hayyim* are such things mentioned.

The *Etz Hayyim*, which conveys the teachings revealed by the Ari z"l, was written by his student Rabbi Hayyim Vital, hence its name. After Rabbi Hayyim Vital's passing, his son Rav Shmuel Vital carefully guarded the *Etz Hayyim*, not letting it leave his room. The holy Shelah was the leading Torah authority at the time. After a trip to Damascus, he wrote in a letter to a leading rabbi:

> *Rav Shmuel Vital allowed me entry to his father's study. There, I saw the original manuscript of the Etz Hayyim. I had great*

difficultly reading it, because it is written in Sephardic script, which I do not understand well.

From the day we received the Five Books of Moses on Mount Sinai, there has never been a book like this!

The *Etz Hayyim* offers no instant solutions. It teaches that the only way for a person to come close to Hashem is by keeping the *mitzvot*, studying His Torah, and correcting his deeds. If a person has a problem, he must face it and find the solution within his actions. He must realize that Hashem doesn't do anything to anyone without a reason. Everything Hashem does is for a purpose. Even if we don't understand it now, we will understand it later. Not only that, but everything is for our good, even what seems not to be good. Nothing bad comes from Hashem.

When we look at life, we are seeing a close-up segment of the total picture. We are so close that all we see is smudges of color. When we move back, everything falls into place. When we see the world in full perspective, as Hashem sees it, then we will understand the true picture. Then we will see why everything happened in the world, and realize that it was good for it to happen. We will then understand that it had to happen exactly that way, and that any other way would not have helped bring the world to its perfection and completion.

At the same time, we must live according to Torah law, as brought in the *Shulhan Aruch*. Wrongdoing is punished, and actions are measured against Divine rules. If a person is a Shabbat desecrator, we are not allowed to drink wine touched by him. We do not say, "Since everything that happens in the world is for the good, then even his wrongdoing is good. This means we can drink the wine."

Hashem, though, sees things differently. Maybe right now that person is not Sabbath observant, but tomorrow he will change. I know people who were involved in drugs and worse, who ended up in jail and eventually did *teshuvah*. Had they not spent time in jail, they would not have done *teshuvah*. Only after first reaching the rock-bottom of society did they come to see the light and do an about-face. We can't say that when they used drugs and committed murder they were doing good things because it led to jail where they did *teshuvah*. We can realize, though, that the final outcome was good, which is the way Hashem sees the world.

As for us, we have to live according to *halachah*. For instance, in the time of the *Sanhedrin*, a person judged to have desecrated the Sabbath publicly was stoned to death. Detailed laws determine what constitutes desecration, and specific conditions must be met for it to be considered such. If two witnesses saw the person and warned him, saying, "That is forbidden," and he replied, "Even so, I will do it," he was guilty. We don't say, "Maybe some good will come of it."

From Hashem's perspective, everything is for the good. The Shabbat desecrator had to be thrown to his death, but he will return in another *gilgul* (incarnation) and come to his *tikun*. It had to be that way.

Everything has to be exactly as it is. That is why there are no ready-made solutions, and self-proclaimed, quick-fix kabbalistic rabbis can never be authentic.

Practical Kabbalah

Within kabbalah, there is a more physical and practical revelation called kabbalah *ma'asit*, practical kabbalah.

Historically, practical kabbalah was used at times by great rabbis when there was a need to save *Klal Yisrael* from terrible decrees. For example, if a community was threatened with annihilation due to a king's decree, the rabbi could use practical kabbalah to bring about a miraculous salvation.

Rabbi Hayyim Vital tells us that anyone who uses the kabbalah to further his own self-interests – whether for money or fame – will be harmed. He might die, lose his mind, feel a sudden compulsion to convert to another religion, or, God forbid, cause his children to die. People who ask a kabbalist which stocks to buy or where they should invest their money are missing the point. Kabbalah is not for making money; kabbalah is for coming close to Hashem.

In our times, anyone who tries to use practical kabbalah is playing with fire. The warnings of the Ari *z"l* against using or misusing *kabbalah ma'asit* were written over four centuries ago, at a time when many people in Zefat had *gilui Eliyahu*, which means the prophet Eliyahu revealed himself to them. In one synagogue in Zefat, the rabbi was Rabbi Joseph Caro, author of the *Shulhan Aruch*; the *darshan* who spoke every Shabbat was the holy Rabbi Moshe Alshich; the kabbalist was the Ari *z"l* himself, and the *shamash* was Rabbi Elazar Azikri, the author of *Sefer Haredim*.

The story is told that one Lag BaOmer, the Ari *z"l* took Rabbi Azikri into the circle with his students and danced with him. His students said, "How can you dance with this ignoramus? He's the *shamash*."

The Ari *z"l* replied, "Don't worry. We know who the *shamash* is." Some say an impressive-looking stranger also joined them in the inner circle. The Ari then told his students that since Rashbi was comfortable dancing with the *shamash*, so was he.

Rabbi Azikri had *gilui Eliyahu* and *ruah hakodesh*. In addition to his book on the 613 *mitzvot*, *Sefer Haredim*, Rabbi Azikri wrote a commentary on the Jerusalem Talmud. The song he composed by Divine inspiration, *Yedid Nefesh*, is sung on Shabbat in Jewish homes around the world.

If such people were warned not to use practical kabbalah, how much more so does this apply to us, who are nowhere near their level of piety and purity. The Ari z"l says that only a person who never sinned – *even unintentionally!* – can make use of practical kabbalah and be guaranteed to survive unharmed.

In practical kabbalah, spiritual forces are bound by an oath. These forces are a mixture of good and evil, like everything else in our physical world. Therefore, anything that is seemingly achieved by controlling these forces is extremely dubious and dangerous because you cannot differentiate and separate between the good and evil.

Take, for example, a kabbalist who makes an amulet and writes a *hashba'ah*, which is binding by oath a certain angel of the *Olam HaAsiyah* to do his will. Let us say, for instance, that he binds the angel to give a childless couple children. Since good and evil are mixed, there is no guarantee that these children will be righteous and not evildoers, God forbid. Second, the person who binds the angel runs the risk of going crazy. The evil forces could destroy him. As soon as they hear their name mentioned in the oath, they say, "Who's binding us?" When they look down and see who it is, they say, "Oh, it's only you," and they finish him off. All this is taught by Rabbi Hayyim Vital. Nor does he suffice with saying such things might happen, but he names specific rabbis. "Like So-and-so," he says, "and So-and-so." He mentions people who made amulets and wrote *hashba'ot*, and tells us what punishment was meted out to them because of it. Rabbi Hayyim Vital says we are not allowed to use this wisdom at all, because no one alive is on the right level. If he said so about his generation, how much more so does this hold true today.

Some kabbalists in our time permit the use of amulets. They claim that in the amulets they write, they are not binding the forces by oath, but just asking them to fulfill a request.[235]

---

235. See Rav Kadouri's letter printed in the beginning of my book *Faith and Folly*.

I disagree with this. If you are making a request, why not make it of Hashem? Why ask an angel? The only reason to write an amulet is to bind the angel by oath. If you are just asking him, what's the point? Some claim there is nothing wrong with doing this. Since the forces are not bound by oath, it is not practical kabbalah anyway. It sounds to me like a new invention. We prefer and recommend only the tried-and-true, traditionally accepted practices of prayer, repentance, and charity.

Tzaddik Nistar

Modern writers have invented a mythical figure they call the *tzaddik nistar*. Unfortunately, he bears little resemblance to the real *tzaddik nistar*.

The fictional *tzaddik nistar*, or "hidden *tzaddik*," is a person who outwardly seems to be a boor and ignoramus but is really a very great person. This is a complete misconception.

If you were to ask me for an example of a *tzaddik nistar* in our times, I would say, "Rav Shach, *ztz"l*, or the Steipler, *ztz"l*."

"What do you mean?" you'll say. "Their greatness and piety were not hidden at all. They were in the headlines every day!"

I would call Rav Shach or the Steipler a *tzaddik nistar* because we knew only a small part, perhaps only one percent, of their righteousness. Truly great people don't show off everything they do. This is a true hidden *tzaddik*.

A *tzaddik nistar* must be one hundred percent pious outwardly. If you see a person who knows Torah and studies Torah day and night, does the *mitzvot*, who prays on time with a *minyan* and never does anything wrong, whose every action is according to the *Shulhan Aruch*, he might be a *tzaddik nistar*. On the other hand, he might not.

Maybe he reveals everything he does. Maybe nothing is hidden. But before this stage is reached, he cannot begin to be a *tzaddik nistar*.

A person should be modest and humble, hiding his good deeds and not revealing everything he does. Not like the person who, in the presence of a guest, said to his wife, "Please bring me my box of snuff. You know where it is – in the room where I say *Tikun Hatzot* every day, next to my *Etz Hayyim*." On the other extreme, somehow the idea also took hold that someone *seen* doing wrong things or being in places no Jew should be, is also a *tzaddik nistar*, because inside, he's a *tzaddik*. There is no such thing. To be a *tzaddik*, the minimum is "*tocho keboro*," his inside should equal his outside.

Previous generations did not have this misconception. The Hatam Sofer, who lived in the nineteenth century, was once *sandak* at a *brit* that took place on Purim. At the moment of the *brit*, he put wine on the lips of the baby and said, *Nichnas yayin, yatza sod*, "When wine goes in, the secret comes out."[236] The baby was named Baruch Mordechai in honor of the day.

Baruch Mordechai grew up into a fine, pious boy and entered the famous Pressburg Yeshivah. However, although he applied himself to his Torah studies diligently, he was not the brightest of students and could not seem to remember what he learned. The *Ktav Sofer*, his rosh yeshivah, suggested to the boy's parents that they send him to Eretz Yisrael. Perhaps there he would find his place, since it is known that "the air of Israel makes one wise."[237]

Baruch Mordechai went to Eretz Yisrael, and after several years married. To support his family, he became a water carrier. Drawing pails of water from the well and carrying them through the streets was not the easiest way to earn a living, but Baruch Mordechai worked at

---

236. *Eruvin* 65a.
237. *Baba Batra* 158b.

this job for decades. People liked him, and almost everyone bought water from him. The one exception was the Brisker Rav, Rav Yehoshua Leib Diskin. He refused to buy water from Baruch Mordechai.

Baruch Mordechai sold water in the mornings and spent the rest of his time in the yeshivah swaying over an open *Gemara* for hours on end. Sometimes, the children would make fun of him by turning his *Gemara* to a different page when he got up to make a cup of tea. No matter how often they did this, he always returned to his seat as if nothing had happened and continued learning at the page opened.

One Purim, when Baruch Mordechai was seventy years old, he joined the festivities in the Old City at a famed rabbi's home. In true Purim spirit, he was made Purim Rav by some of those present.

They plied him with wine, stood him up on the table, and cried out for him to give a speech. Their surprise was total when Baruch Mordechai began spewing forth pearls of Torah wisdom from the *Gemara*, *Midrashim*, *halachah*, and the kabbalah. He was a genius of the highest caliber. The words of the Hatam Sofer seventy years earlier had come true: "When wine goes in, the secret comes out." The *gematria* of the word "wine" is seventy, the same as the *gematria* of the word *sod*, "secret," which was the age of Baruch Mordechai.

Baruch Mordechai might have been a *tzaddik nistar*, for he lived a holy life and did only what was good. The Brisker Rav knew the true value of the water carrier of Yerushalayim and refused to buy from him, since it is improper to use a *talmid hacham* to serve you.

Creating a Golem

I am often asked if it is really possible for man to create a *golem* using kabbalah. The concept is discussed by our sages, who say that a living being could be created according to instructions in *Sefer Yetzirah*. However, knowledge alone is not enough to give a kabbalist the power to do so; it must be accompanied by holiness and merit. A rabbi of the caliber of the Vilna Gaon could have done such a thing, but I strongly believe that no one in our generation is on such a level, especially since each generation is on a lower level than the one preceding it.

Rabbi Hayyim Vital explains the various levels of *ruah hakodesh*, Divine inspiration.[238] Not all the prophets saw with the same clarity. Moshe Rabbeinu, the *Gemara* tells us, saw through a crystal-clear glass, or, some say, in a crystal-clear mirror. The other prophets saw in a tarnished mirror. The image was visible, but less clear.

The early prophets experienced a higher level of revelation than those who followed. From generation to generation, the information transmitted to a prophet came through an increasing number of filters. Moshe Rabbeinu could see even *Olam HaAtzilut*, as it was enclothed, in a passing way, by *Olam HaBeriyah*. The other early prophets saw *Olam HaAtzilut*, but only filtered through *Olam HaBeriyah* (a lower level of vision). The later prophets saw *Olam HaAtzilut* filtered through *Olam HaBeriyah* and *Olam HaYetzirah*. The wisdom of the *Tannaim* and *Amoraim* was only in *Olam HaYetzirah*, the world of the angels.

Today, even this level is no longer accessible to us. After the era of the *Amoraim*, we lost the ashes of the *para adumah*, the red heifer. These ashes were used to purify someone who had become ritually impure. Without these ashes, we are all ritually impure. In this state, it is only possible to access the wisdom of *Olam HaAsiyah*, our world, the lowest of all worlds.

In my book, *Faith and Folly*, I discuss the proliferation of charlatans who pretend to be kabbalists. They claim to perform all

---

238. *Shaarei Kedushah*, part 3, *shaar* 6.

sorts of wonders and miracles using practical kabbalah. Yet which one of them can claim that he never sinned *even accidentally* – the precondition taught by the Ari z"l? To use practical kabbalah, a person's level of purity would have to equal that of the great sages of generations past. Who, today, is on that level?

Our sages taught that Hashem "gives wisdom to the wise."[239] We can explain this to mean that someone who toiled over the words of the revealed Torah will merit knowing the secrets of the Torah.

The right way to grow spiritually is like climbing a ladder. For this reason, Hashem showed Yaakov a ladder in his dream. The ladder was firmly planted on the ground but extended all the way up to the higher heavens. This teaches us that the only way to climb spiritually is rung by rung, starting from the ground upward. If the ladder is not firmly positioned on the ground, it will topple. Similarly, we must climb rung by rung through *peshat*, *remez*, *derash*, and *sod*. Those who don't look for shortcuts will eventually make it all the way up. It's hard work, but the only path to success.

---

239. *Daniel* 2:21.

The Jewish Home

When Hashem gave the Torah to the Jewish people, He told Moshe Rabbeinu: "This is what you should say to the house of Yaakov and relate to the children of Yisrael."[240] The wording might seem repetitious, but the subtle differences reveal important teachings.

The first difference is between "the house of Yaakov" and "the children of Yisrael"; the second is between "say" and "relate." Our sages teach us that "the house of Yaakov" refers to the women, and "the children of Yisrael" refers to the men. The word *say* (*tomar*) means "to speak softly," while the word *relate* (*ta'ged*) means "strong talk." Hashem was giving Moshe Rabbeinu a message: "When you offer the Torah to the Jewish people, and you want to convince the women to accept it, speak to them softly, in a gentle, encouraging manner. Don't frighten them or pressure them. When you talk to the men, though, speak forcefully. Explain to them the seriousness of keeping *mitzvot* and the punishments for failing to do so."[241]

We learn from this that women should be related to in a soft and encouraging manner, never with threats and force.

There is more to be learned from this verse. It would seem that men have a greater portion in Torah and *mitzvot* than women, since many *mitzvot* apply only to men. In particular, men are obligated in the *mitzvah* of Torah study from which women are exempt. Yet when Hashem gave us the Torah, He told Moshe to speak to the women

---

240. *Shemot* 19:3.
241. *Mechilta, parashat behodesh, parasha* 2.

first, before mentioning the men's obligations. Why did the Torah put the women first?

Because the woman is the decisive factor in a Jewish home.

We know that a wife should relate to her husband as a king, respecting him and obeying his wishes. Our sages tell us that a good wife is one who listens to her husband. Nevertheless, the woman is more influential in the home. Hashem knew that even if the men agreed to accept the Torah, unless the women first agreed to cooperate, to be the force behind the receiving of the Torah, it would not work. This is why Hashem told Moshe to speak to the women first. "Make sure the women are going to be happy about it. If they accept the Torah, then, when the men take it on, we can be sure the Torah will be kept properly."[242]

The Torah gives us numerous proofs of the woman's decisive power in the home. For example, when Yaakov went to meet Esav, he hid his daughter Dina out of fear that if Esav would see her, he would want to marry her. Unfortunately, Dina was subsequently taken captive by Shechem, a non-Jew who disgraced her. Her brothers were furious. "Is our sister to be treated like a harlot?" they asked in anger, and went on to kill Shechem's entire clan to punish them for what he did.

Why did Yaakov suffer such a disgrace? How could the daughter of such a holy man fall prey to such a horrible situation?

Our sages tell us that Yaakov was punished for not letting Dina marry his brother Esav. True, Esav was evil. But with a good wife like Dina, he would have changed for the better.

If such a disgraceful punishment was given Yaakov because he did not allow Dina to marry Esav, we have to assume that it was almost

---

242. Shemot 28:2.

guaranteed that had Dina married Esav, Esav would have become a better man. Such is the power of a wife.

We have other examples. Rahel, Rabbi Akiva's wife, built up her husband to become the Torah giant he eventually became. The *Gemara* says that when Moshe went up to heaven to receive the Torah, he saw Hashem tying crowns, *taggim*, on the letters.[243] When Moshe saw Hashem tying these crowns on the letters, he asked Him, "What is the purpose of these crowns?"

Moshe thought the *taggim* served no function. He knew that Hashem gave us a readable Torah, comprised of letters, words, and sentences. We even have *ta'amim* that tell us the melody we should use to sing each verse. But we do not read differently those letters that have crowns on them and those that do not. That is why the crowns seemed to have no significance.

Hashem answered Moshe, "Many generations in the future, a man named Akiva ben Yosef will expound on each and every crown to reveal the priceless secrets of the Torah that they allude to."

Moshe asked to see this person, and Hashem showed him Rabbi Akiva teaching in his yeshivah. Moshe was shocked to realize that he could not understand what Rabbi Akiva was teaching. As Moshe watched, a student asked Rabbi Akiva, "From where did you learn this?" Rabbi Akiva answered, "This is a teaching Moshe received at Sinai." When Moshe heard that, his spirits were restored. Still, he asked Hashem, "You have chosen me to receive the Torah for the Jewish people, yet You are telling me that there will be someone called Rabbi Akiva who will learn hundreds of *halachot* from each crown, and I cannot understand what he is saying." Hashem told Moshe that this was the way He wanted it to be.

---

243. *Menahot* 29b. See Chapter 9, "Lag BaOmer," above.

Such was the greatness of Rabbi Akiva. But how did he attain such a level?

Rabbi Akiva was a forty-year-old unlearned shepherd who worked for one of the richest men of all time. His employer's daughter, Rahel, saw tremendous potential in the ignorant shepherd and wanted to help him become the great rabbi she knew he could be. She gave up everything for this goal, including her father's financial support and her inheritance, for her father disowned her when she insisted on the match.

Rahel married Rabbi Akiva and encouraged him to learn.

We know the result. Rabbi Akiva reached such levels of Torah that even Moshe Rabbeinu was envious.

Rabbi Akiva acknowledged his wife's contribution when he said to his students, "Both my Torah and yours are all hers."

Hashem knew He would need the cooperation of the wives. With all a man's good intentions to keep and study the Torah, if his wife doesn't encourage him, he will not be able to stand up to life's pressures, and he won't learn.

A Woman's Reward in Our Era

The Ari z"l said that women living in the era preceding the coming of Mashiah, which is our generation, will have a unique status. The kabbalists teach us that souls come back many times until they complete the full quota of Torah and *mitzvot* they were supposed to achieve. This is the concept of reincarnation. The souls of the last generation before Mashiah are going to be from the same souls that lived in the time of the *dor hamidbar*, the generation that left Egypt and received the Torah. The sin of the golden calf occurred in that generation, but the women refused to give their jewelry for such a purpose. Their reward will be, the Ari z"l explains, that in the end of days before the coming of Mashiah, women will be given greater control over their husbands. Surely the reward is not meant to be negative; therefore, this must mean that if a wife truly wants her husband to find time to learn Torah and grow, if she sincerely wants to bring the blessings of Torah into her home, she can do it. That is her real reward. Ultimately, as Rabbi Akiva said, everything will be in her merit.

Women have many *mitzvot* to their credit. Yet the major reward given in the next world is for Torah study. Since Hashem exempted women from Torah study to free them for their primary obligations, how will they acquire this most valuable reward given in the next world?

Before answering this question, let us clarify the concept of women's exemption from learning Torah.

The Torah exempted women from responsibilities that would hamper their ability to fulfill their mission. All the positive commandments that have a time limit to them fall into this category, such as wearing *tzitzit* and putting on *tefillin*. A woman's role places her beyond time. Her devoted duty to the home is so tremendous that she doesn't need the perfection these other *mitzvot* bring. Men, on the other hand, do need these *mitzvot*.

There are two parts to the *mitzvah* of learning Torah. One is the *mitzvah* of *v'hagita bo yomam valaylah*, which means that a person must study Torah, the whole Torah, day and night. This implies not only knowing practical *halachah*, but also knowing the laws that do not necessarily pertain to daily life nowadays. Women are exempt from this type of learning.

However, women are obligated by all the negative commandments, the *lo ta'aseh*. A woman may not steal, murder, slander others, lie, and so on. Without knowing the *mitzvot*, it is impossible to keep them, so a woman has to be educated in these *mitzvot*. She also must know the laws that apply specifically to her, in particular, taking *hallah*, maintaining family purity, and lighting the Shabbat candles.

The *Gemara* implies that without being involved in ongoing Torah study one cannot merit the World–to–Come. Since a woman is not commanded to learn, how will she acquire this merit? The *Gemara* answers that there are two ways a woman can earn the same reward: (1) by making sure her sons learn Torah; and (2) by waiting patiently for her husband to return from learning.[244]

When a mother sends her children off to school in the morning, makes sure they do their homework, and follows their progress, she is helping them learn Torah. But what do our sages mean when they say a woman waits patiently for her husband to return home?

A husband can attend a Torah study session or lecture, but if his wife isn't happy about him being out of the house, he won't be able to concentrate. If she gives him the feeling that she will be waiting patiently for him to come home when he finishes his learning, he will be able to concentrate on his studies. The merit of this type of learning is hers, and this is her World–to–Come.

But there is more. A well-run home can give a person *yishuv hada'at*, peace of mind. When a husband knows that his children are well cared for, that his house is a comfortable place to come home to, a warm place, full of love and happiness, he has peace of mind. He knows he can rely on his wife to take care of the children and to educate them in the right way. All this gives him the right frame of mind to venture into the world to learn or work. King Solomon praised this kind of a wife: "Her husband trusts her."[245] A husband

---

244. *Sotah* 21a.
245. *Mishle* 31:11.

blessed with such a partner knows that everything is taken care of and running as it should be.

Eshet Hayil

Every Friday night, we sing the last chapter of *Mishle*, "*Eshet Hayil*," written by King Solomon. In it, he enumerates the virtues of a Jewish wife. Friday night is an especially appropriate time for a husband to show his appreciation to his wife, since she worked so hard to make a beautiful Shabbat.

King Solomon lists the praises of the Jewish wife alphabetically. Since a wife does everything from a to z, she deserves full credit from a to z. There is a much deeper meaning, though. King Solomon is telling us that the study of Torah, which is written using every letter of the alphabet, depends on the wife.

The *Ashrei* prayer,[246] in which we sing the praises of Hashem, also follows the alphabet. However, one letter is missing: *nun*. The *Gemara* explains that *nun* stands for *nefilah*, falling.[247] The Jewish people are suffering in exile, and the *Shechinah*, the Divine Presence, is suffering with them. Because King David did not want to mention the fall of the Divine Presence, no sentence in *Ashrei* starts with the letter *nun*. Yet the next sentence, which begins with the letter *samech*, says, "Hashem supports up all the falling," alluding to the missing *nun*.

The *nun* appears in *Eshet Hayil*, yet a close look at its verse reveals an interesting point. All the other letters begin verses of praise for the wife, but the verse beginning with *nun* seems to be praising the husband: *Noda b'she'arim ba'alah b'shivto im ziknei aretz*, "The husband is famous when he sits with the elders of the land."

---

246. *Tehillim* 84:5; 145:1-21
247. *Berachot* 4b.

We can ask two questions. First, why does the *nun* appear in *Eshet Hayil* but not in *Ashrei*? Both of them follow the Hebrew alphabet. Second, why does the verse beginning with *nun* praise the husband and not the wife?

An answer to these questions can be found in the words of the Ramak, Rabbi Moshe Cordovero, a great kabbalist who lived in Zefat almost five hundred years ago. In his book *Tomer Devora*, he writes that the Divine Presence, which is revealed in this world to those who merit such a revelation and dwells in a Jewish home, is represented as a wife. (Obviously, this should not be taken literally in any way, as we explained in the chapter on kabbalah.) The higher revelations of the Creator are beyond our comprehension, but when Hashem reveals Himself in this lowly world, He reveals Himself in, let us say, a limited form.

This is a very fine point. How can we say that Hashem is minimizing Himself or His greatness, God forbid? Rather, it is our comprehension that is limited. What we can comprehend in this world of the Divine Presence is a very limited revelation.

For example, you cannot look directly at a strong light, but you can see the aura of light around it. In the same way, so to speak, the Divine Presence that is revealed to us in this world is a filtered presence that we are able to comprehend and understand. If we refer to the full bright light in the masculine, then the aura that extends beyond it, which is a weaker revelation, can be considered the feminine form. So the *Shechinah*, the Divine Presence that reveals itself in this world, is always referred to in the feminine form.

The Ramak tells us a very deep idea. He says that a person should honor his wife with clothes and all her necessities even beyond his means. He should minimize his own needs and extend himself to take care of his wife's needs. He also says that when a husband buys his wife jewelry or good quality clothing he should have in mind that the respect he is showing his wife is actually being shown to the *Shechinah*, because the *Shechinah* rests in a Jewish home as a result of the wife's deeds.

"When a husband and wife are worthy, the *Shechinah* is with them."[248] A husband and a wife who have succeeded in setting up a good Jewish home based on Torah, *halachah*, and good behavior, will have the Divine Presence in their home.

King Solomon is teaching us concerning the verse that starts with the letter *nun* that if the husband is sitting with the elders of the land and studying Torah, it is really to his wife's credit. This is the link between this *nun* and the missing *nun* in *Ashrei*. By our actions, we can uplift the Divine Presence, which is the highest act we can perform. When the husband learns Torah and sits among the great rabbis, he uplifts the *Shechinah*. The *nun* of *Eshet Hayil* is the force that will uplift the *nun* missing from *Ashrei*. When a Jewish home is as it should be, the *Shechinah* is uplifted, and then the problem of the falling of the Divine Presence is rectified. Who is credited with all of this? The wife, for she is the one supporting and encouraging her husband's learning.

While we are still discussing *Eshet Hayil*, there is another verse that needs clarification: "She does for him good – and not bad – all the days of her life." What is this telling us? If she is doing good doesn't that automatically exclude doing bad? I understand this as follows: sometimes a wife loves her husband very much, and she really wants to do good to him. So when he comes back from work, she has a beautiful dinner ready and waiting. She wants to spend time with him and shower him with love and affection. She is doing good to him.

But the outcome might not be so good. If he is so comfortable at home, he might not go to his evening class. With such a loving wife

---

248. *Sotah* 17a.

showering him with affection, he is happier at home. A wife has to know how to gauge this. Yes, of course she should do good to her husband. But she must also make sure that no bad comes from that good, for too much good can have, at times, a negative result.

We have discussed the importance of a wife in a Jewish home, and we have seen that she is without doubt the determining factor behind the success of the home. But on the other hand, a husband must make certain decisions and take the lead. After all, the husband studies Torah, and as a result he knows his obligations, and his wife's and children's obligations. Obviously, when discussing such important decisions as which school to enroll the children in or which synagogue to belong to, both husband and wife should give their input. However, the final decision rests in the husband's hands. We rely upon him to make the proper inquiries and know what is best. As the *Gemara* says, in spiritual matters the husband's decisions take precedence. If the topic has more to do with material matters, from a wife running her own business down to decorating the house, the woman's decision should take precedence.

Show a United Front

When it comes to educating the children, parents must always show a united front. This is very important. For example, if a child did something wrong, the mother may feel very strongly that he should be punished. The father, though, for some reason, does not want to punish the child. If the child senses the division in how his parents are relating to him – one being agitated, the other less so – he becomes confused. This is not good *hinuch*. Children must see very decisive reactions from the parents concerning what is good and what is bad. When husband and wife have a difference of opinion on matters of *hinuch*, one or the other should give in at the moment. Later, the issue can be discussed with the spouse privately.

For example, let's say the husband felt that the wife took too strict an attitude toward a certain matter. When the wife is disciplining the son, her husband should not express any criticism or disagreement. Later, he can talk to her in private and say, "By the way, I didn't agree with how you handled that episode this afternoon. I think you carried it a little too far." He should explain why he feels that way. The opposite is true as well. Sometimes a wife has to cooperate with her husband's decision for the sake of the children's *hinuch*. Later, she can discuss the incident with him and talk over how such things might be handled.

Unless there is a united front, children will not get the proper *hinuch*. It is of utmost importance that the children get a clear message that their parents always cooperate with each other.

Another axiom in raising children is that the most powerful form of teaching is by good example. There is the father who constantly tells his son, "You have to learn." But then the son sees his father come home from work and sit down to read a newspaper. The son thinks to himself, "If learning is so important, why don't *you* learn?" But if the son sees that his father respects his time and puts aside at least some of his time for studying Torah, he will learn to appreciate the importance of Torah study.

It is very easy to tell children "do this, do that." Parents have many demands. But the child must see these wonderful things being done in his own home. Setting a good example is the most effective way to educate. One can see this idea in the *Shema*, where we are told, "*v'shinantam l'vanecha, v'dibarta bam*," "And you shall teach them diligently to your children, and you shall speak of them…." This is referring to the *mitzvah* of Torah study. How should a parent teach his child? He can put his child in the best school, hire the best tutor, and buy him plenty of books. He might think he is fulfilling the *mitzvah* of "*v'shinantam l'vanecha*," but if he doesn't learn himself, they will not get the message. *V'dibarta bam* is the main lesson. *You* speak the words of Torah. If your child sees *you* involved with learning, he will learn to appreciate how important Torah study is. Just telling him to study will not work.

Times Have Changed

Another point to remember is that in this day and age things are not the way they were in previous generations. Once upon a time, the general culture was less educated and people accepted things the way they were without asking questions. In such a climate, Torah and *mitzvot* could be taught as givens: this is our way, that is their way. But nowadays, it is not like that. The world is so advanced, science and technology have developed so much, and the younger generations are taught to be inquisitive and to ask the reason for everything.

If a child asks, "Why can't I put on the light on Shabbat?" and the father answers, "It's forbidden; it's work," with no explanation, the child may ask, "What do you mean it's work? I don't sweat, there is no effort involved, so what's the problem?" If a parent is not educated enough in Torah, he won't have the proper answers. He has to be able to explain the essence of work, to understand why carrying a chest of drawers up and down the stairs thirty times on Shabbat is not considered desecrating Shabbat but carrying a handkerchief out to the street (where there is no kosher *eruv*) is. The concept of work is not necessarily just labor or sweating or doing something physically difficult. It may not be in the spirit of Shabbat, but it's not *hilul Shabbat*. A small act might be forbidden and doing it would cause *hilul Shabbat*, while an act that seems more strenuous or more like work might be permitted. A parent must be knowledgeable enough to explain this to his children.

In our generation, we cannot bring up children on tradition alone. We cannot tell a child, "This is how we do it," and nothing more. It doesn't work anymore. We have to give them explanations. We have to be able to prove it to them and to make them understand the concepts. Then they will do *mitzvot* happily. Anything a person does without understanding is a burden and brings no fulfillment. But even the most difficult things are easy to do when we understand why we are doing them.

It is not enough for a father or mother to know how to read the *parashah* and say *Tehillim*. This will not answer their children's questions. Parents today have to be able to understand the meaning behind the laws and the explanations of the Torah, and they must be able to explain this to their children. Furthermore, if parents cannot relate to what their child learned in school, he will lose interest in the material. A child must see the Torah concepts he learns in school put into practice in his home. If he learns all about Shabbat but doesn't see it at home, he will be confused.

Parents must relate not only to what their children learn, but also should encourage their children by listening to them when they share what they have learned and by praising their accomplishments. Parents should be able to add to what the children tell them and to take the topic beyond what was learned in school, to show them that this is our way of life and that it is meaningful for us. When the child receives instructions in such a way that he understands what lies behind what he is doing, and he sees the significance of these practices in his own home, Judaism gets a stamp of truth. It is very important that the education at home be a continuation of what he learned in school. Seeing his father and mother taking an interest in his studies will build up the correct attitude in the child.

The Shabbat Table

During the week, many of us are busy people, working hard for a living. Hopefully, we pray *Shaharit* with a *minyan*, *Minhah* and

Maariv, too. Maybe we can go to a *shiur* a few times a week. But quite often, by the time the father comes home, the children are already asleep. When do they get to enjoy the presence of their father and learn from him? The best time for this is on Shabbat. Shabbat has tremendous importance, as the day when the major part of all the education of a Jewish home is going to be transmitted. Of primary importance is that the children see the harmony between the husband and the wife. They should see how the mother respects the father and how the husband respects his wife. Shabbat is the opportunity when we can show our children our belief in the Torah, our belief in the sages, and our involvement in the *mitzvot*. When we keep Shabbat, we declare that Hashem created the world in six days and rested on the seventh. We demonstrate our belief that Hashem created the world, that He gave us the Torah, and that He commanded us to keep the Shabbat and to keep the *mitzvot*. Shabbat shines with the beauty of a spiritual day.

There is an unbelievable amount of *emunah* a person can instill in his children on Shabbat. When the children see the atmosphere of Shabbat as it should be, singing *zemirot*, and hearing *divrei Torah* at the table that add to what they have learned, they will learn the importance of Torah and experience the beauty of Shabbat. Today there are many books available in English as well, so everyone should be able to say over some interesting observations from these books.

When we sit at the table, it should not be a quick job. It is a wonderful opportunity that we should not waste but utilize to the fullest. I always use the opportunity of the Shabbat table to give over *hashkafah*, the Jewish outlook, to my children. I talk about the *parashah*, but I take the ideas beyond that to teach the correct attitudes to the situations in our lives and to current events. This helps the children develop the correct way of looking at things. It strengthens them to handle the trials and tribulations that arise in their own lives and to know how to be able to relate to them according to the Torah's outlook. There is no better opportunity than Shabbat, when the family is united in an atmosphere of warmth and happiness.

In our generation, many people pick and choose what they do according to their convenience. Let me explain. The Ari *z"l* taught the way of piety, of going beyond the call of duty of the *Shulhan Aruch*. Some people say they follow the Ari's way. How? Well, the Ari was very particular on Shabbat to sleep at least three hours. In this, they follow the *minhag* of the Ari. But the Hida wrote in his book, *Moreh Be'etzba*, that the Ari *z"l* received greater prophetic visions in his sleep than we can achieve when we are awake.

On our level, we should make sure that on Shabbat more of our time is used for service of Hashem. During the week, a person is busy earning a living. That is also very important, as our sages say, "A person who benefits from the sweat of his brow—" in other words, he earns his own living "–is considered greater than a God-fearing person." But when Shabbat arrives, we have to be able to demonstrate that when we have the chance, we readily adopt a more spiritual mode, with more time for learning and more time for the education of our children. Once a week we can recharge our batteries with a feeling for Torah, *mitzvot*, and spiritual matters.

Shabbat is also an ideal time for strengthening the relationship between husband and wife. It is the nature of a wife to expect attention from her husband. She needs to feel that her husband is thinking about her. Shabbat is a golden opportunity.

Strengthening the Marriage

There are many small, subtle ways a husband can strengthen the bond of marriage. For example, he should make a habit of picking up the telephone when he's at work and calling home to ask, "How are you? How are you managing?" He'll find the time to call his broker ten times a day to see how his stocks are doing, but it's more important to give his wife some attention. I am speaking as a rabbi, and I personally do this because I know how important it is. When a wife feels that her husband is thinking about her and is a partner with her even from afar, it gives her confidence and strength.

A well-known rabbi was a tremendous *masmid*, who learned day and night. People used to wonder, "If he learns so much, how can he have any time for his wife?" That's what they thought until they had a chance to observe the rabbi and his wife on a vacation. He continued to learn night and day, but now people had the opportunity to gain a glimpse into his private life. They saw how he sat down for breakfast with his wife for about fifteen minutes. While they were eating, he engaged her in an ongoing animated conversation, sharing ideas and experiences. He gave her his focused attention, giving her what we would call "quality time." He took an interest in everything. In fifteen minutes, he filled his wife with a tremendous feeling. After that, she let him go learn for the rest of the day.

No matter how engrossed a man is in his business and how preoccupied he is with his own activities, he has to know that his wife needs his attention. A wife has to feel that her husband loves her and is thinking about her even when they are not together. Every woman needs this encouragement and recognition from her husband. This is what gives her the strength to carry on and to accomplish what she must. Even if a husband is highly pressured for time, he must make sure that during the time he does spend with his wife, he gives her his full attention and shows a sincere interest in her life.

Though a husband should find time for this every day of the week, Shabbat especially is a prime time to show his wife that he appreciates her. Shabbat is not just a day to eat, sleep, and talk about anything and everything. Shabbat should be a day full of life, full of respect and honor for the wife, with her husband showing appreciation for how much effort she put into preparing such a beautiful Shabbat. A husband sings *Eshet Hayil* for his wife to show his appreciation and to uplift the home once a week in a way that will bring the light of the Torah into the whole week.

Nowadays, seminars take place all over the world. What is a seminar? It takes people away from their daily routine and frees them from the weight of their problems. When people are in a hotel where they have no need to worry about anything, they use the time to think things over. The time made available becomes an opportunity to tackle issues they do not normally get around to considering. If we think about it, every Shabbat is like a mini-seminar for the family. It is a time when the business is closed, there is no phone, no driving, and no going out. It's a time when we can disconnect ourselves from worldly matters and devote ourselves to the main part of our life, which is the spiritual side of existence.

Some people make the mistake of thinking that when they go to the *bet knesset*, that's spiritual; when they put on *tefillin* and *tzitzit* or do a *mitzvah*, that is spirituality. They wonder what could be spiritual about eating. Isn't that just enjoying oneself? The same goes for such things as sleep. When a person is tired, he falls asleep. What's spiritual about that? All such things are a matter of filling our necessities.

But that is not the right way to look at it. King Solomon said, "Know Hashem in all your ways…"[249] Everything we do can be service of Hashem. This is really and truly the difference between our religion and all other religions. That is why the Jewish religion does not encourage cutting oneself off from any form of pleasure. The sages tell us that someone who took an oath to be a nazarite is called a sinner. In other words, Hashem created us with a sense of taste and a sense of smell, and He created all types of fruits. Each one has a different shape, a different color, and each fruit has a different smell

---

249. *Mishle* 3:6.

and a different taste. Hashem created us with the capacity to sense all these things, so of course He wants us to enjoy this world and to thank Him for these pleasures by making a blessing on the food we eat and other benefits we enjoy. But to use Hashem's food only for our own pleasure and our own fulfillment is wrong. We have to know how to make use of the world in the correct way, and thereby uplift it to a spiritual level.

You can be involved in business. In fact, the Torah expects a man to earn a living and to support his wife and family. But he has to conduct his business affairs honestly. His word must be binding, he can't lie or cheat, he can't overcharge or take interest.

It's the same with eating. If you want to eat, go ahead and enjoy yourself. But first make sure the meat is properly slaughtered and has been salted to take out the blood. Don't eat milk and meat together. If you're eating fruits or vegetables that grew in Eretz Yisrael, make sure terumot and ma'aserot, shemittah and orlah were properly observed before eating the produce grown there.

The bottom line is that you can have whatever you want, but do it in the proper way. This is the meaning of "Know Hashem in all Your ways."[250] There is no basic division that says that when you are in the synagogue it is spiritual, but when you are at home or at work that is not spiritual. Work is also spiritual. A person can make a tremendous kiddush Hashem if he earns his money honestly, and gives ma'aser and does good things with it.

This was the message Hashem gave Yaakov Avinu when he left the yeshivah of Shem and Ever after learning there fourteen years. Yaakov was on his way to get married, not only to one wife but to four, and he was going to have a large family – twelve tribes. He was going to have to deal with Lavan and Lavan's sheep and with many more worldly

---

250. Ibid.

matters. Yaakov was just a simple yeshivah boy, unfamiliar with all these worldly matters. He didn't know what business was, he didn't know what marriage was, he hadn't yet experienced what real life was all about, and he was worried and apprehensive about how he was going to cope. How was all of this connected with the spiritual world?

Yaakov fell asleep, and Hashem showed him a ladder standing on earth reaching up to Heaven. Hashem showed Yaakov that he was wrong. It's as if Hashem said to him, "You thought that learning in yeshivah is spirituality, but now that you are going out to the world, into the jungle, there is no more spirituality. You are wrong. Here, you will find the spirituality. There is a *mitzvah* in everything you are going to do in the outside world. It is all serving Hashem."

If you get married in the right way and raise your children in the right way, everything becomes a *mitzvah*. Outwardly, though, your life may look no different than that of a non-Jew. He also eats, he also has children, he also earns a living. The difference is that you work, but you transform it into spirituality.

Hashem showed Yaakov what a human being is all about. True, your body is rooted in this world. This is symbolized by the ladder that stands in this world. But the top of this ladder reaches the heavens. This refers to our soul, which is always connected to the higher worlds. All the challenges awaiting Yaakov – his dealings with Lavan the trickster, his tending the sheep, his marriages – are there for him to uplift to a spiritual level.

When Yaakov woke up from his dream about the ladder, he said, "God is truly in this place, and I did not know it."[251] Yaakov was in effect saying, "I made a big mistake. I thought that to be connected to Hashem means learning Torah, praying, putting on *tefillin*, wearing *tzitzit* and so on, but now I see that Hashem is everywhere, and that I

---

251. *Bereshit* 28:16.

can serve Him with whatever I do, even out there in the material world, out there in the jungle."

That is an entirely new perspective on life, and this is the secret of the Jewish home. People should not think that building a home is merely a physical and material matter of finding a wife who cooks good food or a husband who earns well, renting or buying a nice home, having a comfortable bed to sleep in, and all the other physical amenities. We must understand that a Jewish home is actually a miniature *Bet HaMikdash*. People say a man's home is his castle. We Jews say a man's home is a sanctuary. Hashem said, "Make for a Me a sanctuary, and I will dwell among them." The Alshich explains that "I will dwell among them," means among the Jewish people. In other words, every single Jewish home is a home for the Divine Presence. When a husband and wife merit it, the Divine Presence dwells in their home. If their home is used as a place to serve Hashem, a place of *mitzvot*, prayer, charity and *hesed*, and Torah study, it becomes uplifted to something spiritual. It has something beyond its real estate value – it has *kedushah*. This is a Jewish home, and Hashem is truly in this place, too.

The truth is that Hashem is everywhere. He is constantly with us. Every Jewish person should train himself to live according to this concept. Don't think that doing so is a *middat hassidut* only for the super *frum*. It's the first *halachah* in the *Shulhan Aruch*: "'I have placed Hashem before me always' – this is a major principle of the Torah." The Rema quotes the Rambam in *Moreh Nevuchim* about how a person should know that wherever he is and whatever he is doing, Hashem is with him. This applies to whatever he is doing, even things that may seem to be trivial and material. A woman may think, "What am I doing when I am preparing for Shabbat? Making salads, peeling vegetables, cooking – what's so special about that? Why can't I be involved with Torah and *mitzvot* like my husband?" The truth is that if she understood what she was doing, she would realize that her actions are no less than those of the *kohen gadol* in the Holy of Holies, bringing the *ketoret* or doing the *avodah*, because that is really what she is doing.

The *Zohar* says that not only are we on a higher level every Shabbat, but all the created worlds, even the physical, are uplifted to a higher spiritual level. When we receive Shabbat during *kabbalat Shabbat*, all the worlds transcend to a higher plane. When this happens, the forces of evil also want to link up to the *kedushah* and rise up, but a great light streams forth from the higher worlds of holiness and smashes them and throws them down. What creates this force that throws down all the evil forces? The *Zohar* says that in preparing for Shabbat, women arrange the table and taste the food to see if it lacks seasoning. These *mitzvot* are what creates the powerful spiritual force that pushes away the *kochot hatumah*, the *Sitra Ahra*. These seemingly trivial actions have the power to push away the forces of impurity so that they can't rise with the worlds of holiness that ascend on Shabbat.

A person could think, "What value is there in such a little thing as tasting the food for Shabbat to see that it has the right taste?" Yet, if it is done *lichvod Shabbat*, in honor of Shabbat, it is a great *mitzvah*. Arranging the table nicely, choosing a pretty tablecloth, setting out special Shabbat silverware – whatever you do to make the table beautiful and attractive – has great power.

The *Gemara* says that it is a *mitzvah* to make the beds, set the table, and tidy the house before Shabbat, so that Shabbat comes into a beautifully prepared home. So we see, "Hashem is truly in this place" – even in mundane things.

When a person is educated in Torah, he knows that with every action he does, he can fulfill a *mitzvah*. If you meet someone in the street and say, "Hello. How are you? How do you feel today? Can I help you?" you can change his life. This man may have felt lonely and neglected, he may have felt that no one cares for him, and your words gave him a little bit of hope and encouragement. There are millions of things that you can do no matter where you are. Every single step we take every single day can be transformed into a *mitzvah*.

I think these ideas can strengthen us to realize that this world is a world where the main demand made of us is in spiritual matters. The physical, the material, is more or less arranged for us. We say in our prayers, *Mashiv haruah u'morid hageshem*, "You cause the wind to blow and the rain to fall." What does Hashem want from us? If we are *mashiv haruah*, if we send up our spirituality, our *ruhaniyut*, to Hashem, then He will be *morid hageshem*, He will give us all the material blessings, the *gashmiyut* that we need. As the Torah says, "If you follow My statutes and keep My commandments, and you fulfill them, I will provide your rains in their proper time...."[252] One of the great sages explains it this way: You may be worried that if you toil in Torah day and night non-stop, you will become so spiritual that you may not be able to relate to the physical world. Hashem reassures you by promising to give you "*geshem*," which refers to *gashmiyut*, all our physical and material needs, whenever you need it.

No matter how spiritual we are, Hashem will give us what we need to live our physical lives in the correct way with *berachah* and *hatzlahah*.

---

252. *Vayikra* 26:3–4.

The Jewish Woman

Discovering Your Identity and Your Mission

With the destruction of the *Bet HaMikdash*, the Jewish people were sent into a long, painful exile that has lasted almost two thousand years. All our suffering – from the personal anguish of individuals to the trials and tribulations of the nation – has its source in this tragic event.

When the *Bet HaMikdash* still stood, it was the dwelling place of the *Shechinah*, the Divine Presence. From within it, the *Shechinah* radiated outward to all corners of the world, filling Jewish homes with light. When the *Bet HaMikdash* was reduced to ruins, the *Shechinah* was driven into exile along with Hashem's chosen people. As painful as the *galut* (exile) is for us, it is far more painful for the *Shechinah*, which remains without a home.

Yes, Hashem is everywhere. He is Omnipresent. But He longs to be where there is sanctity and purity. In today's world, is there any place fit for the *Shechinah*?

The *Shechinah* can only find a place among people who are learning Torah and doing *mitzvot*. This can be in a *shul*, a yeshivah, a *bet medrash*, a *kollel* – or a Jewish home. When a husband and wife are worthy of it, the *Shechinah* will dwell in their home.

The responsibility for making a home fit for the *Shechinah* falls on the Jewish wife, because she creates the home. If a home is run properly by the wife, it becomes a place for the *Shechinah*, and there can be no greater source of blessing. Even when the *Bet HaMikdash* stands, the ultimate goal is not for the *Shechinah* to remain centered in the Holy Temple, but for it to radiate outward into every Jewish home. The *Shechinah* wants to be among us and part of us.

Having a Happy Marriage

Our sages teach us that anyone who makes a bride and groom happy is considered to have rebuilt one of the ruins of Yerushalayim.[253] We can ask three questions about this: (1) Why should credit be given to the person who makes them happy and not to the *shadchan* who introduced them? (2) When a bride and groom marry, they create a *new* home; how is that connected with rebuilding a ruin? (3) Why a ruin in Yerushalayim?

The *Zohar* tells us that the souls of a husband and wife are really two halves of one soul. In the higher worlds, before the souls came down into this world, they were joined together. When the time came for that couple to enter this world, Hashem separated them. The male soul entered the body of a man, and the female soul entered the body of a woman. When these two people meet each other and marry, it really is as if they were rebuilding a ruin, since they were united in the past.

Why a ruin in Yerushalayim? Actually, the sages are referring to *the* ruin in Yerushalayim, the *Bet HaMikdash*. Every single Jewish home is like another stone in the future *Bet HaMikdash*. There is an opinion in the *Rishonim* that the third *Bet HaMikdash* will not be built by man, but will descend from the heavens fully built. For almost two thousand years, we have been rebuilding the *Bet HaMikdash* every day through Torah, *mitzvot*, good deeds, and, especially, with every new Jewish home. Every Jewish home established as it should be adds another stone in the third *Bet HaMikdash*. When all the Jewish

---

253. *Yalkut Shimoni, Yirmiyahu* 7:277.

homes have been brought to completion, the building of the spiritual *Bet HaMikdash* in the higher world will also be complete, and it will come down into the physical world.

Now that we know what the ruin was and why a bride and groom are rebuilding it, we can answer the first question: Why is credit given to the person who makes them happy?

The answer is that when there is no happiness, the *Shechinah* departs. Someone who makes a bride and groom happy at their wedding brings the *Shechinah* into their home right at the beginning. At the beginning of building a new Jewish home, the most important thing is to bring *simhah* into that home. That's the whole concept of making the bride and groom happy. The *Gemara* tells how the great sages of the time would dance in front of them, or juggle. Their purpose was to bring them happiness, which would bring the *Shechinah* into their home.

Bilaam's Scheme

In our day and age, it's very difficult to create a home suitable for the *Shechinah* to dwell in. In previous generations, a Jewish home was, more or less, a good Jewish home. All the bad things were outside, and it was very difficult for evil to penetrate it.

When the evil Bilaam tried to curse the Jewish people, Hashem didn't let him. He transformed all of Bilaam's curses into blessings. We can learn from the blessings uttered by him what he intended to curse. One of his greatest blessings was "How good are your tents, Yaakov, your dwelling-places, Yisrael!"[254] What beautiful homes you have, what good homes full of holiness. Our sages tell us that Bilaam saw the modesty of the Jewish family. Their tents were arranged so

---

254. *Bamidbar* 24:5.

that no opening faced another, giving each person his privacy. Having seen this wonderful aspect of Jewish homes, Bilaam sought to curse them, for he recognized this as the source of all their blessings. But Hashem wouldn't let him, and the curse became a blessing.

Bilaam's words seem repetitious: "How good are your tents...your dwelling-places...." The first statement refers to private homes, and the second, to public dwellings: synagogues, yeshivot, *hadarim*, schools, *kollels*. If the homes are good, then the synagogues and the yeshivot are going to be good as well. It all begins in the home.

How can we make the home a place that is really acceptable to the Divine Presence?

When Bilaam saw that he couldn't curse the Jewish people, he decided to cause them to sin through immorality, hoping this would lead them to idolatry, which would ensure that his curse could take effect. To entice them to sin, he devised a wicked plan. Opposite the Jewish encampment, he set up a large fairground attractively laid out to draw shoppers. He advertised a big sale, with beautiful goods being sold at half price. When people came to shop, they found numerous tents, each with an old lady sitting at the entrance. "Please come inside," she would say. "The real bargains are inside the tent." In this way, she would tempt the men to step inside, where a young Midianite girl awaited the unsuspecting customer. This girl would charm the Jewish customer and entice him to sin. Finally, she would say, "I have only one request. Before we sin, just bow down to the idol over there." In this way, the Jewish people would come to commit the sin of immorality as well as idol worship.

We know the outcome. Bilaam's nefarious plan was successful. How did he do it? By drawing the people outside! Inside our homes, the *Shechinah* dwelled. But outside, Bilaam could get hold of them. The situation remained this way almost to our times.

However, in this day and age, our tremendous test is that Bilaam's plan is no longer outside. It's all inside. There are CDs, television, DVDs, videos, and the Internet. We have all sorts of newspapers and magazines, all filled with immorality, murder, and idolatry – the three cardinal sins that every Jew must be willing to die for rather than transgress. It is unbelievable how all this has penetrated our homes.

Unfortunately, homes are already full of this garbage, because people don't realize the dangers. What can the children do when they are being brought up in such an environment?[255] How do we expect them not to sin?

The evil inclination doesn't recognize any geographical boundaries. He works in America, in Europe and even in Eretz Yisrael.

People say to me, "Rabbi, you should have a computer."

"What do I need a computer for?" I ask them.

"If you have a computer," they say, "you have all of *Shas*, the Talmud *Bavli* and *Yerushalmi*, the *Zohar*, and all the writings of the Ari *z"l* at your fingertips! You have the *Shulhan Aruch*, the *baalei mussar*, all the hassidic works, *halachic* rulings – everything with just a click of the mouse. It's like having Rabbi Moshe Feinstein as your *havruta*."

They say if you've got a computer, you've got everything. But they don't say that one click can take you to the depths of depravity. Who knows where a person can end up? Bilaam's evil plan is penetrating our homes, brainwashing us and our children. We have to stop and think. Who is making the decisions in our life?

We Are All Affected

We are so influenced by the world around us. Our minds and value systems are tainted by non-Jewish ways of thinking. Exposure

---

255. *Berachot* 32a.

to foreign ideas and understandings is affecting our Jewish concept of living.

For instance, people read all sorts of secular novels. What happens to young girls who read such novels? How will they grow up? What expectations of marriage will they have? Will they be satisfied to be *neshot hayil* married to *talmidei hachamim*? All sorts of non-Jewish ideas have penetrated their minds. What do they expect from a husband? Will they be being satisfied with a modest home and a modest lifestyle?

Such things affect us in a very dangerous way. And it's all part of Bilaam's evil plan, except that now it's inside our homes. Today, you can even have it in the palm of your hand. You can have a tiny, little computer that sits in your pocket next to your heart, and whenever you want, you can go from your *Gemara* to Hollywood or even worse. In one second you're there, and that's it.

The technology is so cheap that anyone can afford it, and it's so easy to use that even a child can figure it out – and it's so contaminating that it destroys people's minds, hearts, and souls. It's burning up their *neshamot*, destroying their homes, and driving the *Shechinah* away.

The *Shechinah* wants to come into holy homes, where people live pure Jewish lives, where there's Torah and *hesed*. All good Jewish homes have Torah and *hesed*, but, unfortunately, many homes are still hooked up to these forms of degradation. Can a person really not be affected? How can a person be so naïve as to say, "Oh no, it doesn't affect us"?

We have to know that we are being completely brainwashed by alien ways of thinking. Keeping up with the Joneses is very destructive, but it is the least of all evils. The worst is to be impressed by their behavior. We have to know that serving Hashem is not only limited to the husband going to *shul*, praying three times a day, wearing *tallit* and *tefillin*, going to a *Daf Yomi shiur* and giving *tzedakah*. The values of the outside world are not our values. Our sages tell us that a Jew is recognized by three outstanding traits: he is merciful, modest, and kind. In today's world, someone who is shy is considered lacking. He's going to have a problem finding a *shidduch*. He blushes. Something must not be normal. He's so quiet. In Israel, they like chutzpa. A person has to be brazen and rude. That's thought of as being "a real man."

We should be changing ourselves to be better people. We have no chance when we're influenced by the outside world, because then we see things the way they see things. We see success the way they see success. The sages tell us that everything is the opposite of what we see. Who is a strong person? Not Mr. Universe with huge biceps. Who is rich? Not Bill Gates with his billions. Who is wise? Not the biggest talker. The sages tell us that a strong person is someone who can control himself. That takes real strength. Strength comes from within. All other forms of strength are meaningless. Why? Because if a person can control himself, he has control over the world as well. A righteous person rules through his fear of Hashem.[256] The world will look up to a person who is a real *tzaddik*, and they're willing to humble themselves before him. So a *tzaddik* can rule because of the fact that he has bearing. But to be able to rule over the world, first he has to be able to rule over himself – that is, to control all his desires and channel all his powers and talents to serving Hashem. That's real strength.

Who is rich? One who is happy with what he has. A beggar is someone who lacks. So if someone has a hundred million, let's say, and he still feels he is lacking the next hundred, then he's the biggest beggar around. A small beggar may lack a quarter to buy a cup of coffee, but a person who lacks a hundred million is a big beggar. So

---

256. *II Shmuel* 23:3.

who is rich? Someone who is happy with what he has, someone who feels he lacks nothing. The more you lack, the poorer you are. If you don't feel yourself lacking, you are rich.

Who is wise? Someone who loves wisdom and Torah so much that he learns from anyone. Such a person is not too proud to listen to a small child saying something interesting, because he might just learn something from him. If you truly love wisdom, you won't miss turning over a stone to reveal the diamond that might be under it.

Our concepts are different from those of the outside world. Our sages tell us, for example, that the wicked are considered dead even while they're alive, while the righteous are considered alive even when they're dead. But what do people say? They say, "That guy's having the time of his life." In Israel, they say, "Hu oseh hayyim!" What do they mean? That the person is enjoying all sorts of worldly pleasures – that's considered living! And what's considered dying? When a person dies, his soul leaves his body and he dies. That's considered dying. But our sages say this view is completely wrong. Who is alive? Someone who cleaves to Hashem, the source of all life. And who is dead? Someone who is far from Hashem; who isn't connected to the source of life. Even when the righteous die, they cleave to Hashem, so they are alive. As for the wicked, even when they are alive and kicking, they're really dead, because they're far from Hashem.

Torah concepts are different from those of the outside world. But if we allow ourselves to be influenced by reading all sorts of non-Jewish literature, our minds will absorb their concepts. Our systems become polluted by their ways of thinking, and, since all the so-called "wise" people think that way, these beliefs are accepted as truth. No one dares to question these accepted beliefs, and so our thinking becomes distorted. From there it follows that our actions and the way we live our lives are distorted as well, because we are open to this alien influence of Bilaam.

This was Bilaam's plan. Instead of enticing us into those little booths at his carnival, he's gotten a foothold in our homes. He has entered the minds, hearts, and souls of us and our children.

The Woman Is the Home

How can we protect ourselves from the evil influence of the world outside? The destruction that's taking place is causing the *Shechinah* to leave us. The Divine Presence is in *galut* because of us. If we really want to remedy the situation, the way to do it is for each woman to understand that the Jewish home *is* the woman. It's up to her to make the home a fitting place for the *Shechinah*.

In some ways, a woman is more susceptible to these types of influences. Our sages say, "A woman was created for beauty."[257] A woman can invest her whole life in externals if she looks at things superficially. In doing so, she will lose all the wonderful blessings of a Torah way of life, of a Jewish home that will bring the *Shechinah* into it, of children following the right path.

How degrading and cheap it is for fine Jewish daughters, the protégées of Sarah, Rivka, Rahel, and Leah, to have their fashions, their customs, and their characters molded by perverts from Paris or Hollywood. What do these vulgar people have in mind when they create and design? Their ultimate purpose is to encourage immorality and to make money by taking advantage of gullibility and naïveté. Everyone knows the story of the emperor whose tailors fooled him into appearing naked before his subjects, all the while praising his beautiful new royal garment. So, too, our modern cultured and naïve Jewish daughters are dressed in fancy rags while being led to believe that they are dressed according to the latest fashions, paying huge amounts of money for clothes,

---

257. *Ketubot* 59b.

which, to our shame and disgrace, leave them looking as if undressed. How foolish can we be?

Modesty is the very essence of a Jewish daughter. Her true beauty is reflected through her modesty. Just as a beautiful priceless diamond necklace is not dangled out of the window but is protected and guarded in a plush leather box hidden away in a safe, so modest clothing protects the beauty of a Jewish daughter from the prying eyes of evil, lustful wrongdoers who plot how to desecrate her sanctity and the holiness of her family and home.

The ways of the pervert and immoral are very cunning and misleading. Sometimes a woman can be completely covered and yet she is considered undressed. Tight revealing garments merely lead her to believe she is modestly dressed. What a pity that people do not realize that the body merely clothes the dazzling radiant beauty of the soul. The more the body is revealed and expressed, the more the soul is dejected and repressed.

Let us come to our senses, and the sooner the better, to recognize the true beauty and fineness that accompanies a life of modesty.

External influences have a profound effect. A woman who knows this will use it to instill Torah values in her children. The daughter-in-law of Shammai used to take her infant son into the study hall so that he could hear words of Torah. Though the baby could not understand what was being said, the voices learning Torah had a good influence on him, purifying him with the holiness of the Torah.

Some children are brought up listening to jazz, pop, and who knows what else. This has a bad influence on them. What about things like classical music, Beethoven, Tchaikovsky and so on? What's the problem? It's not pop, and there are no improper lyrics, which are obviously harmful. What could be wrong with classical music?

Our sages tell us that even an inanimate object made by an evil person has evil in it, and that anything that came to being through a God-fearing person will have *kedushah*. One example of this was the field that Avraham bought from Ephron as a burial site for Sarah. The Torah tells us that at the time of the purchase, "Ephron's field stood up."[258] Rashi explains this to mean that the field was uplifted. By leaving the dominion of an ordinary person to become the possession of a *tzaddik*, an inanimate object, a field, became holy.

An example of how evil can corrupt inanimate objects is the earth at the time of the flood. At that time, the entire world was steeped in immorality. The evil corrupted the earth's crust to a depth of three *tefahim* (three handbreadths, about nine to twelve inches). This layer of the earth was swept away by the floodwaters to remove the power of sin with which it was contaminated.

The rocks that fought for a place under Yaakov's head are an example of inanimate objects that sought to be uplifted by a *tzaddik*. After studying in yeshivah for fourteen years nonstop, Yaakov came to the place where the *Bet HaMikdash* was going to be built. During his years of study, he never lay down to sleep. Now, for first time, he was going to do so. He took some rocks and put them around his head to protect him. All of a sudden, the stones started arguing among themselves for the privilege of having Yaakov rest his head on them. When Hashem saw this, he fused them into one stone, which Yaakov used as a pillow. Though rocks are inanimate objects, they wanted to have a connection with a *tzaddik*. And they became uplifted through that connection.

These are just a few of the many examples that could be brought to demonstrate the point – which brings us back to classical music. We have to ask ourselves what all the non-Jewish composers had in mind when they composed their music. Most early classical music was

---

258. *Bereshit* 23:17.

church music. The purpose of composing it was to honor their so-called gods, which makes it part of idol worship. The composer's intentions are in that music, and this has a negative influence.

But what about the other classical music? What made the composers happy or sad? They certainly weren't happy about understanding a difficult *Gemara* or sad about the *Shechinah* being in exile. They were happy about sinning, and they were unhappy when they couldn't sin – and this is what comes out in their music. This is their music, their art, their literature, their everything. Everything is idolatry, bloodshed, and immorality.

All this can harm us. A person can't say, "What's wrong if I just listen to some music? What's wrong if I just read these books?" All sorts of wrong forms of understanding can penetrate the mind. Wrong feelings can penetrate, too. Children, especially, are very easily influenced. Their minds and hearts could be warped.

The *Gemara* tells us that Rabbi Yochanan, who was very beautiful, used to sit outside the entrance to the *mikveh*. In this way, he would be the first person a woman saw as she left, and she would merit having children of his caliber of holiness and beauty.

If just seeing a *tzaddik* like Rabbi Yochanan can have an influence on how a Jewish wife conceives and gives birth, what effect does watching television, with all its immorality, have on an expectant Jewish woman? What will she think and feel? What influence will this have on her unborn child?

"All the honor of a Jewish wife, who is like a princess, is inside." [259] We can infer something very interesting about this verse. Only the *Kohen Gadol* on Yom Kippur could enter the Holy of Holies, which is the innermost sanctuary in the *Bet HaMikdash*. Also, only the *Kohen Gadol* wears four golden garments when he serves in the *Bet*

---

259. *Tehillim* 45:14.

HaMikdash. This verse uses the same imagery to describe a wife. The honor of a Jewish princess is inside, an allusion to the innermost sanctuary, the Holy of Holies. The verse goes on to say that her clothes are golden, an allusion to those of the *Kohen Gadol*. And just as the *Kohen Gadol* enters the Holy of Holies, so the Jewish wife is considered to be the Holy of Holies (see *Tanhuma Vayishlah* 6).

A premature baby needs to be in a protected environment. Since exposure to germs could be fatal, this environment must be as sterile as possible. Only an incubator can provide the maximum protection to ensure the baby's physical well-being.

But what about the baby's spiritual environment?

For this, you need a Jewish mother. She is the spiritual incubator. And she has to be completely pure and sterile. She is a *Bet HaMikdash*. Our sages call the Holy of Holies "*heder hamitot*," the bedroom. In the Holy of Holies, the Jewish people and Hashem become one, so to speak. It is the place where they are united. Their becoming one was symbolized by the *cherubim*, in the forms of golden angels, which were on top of the *aron hakodesh*.

People of shallow understanding, like the gentiles who destroyed the *Bet HaMikdash*, could never understand and appreciate the depths of these sublime concepts. Our rabbis relate that when they found the golden angels in the Holy of Holies intertwined one with another, they took them out to show them off publicly.[260] "Aha!" they said. "We discovered that the Jews also worshipped idols! We found their statues hidden inside the Holy of Holies."

But our sages tell us that those two *cherubim*, those two little angels that were intertwined, represented the relationship between Hashem and *Knesset Yisrael*. When we served Hashem correctly,

---

260. *Yoma* 54b.

they were intertwined. When we sinned, they actually turned away from each other. Their message to us is similar to the message embedded deeply in *Shir Hashirim*.

If we understand that the Jewish housewife is the Holy of Holies, and she is a holy incubator for her children, then she has to be untainted and pure, the purest of pure. Anything can be harmful to a Jewish wife, even things that are inanimate and seem to have no influence. It depends on where it comes from. If it comes from a holy source, it has a good influence. If it comes from an evil source, it has a bad influence.

So if we want to have Jewish homes, if we want to be *nashot hayil*, if we want our children to be good, God fearing *tzaddikim*, if we want all the wonderful things for our family, we have to make sure that our homes are going to be pure, and that we are going to be pure.

In this merit, the *Shechinah* will be in our homes and with us – and this is the biggest blessing we can bring to ourselves and to all *Klal Yisrael*.

Glossary

Aharonim – Rabbis and legal deciders from the fifteenth to nineteenth centuries.

Ahavat Yisrael – Love of fellow Jews.

Al Hanisim – Prayer inserted in the *Shemonah Esre* and *birchat hamazon* during Purim and Hanukah.

Amal – Effort (in Torah).

Amoraim – Third to fifth century Sages whose arguments and opinions are recorded in the Talmud.

Apikorus – A heretic.

Aron Hakodesh – The ark that in which Moshe placed the Tablets of the Covenant. Likewise, the cabinet where the *sefer Torah* is kept in the synagogue.

Ashkenazi – Jews primarily from Northern and Eastern parts of Europe and Russia.

Av bet din – Head of the religious court.

Avinu – Our father.

Avodah – Service, such as in *avodat Hashem* – service of God.

Avodah zarah – Idol worship.

Baalei teshuvah – Returnees to Judaism.

Baruch Hashem – "Blessed is God."

Basar veyayin – Meat and wine.

Batim – The boxes of *tefillin* that hold the written parchment (literally, "houses").

Bet din – A religious court.

Bet HaMikdash – The Holy Temple in Jerusalem.

Ben Torah – A student of Torah (literally, "a son of the Torah").

Berachah (berachot) – Blessing.

Bereshit – The book of Genesis. Also, the first word of that book: "In the beginning."

Birkot hashahar – The morning blessings.

Bitahon – Trust in God.

Bitul Torah – Time wasted from Torah study.

Blatt – A page of *Gemara* (both sides).

Bor – A pit.

Brit kodesh – The Holy Covenant.

Brit milah – Circumcision.

Darshan – A public speaker on popular, homiletic topics.

Derash – One of the principle methods of Torah interpretation – the homiletic.

Derech Hashem – Translated as *The Way of God*, by Rabbi Moshe Hayyim Luzzatto.

Dor hamidbar – The generation of the desert, who left Egypt but did not enter the Land of Israel.

Emunah – Faith in God.

Eretz Yisrael – The Land of Israel.

Eruv – A rabbinic enactment that transforms a public domain into a private one, allowing for carrying in the street on Shabbat.

Eshet Hayil – A woman of valour, from *Mishle* 31:10.

Frum – To be pious or devout (Yiddish).

Galut – Exile.

Gan Eden – The Garden of Eden.

Gedolei Yisrael – The leaders (literally, "great men") of Israel.

Gehinom – Hell, where the soul is sent after death for purification, before ascending to *Gan Eden*.

Gemara – *Halachic* and *aggadic* material which comprises the later portion of the Talmud.

Gematria – The numerical equivalent of a Hebrew word. (The Hebrew alphabet also serves as numbers, from *aleph*=1 to *tav*=400.)

Gemilut hassadim – Acts of kindness to the needy.

Geonim – Leaders of the great Babylonian yeshivot from 650–1250.

Golem – A man-like creature, created and animated through the use of Divine Names.

Hacham (hachamim, hachmei Yisrael) – The sages of Israel.

Hafetz Hayyim -- Rabbi Israel Meir HaCohen Kagan (1838-1933). One of the most famous and beloved sages of recent times. Known after his work on *lashon hara*, author of the *Mishnah Berurah*.

Hagshamah – Attributing material qualities to God.

HaKadosh Baruch Hu – The Holy One, blessed be He.

Halachah (halachot) – Jewish law.

Halilah – "God forbid."

Hanukat habayit – The dedication of a home, or of the Holy Temple.

Hashba'ah – An oath made to bind some spiritual force.

Hashem – Literally, "the Name"; God.

Hashgahah pratit – Divine providence.

Hashkafah – Jewish philosophy and approach to life.

Hatam Sofer – Rabbi Moshe Schreiber (1762-1839). A leading sage of European Jewry, called after his books of responsa and exegesis.

Hatan – Groom.

Havruta – A study partner.

Hayyot – Living creatures, as in Yehezkel's vision.

Hazon Ish – Rabbi Avraham Yeshayahu Karelitz (1878-1953). One of the leading sages in the Land of Israel, known after his famous work.

Hechal – The outer chamber of the Holy Temple.

Heder (hadarim) – An elementary school for Torah study.

Hefker – Ownerless.

Hesed – Lovingkindness.

Hiddush (hiddushim) – Original Torah thoughts.

Hilul Shabbat – Desecration of Shabbat.

Hinuch – Jewish education.

Hishtadlut – Human effort.

Hochmat hanistar – Hidden wisdom (of kabbalah).

Hochmat hasod – Secret wisdom.

Hovot HaLevavot – Translated as *Duties of the Heart*, by Rabbi Bahya ben Joseph Ibn Pakuda.

Hulin – The profane or secular.

Hurban habayit – The destruction of the Holy Temple.

Kabbalah – Esoteric teachings of the Torah.

Kabbalat haTorah – The receiving of the Torah.

Kallah – A bride.

Kaparah – An atonement.

Kavanat halev – The intention of the heart.

Kedushah – Holiness.

Kefirah – Heresy.

Kemitzah – Scooping up a handful of flour for the meal offering in the Temple.

Keri – Arbitrarily, related to the word *mikrah*, a chance event.

Ketubah – A marriage contract.

Kiddush – The blessing made over the wine at the onset of Shabbat and festivals.

Klal Yisrael – The Jewish people as a whole.

Klei hakodesh – The vessels used in the Holy Temple.

Klipah – Literally, a "shell"; referring to the forces of evil that obscure holiness.

Knesset Yisrael – The community of Israel.

Kodesh Hakodashim – The Holy of Holies.

Kohen gadol – The High Priest in the Temple.

Kollel – A yeshivah for married men.

Korbanot – Sacrifices in the Temple.

Kotel – The Western Wall.

Kove'a itim laTorah – Establishing set times for Torah study.

L'shem yihud – For the sake of the union [of the Holy One and His *Shechinah*]. A Kabbalistic phrase recited before the performance of certain mitzvot.

Lashon hara – Literally, "evil speech," such as slander, gossip, talebearing.

Lashon kodesh – The Holy Tongue.

Luhot habrit – The Tablets of the Covenant.

Lulav – The palm branch waved on Sukkot.

Mahshavah – Thought.

Maran – "Our teacher."

Mashiah – The Messiah.

Mazal – One's fate or spiritual destiny.

Mehilah – Forgiveness.

Melaveh malka – A festive meal made after the conclusion of Shabbat.

Menorah – The seven-branched candelabrum used in the *Bet HaMikdash*, or the eight-branched one lit during Hanukah.

Menuhah – Rest.

Mesillat Yesharim – Translated as *The Path of the Just*, by Rabbi Moshe Hayyim Luzzatto.

Middat Hassidut – To go beyond the letter of the law.

Middot – Character traits.

Midrash – The anecdotal and homiletic teaching of the Oral Torah.

Mikdash – The Sanctuary.

Mikveh – A ritual bath.

Minhag (minhagim) – Jewish customs.

Minhah – The afternoon prayer.

Minyan – A quorum of ten Jewish men.

Mishkan – The desert Sanctuary.

Mishnah – Brief, *halachic* statements that comprise the earliest transcription of the Oral Torah. Compiled by R. Yehuda HaNasi.

Mitzvah – The Torah's commandments.

Moreh Nevuchim – Translated as *A Guide for the Perplexed*, by the Rambam (Maimonides).

Motzaei Shabbat – Saturday night.

Muktzeh – Things that one is forbidden to move on Shabbat.

Mussar – Ethical teachings directed toward moral improvement. The *mussar* movement was founded by Rabbi Yisrael Salanter in the 19th century.

Nefesh habehamit – The animal soul in a person.

Neilah – The closing prayer of Yom Kippur.

Neshamah yeterah – The extra soul of Sabbath.

Neshamot – Souls.

Nusah – The liturgy unique to each Jewish community, such as *nusah Sefard or nusah Ashkenaz*.

Olam HaAsiyah – The World of Action.

Olam HaAtzilut – The World of Emanation.

Olam Haba – The World–to–Come.

Olam HaBeriyah – The World–to–Come.

Olam HaYetzirah – The World of Formation.

Oneg – Pleasure.

Parashah – The weekly Torah reading.

Parnassah – Livelihood.

Parochet – The curtain in the Temple that separated the *hechal* from the Holy of Holies.

Pele Yoetz – A *sefer* of ethical teachings by Rabbi Eliezer Papo (1785-1826).

Peyot – Side-locks worn by religious Jewish men.

Pirkei Avot – Translated as "Ethics of the Fathers."

Poskim – *Halachic* decision makers.

Pshat – The literal interpretation of the Torah.

Rabbanim – The rabbis.

Rabbeinu – Our rabbi.

Rabbeinu Hakodesh – "Our Holy Rabbi"; a designation for Rabbi Yehuda Hanasi, the second century leader of the Jewish people, and descendent of David Hamelech.

Ramhal – Rabbi Moshe Hayyim Luzzatto ((1707-1746).

Rashei tevot – The first letters of a series of Hebrew words.

Rema – An acronym for Rabbi Moshe Isserles (1530 - 1572), rabbi of Cracow, whose glosses on the *Shulhan Aruch* constitute the authoritative *halachah* for Ashkenai Jewry.

Remez – The symbolic meaning: one of the principle forms of Torah interpretation.

Reshit – "The beginning."

Rishonim – Jewish sages from approximately 1250 to 1500, following the period of the Geonim.

Rosh Hodesh – The first of the Hebrew month. *Erev Rosh Hodesh* is the day before.

Rosh yeshivah (roshe yeshivot) – Head of a yeshivah.

Ruah hakodesh – Divine inspiration, a lesser form of prophecy.

Ruhaniyut – Spirituality.

Sandak – The individual who holds the baby during the circumcision.

Sanhedrin – The supreme court and legislative body of Israel. The Great Sanhedrin had seventy-one elders, and the Lesser Sanhedrin had twenty-three.

Schach – The leaves and branches that make up the roof of a *sukkah*.

Seder Kodashim – The Talmudic order of Kodashim, that concerns the Temple services and sacrifices.

Sefarim – Holy, Jewish texts.

Sefirat haomer – The counting of the *omer* – the forty-nine days between Pesah and Shavuot.

Shabbat Shuva – The Shabbat between Rosh Hashana and Yom Kippur.

Shadchan – A matchmaker.

Shamash – The caretaker of a synagogue.

Shamor v'zachor – "Keep and remember."

Shas – An acronym for *shishah sedarim*: the "six orders" of the Mishnah and Talmud.

Shechinah – The Divine Presence.

Shelomei emunei – Those of perfect faith.

Shem Havaya – God's four-letter Name. The Tetragrammaton.

Shema – The *Shema* prayer: "Here O Israel, the L-rd is our God, the L-rd is One."

Shemoneh Esre – The "Eighteen Blessings" (really nineteen) that is at the center of the daily prayer service. Also known as the *Amidah* ("standing prayer").

Sheva berachot – The "Seven Blessing" made under the *chuppah* and at each festive meal for the seven days following the wedding.

Shidduch – A match.

Shir Hashirim – The Song of Songs, by Shlomo Hamelech.

Shiur (shiurim) – A Torah class.

Shor – An ox.

Shtender – A raised table for placing prayer books or study books.

Siddur – A Jewish prayerbook.

Simchah – Joy, happiness.

Sitra Ahra – Literally, the "Other Side"; the forces of evil and impurity.

Siyatta diShemaya – Heavenly assistance.

Sod – Secret. One of the methods of Torah interpretation.

Sofei tevot – The last letters of a Hebrew phrase or sentence.

Sugya – A topic of study.

Sukkah – The temporary dwelling used on Sukkot.

Ta'amei hamikra (ta'amim) – Cantillation marks for Torah and Prophets.

Ta'amei hamitzvot – The reason for the mitzvot.

Tahanun – A supplicatory prayer for forgiveness.

Taharah – Spiritual purity.

Tahtit – The bottom part.

Takanah – An rabbinic ordinance.

Tannaim – Sages of the Mishnah (pre-Talmudic period).

Tefillah – Prayer.

Tehillim – Psalms.

Teshuvah – Repentance.

Teshuvah shelemah – Perfect repentance.

Tikun – Repair, rectification. Kabbalistic term for rectification on an esoteric level.

Tikun Hatzot – The midnight prayer over the destruction of the Temple.

Tosaphot – A commentary on the Talmud, written by some of the *Rishonim* (primarily in France), from the 12th to 14th centuries.

Tzedakah – Charity.

Ushpizin – Guests (Aramaic). Referring usually to the seven holy guests who visit the *sukkah*.

Vanahafoch hu – "It was turned around" (*Megillat Esther* 9:1).

Vayachel – Literally, "And he began..."

Vidui – Confessionary prayer.

Yahrtzeit – The anniversay of a person's death.

Yegia – Strenuous effort.

Yerushalayim – Jerusalem.

Yesh me'ayin – Literally, "something out of nothing," referring to creatino *ex nihilo*.

Yeshivah – A school of Talmudic study.

Yetzer hara – The evil inclination in a person.

Yetzer hatov – The good inclination.

Yiddishkeit – Judaism (in Yiddish).

Yirat shamayim – Fear of God (literally, "fear of heaven").

Yisrael – Israel.

Yom Tov – A festival.

Yomam valayla – Day and night.

z"l – An acronym for *zichrono livrachah*, "may he be remembered for a blessing."

Zechut – Merit.

Zefat – A city in the mountains of Northern Israel, famous for its Kabbalistic masters.

ztz"l – An acronym for *zecher tzaddik livrachah*, "may the righteous be remembered for a blessing."